The Character of Logic in India

BIMAL KRISHNA MATILAL
(COURTESY OF MRS. KARABI MATILAL)

THE CHARACTER OF LOGIC IN INDIA

BIMAL KRISHNA MATILAL

Edited by Jonardon Ganeri and Heeraman Tiwari

STATE UNIVERSITY OF NEW YORK PRESS

SUNY Series in Indian Thought:
Texts and Studies
Wilhelm Halbfass, Editor

Published by
State University of New York Press, Albany

Printed in the United States of America

For information, address State University of New York
Press, State University Plaza, Albany, N.Y., 12246

Production by E. Moore
Marketing by Anne M. Valentine

Library of Congress Cataloging-in-Publication Data

Matilal, Bimal Krishna.
The character of logic in India/Bimal Krishna Matilal : edited by Jonardon Ganeri and Heeraman Tiwari.
p. cm. — (SUNY series in Indian thought)
Includes bibliographical references and index.
ISBN 0-7914-3739-6 (hc : acid free). — ISBN 0-7914-3740-X (pb : acid free)
1. Logic—India—History. I. Ganeri, Jonardon. II. Tiwari Heeraman. III. Title. IV. Series.
160'.954—dc21 97-19873
CIP

10 9 8 7 6 5 4 3 2 1

Contents

Editors' Foreword *vii*

1. Introducing Indian Logic *1*

2. Debates and Directives *31*

3. Tricks and Checks in Debate *60*

4. Diṅnāga: A New Era in Logical Thinking *88*

5. Dharmakīrti and the Problem of Induction in India *108*

6. The Jaina Contribution to Logic *127*

7. Navya-Nyāya: Technical Developments in the New School since 1300 AD *140*

Philosophers Discussed *169*

Bibliography *171*

Index *177*

Editors' Foreword

Matilal planned this book around 1988, in conjunction with the Institut International de Philosophie in Paris. He wrote most of it during the years 1989 to 1991. The structure of the book suggests comparison with Kneale and Kneale's *The Development of Logic*; that is, to be a book in which the origins of logical theory in India are traced chronologically, while paying at the same time careful attention to their philosophical significance. He would perhaps have agreed with Kneale and Kneale, who described the primary purpose of their work as having been "to record the first appearances of those ideas which seem to us most important in the logic of our own day" (1964: v). Writing this book provided Matilal with an opportunity to present what he took to be the most distinctive features of Indian logic, and to elaborate his views on the nature of philosophical activity in classical India. There is, however, a single central theme to this book, namely an inquiry into the origins, development, and nature of the Indian concept of an "inference-warranting relation" (vy*āpti*), often called the relation of "concomitance" or "pervasion," between the reason or evidence and the inferred conclusion. Matilal traces the origins of this concept to the early debating manuals, where the first attempts to demarcate the good or rational patterns of argument from the bad or irrational ones are to be found. He traces its development to two Buddhist logicians, Diṅnāga and Dharmakīrti, who were largely responsible for the construction of a clearly-articulated theory of the relation, as well as to Gaṅgeśa and his Navya-nyāya school, where the proper definition and analysis of the relation came to be an all-important concern.

The following brief outline charts the course taken in the book. In the first chapter, having given an introductory overview of the topics to be discussed in later chapters, Matilal reconstructs the Indian theory of inference in its essential characteristics, and examines the concepts it employs by comparing them with western logical theory. Chapters 2 and 3 describe how certain logical concepts came to develop within early debating theory. Among the examples discussed are the logic of implication in the Buddhist debating manual, the *Kathāvatthu*; the emergence of the idea of a logically-warranted inference from the analysis of such notions as "quibbling," "sophistical rejoinders," and "checks" in debate; and how studying the type of debate known as 'refutation-only' (*vitaṇḍā*) debate leads to a clarification of the concept of negation and the logical basis of skepticism. Chapters 4 and 5 are to do with the works of Diṅnāga and Dharmakīrti. In particular, Diṅnāga's celebrated "triple-condition" (*trairūpya*) theory of the inferential sign is examined, together with its relations to his equally celebrated "exclusion" (*apoha*) theory of meaning, and Dharmakīrti's attempts to explain how we can know by induction that the inference-warranting relation obtains between two properties if and when it does. Chapter 6, "The Jaina Contribution to Logic," is somewhat tangential to the main theme. It concerns the Jainas' attempt to ground their pluralism in a seven-valued logic (*saptabhaṅgī*), in which both a sentence and its negation could be simultaneously asserted as true. The manuscript indicates only that chapter 6 is to have the title it does, and the text for this chapter comes from a lecture Matilal presented in 1990. It is possible, therefore, that Matilal intended to write a new piece on Jaina logic, specifically on the Jaina theory of the inference-warranting relation, for this book. Those who are interested may refer to Matilal's essay entitled "Necessity and Indian Logic," in his *Logical and Ethical Issues in Religious Belief* (Calcutta, 1982), wherein the Jaina theory is briefly discussed. Chapter 7 deals with the philosophical logic of the Navya-naiyāyikas, particularly as it bears upon their new definitions of the inference-warranting relation, and their attempts to handle certain problem-cases to do with "ever-present" (*kevalānvayin*) and "partially locatable" (*avyāpya-vṛtti*) properties.

The intended layout of the book is indicated clearly in the manuscript, and we have not, with two exceptions, had to speculate on the order of material or what was to be included. One exception is, as already noted, the contents of Chapter 6. The other concerns Chapter 7: Matilal had originally included in this chapter the biographical material on Navya-nyāya authors which appeared in his history of Nyāya-Vaiśeṣika (1977a). We felt, however, that twenty or so pages of dates, names, and places impeded the flow of the work, and decided against reproducing them here. The manuscript itself was a first draft, and required a considerable ammount of editing. We have reorganized sections, and made such grammatical and stylistic alterations as deemed necessary to improve the readability of the text. We have added an editorial footnote here and there (and there are no footnotes other than editorial ones), and have inserted all bibliographical references as far as we can trace them.

We have also added a bibliography, index, table of philosophers discussed, and provided the sections in Chapter 6 heading titles. Matilal had provisionally given the book the title *The Development of Logic in India.* However, this could be (and has been) found to suggest a work of a more historical nature, and for this reason we have slightly altered the title to its present one. Matilal planned to write a final chapter, entitled "Concluding Remarks and Appraisal." We have moved what is now the final paragraph of Chapter 7 from its original position near the middle of that chapter; this will serve, we hope, as a fitting conclusion to the book.

Certain parts of this book have appeared in print before. Most of §1.2 was originally written for the volume *Semiotics* in the Walter de Gruyter series, *Handbooks of Linguistics and Communication Science*, and appeared as Appendix 2 in Matilal's *The Word and the World* (1990). Chapter 4 includes Matilal's article "Buddhist Logic and Epistemology" in Matilal and Evans (1986). It seems that he had intended to rework his interpretation of Diṅnāga, but did not get very far. Parts of Chapter 5 were prepared for the Second International Dharmakīrti Conference in Vienna, 1989, and later published in the volume of its proceedings (*Studies in the Buddhist Epistemological Tradition;* Steinkellner, 1991). What is now Chapter 6 was presented as the keynote address to the Bhogilal Leharchand Institute of Indology Conference on Jainism in Delhi, 1990, and subsequently printed as "*Anekānta*: both yes and no?," in the *Journal of Indian Council of Philosophical Research* (vol. viii, no. 2, January–April 1991). Finally, part of Chapter 7 derives with little alteration from §§ 2.3–2.5 of Matilal (1985).

Among the many people who have wished us well during our editing of this volume, we would like especially to thank Richard Sorabji for his sustained encouragement and practical assistance throughout, and Karabi Matilal for her perseverance and cooperation. We would also like to thank Alexis Sanderson, of All Souls College, Oxford, for going through the manuscript and making many helpful suggestions, as well as Wilhelm Halbfass, and Bill Eastman at S.U.N.Y. Press. We must thank, too, the editor of the *Journal of Indian Council of Philosophical Research* for permission to reprint "*Anekānta*: both yes and no?," and the editor of *Studies in the Buddhist Epistemological Tradition* (1991), and the Institut für Tibetologie und Buddhismuskunde der Universität Wien, for permission to reprint the article "Dharmakīrti and the universally negative inference."

J.G.
H.T.

CHAPTER 1

INTRODUCING INDIAN LOGIC

1.1 "LOGIC" IN WHAT SENSE?

"Logic" I shall here understand to be the systematic study of informal inference-patterns, the rules of debate, the identification of sound inference vis-à-vis sophistical argument, and similar topics. One may feel somewhat apologetic today to use the term "logic" in the context of classical Indian philosophy, for "logic" has acquired a very specific connotation in modern philosophical parlance. Nevertheless, the list supplied in the opening sentence is, I believe, a legitimate usage of the term, especially when its older senses are taken into account. S.C. Vidyabhusana's monumental, but by now dated, work *A History of Indian Logic* (1921), has misled many non-Sanskritists. For both he, and scholars such as H. N. Randle and T. Stcherbatsky, used such terms as "Indian logic" and "Buddhist logic" when their intention was to write about the theory of *pramāṇas* or accredited means of knowing in general, perhaps with particular emphasis upon the specific theory of *anumāna*, inference considered as means of knowing. I have chosen not to follow the same path; instead, I shall take "logic" in its extended and older sense in order to carve out a way for my own investigation. I shall use the traditional *śāstras* and try to explain their significance and relevance to our modern discussion of the area sometimes called "philosophical logic." I shall include much else besides, as the initial list shows, but will try to remain faithful to the topic of logic, debate, and the study of inference. I. M. Bochenski included a separate, albeit sketchy chapter called "The Indian Variety of Logic," in his great work *A History of Formal Logic* (1956). This will, perhaps, be enough to justify my use of the term "logic" when I am trying to cover similar ground.

Logic as the study of the form of correct arguments and inference-patterns, developed in India from the methodology of philosophical debate. The art of conducting a philosophical debate was prevalent probably as early as the time of the Buddha and the Mahāvīra (Jina), but it became more systematic and methodical a few hundred years later. By the second century BC, the intellectual climate in India was bristling with controversy and criticism. At the center of controversy were certain dominant religious and ethical issues. Nothing was too sacred for criticism. Such questions as: "Is there a soul different from body?", "Is the world (*loka*) eternal?", "What is the meaning, goal, or purpose of life?", and, "Is renunciation preferable to enjoyment?", were of major concern. While teachers and thinkers argued about such matters, there arose a gradual awareness of the characteristics or patterns of correct—that is, acceptable and sound—reasoning, and concern about how it differs from the kind of reasoning that is unacceptable.

1.2 AN HISTORICAL SKETCH OF LOGICAL ISSUES IN INDIA: DEBATE AND LOGIC

Logic developed in ancient India from the tradition of *vādavidyā*, a discipline dealing with the categories of debate over various religious, philosophical, moral, and doctrinal issues. There were several *vāda* manuals available around the beginning of the Christian era. They were meant for students who wanted to learn how to conduct debates successfully, what tricks to learn, how to find loopholes in the opponent's position, and what pitfalls to be wary of. We will examine some of these manuals in chapters 2 and 3. Of these manuals, the one found in the *Nyāyasūtras* of Akṣapāda Gautama (circa 150 AD) is comparatively more systematic than others. We shall hence follow it in this introductory exposition.

Debates, in Akṣapāda's view, can be of three types: (i) an honest debate (called *vāda*) where both sides, proponent and opponent, are seeking the truth, that is, wanting to establish the right view; (ii) a tricky-debate (called *jalpa*) where the goal is to win by fair means or foul; and (iii) a destructive debate (called *vitaṇḍā*) where the goal is to defeat or demolish the opponent, no matter how. This almost corresponds to the cliché in English: the good, the bad and the ugly. The first kind signals the employment of logical arguments, and use of rational means and proper evidence to establish a thesis. It is said that the participants in this kind of debate were the teacher and the student, or the students themselves, belonging to the same school.

The second was, in fact, a winner-takes-all situation. The name of the game was wit or intelligence. Tricks, false moves, and unfair means were allowed according to the rules of the game. But if both the debaters were equally clever and competent, this could be kept within the bounds of logic and reasoning. Usually two teachers of different schools would be participants. This used to take place before a board or jury called the *madhyastha* (the mediators or adjudicators) and a chairman, usually a king or a man with power and money who would organize the debate. The winner would be declared at the end by the consensus of the adjudicators.

The third type was a variety of the second type, where the winner was not supposed to establish his own position (he may not even have had a position) but only to defeat the opponent using logical arguments, or as the case was, tricks or clever devices. It was explicitly destructive and negative; hence philosophers like Vātsyāyana (circa 350 AD) denounced this form of debate in unambiguous language. Again, a clever and competent opponent might force the other side into admitting a counter-position ("If you deny my thesis *p*, then you must admit the thesis not-*p*; therefore, please establish your thesis"), and if the other side yielded, the debate was decided in favor of the former, or it would turn into the second form of debate.

The notoriety of the third type was universal, although some philosophers (for example, Nāgārjuna, Śrīharṣa) maintained that if the refutations of the opponent were done on the basis of good reason and evidence (in other words, if it followed the model of the first type, rather than the second type) then lack of a counter-thesis, or non-establishment of a counter-thesis, would not be a great drawback. In fact, it could be made acceptable and even philosophically respectable. That is why Gauḍa Sānātani (quoted by Udayana; see Matilal, 1986: 87) divided the debates into four types: (i) the honest type (*vāda*), (ii) the tricky type (*jalpa*), (iii) the type modeled after the tricky type but for which only refutation is needed, and (iv) the type modeled after the honest one where only the refutation of a thesis is needed. Even the mystics would prefer this last kind, which would end with a negative result. The different types of debate, and the philosophical significance of the 'refutation-only' type, are discussed in depth in chapter 2.

Apart from developing a theory of evidence (*pramāṇa*) and argument (*tarka*) needed for the first type of debate, the manuals go on to list a number of cases, or situation-types, where the debate will be concluded and one side will be declared as "defeated" (or *nigraha-sthāna*, the defeat situation or the clinchers). The *Nyāyasūtra* lists 22 of them. For example, (a) if the opponent cannot understand the proponent's argument, or (b) if he is confused, or (c) if he cannot reply within a reasonable time limit—all these will be cases of defeat. Besides, these manuals identify several standard "false" rejoinders or *jāti* (24 of them are listed in the *Nyāyasūtra*), as well as some underhand tricks (*chala*) like equivocation and confusion of a metaphor for the literal. These "tricks," "false rejoinders," and "defeat situations" are examined in detail in chapter 3. Now we may survey the type of logical theorizing that arose out of the study of debate in India.

The Nyāya *Model*

Akṣapāda defined a method of philosophical argumentation, called the *nyāya* method or the *nyāya* model. This was the standard for an ideally-organized philosophical disputation. Seven categories are identified as constituting the "prior" stage of a *nyāya*. A *nyāya* starts with an initial doubt, as to whether *p* or not-*p* is the case, and ends with a decision, that *p* (or not-*p*, as the case may be). The seven categories, including Doubt, are: Purpose, Example, Basic Tenets, the "limbs" of the formulated reasoning, Supportive Argument (*tarka*), and Decision. Purpose is self-explanatory. The example is needed to ensure that the arguments would not be just empty talk. Some of the basic tenets supply the ground rules for the argumentation.

The "limbs" were the most important formulation of the structure of a logical reasoning; these are a landmark in the history of Indian logic. According to the *Nyāyasūtras*, there are five "limbs" or "steps" in a structured reasoning. They should all be articulated linguistically. The first step is the statement of the thesis, the second the statement of reason or evidence, the third citation of an example (a particular case, well-recognized and acceptable to both sides) that illustrates the underlying (general) principle and thereby supports the reason or evidence. The fourth is the showing of the present thesis as a case that belongs to the general case, for reason or evidence is essentially similar to the example cited. The fifth is the assertion of the thesis again as proven or established. Here is the time-honored illustration:

Step 1. There is fire on the hill.
Step 2. For there is smoke.
Step 3. (Wherever there is smoke, there is fire), as in the kitchen.
Step 4. This is such a case (smoke on the hill).
Step 5. Therefore it is so, i.e., there is fire on the hill.

The Buddhists and others argued that this was too elaborate for capturing the essential structure. All we need would be the first two or the first three. The rest would be redundant. But the Nyāya school asserted all along that this *nyāya* method is used by the arguer to convince others, and to satisfy completely the "expectation" (*ākāṃkṣā*) of another, you need all the five "limbs" or steps. This is in fact a full-fledged articulation of an inference schema.

Returning to the *nyāya* method itself, the supportive argument (*tarka*) is needed when doubts are raised about the implication of the middle part of the above inference schema. Is the example right? Does it support the evidence? Is the general principle right? Is it adequate? The "supportive arguments" would examine the alternative possibilities, and try to resolve all these questions. After the supportive argument comes the decision, one way or another.

Another seven categories were identified as constituting the "posterior stage" of the *nyāya* method. They consist of three types of debate (already mentioned), the group of tricks, false rejoinders, and clinchers or defeat situations, and another important logical category, that of pseudo-reason or pseudo-evidence.

Pseudo-evidence is similar to evidence or reason, but it lacks adequacy or the logical force to prove the thesis adduced. It is in fact an "impostor." The *Nyāyasūtra* notes five such varieties. Although these five varieties were mentioned throughout the history of the Nyāya tradition (with occasional disagreement, for example, Bhāsarvajña, who had six), they were constantly redefined to fit the developing logical theories of individual authors. The five types of pseudo-evidence were: the *deviating*, the *contradictory*, the *unestablished* or *unproven*, the *counter-balanced*, and the *untimely*.

Since there can be fire without smoke (as in a red-hot iron ring), if somebody wants to infer presence of smoke in the kitchen on the basis of the presence of fire there, his evidence would be pseudo-evidence called the "deviating." Where the evidence (say a pool of water) is usually the sign for the absence of fire, rather than its presence, it is called the contradictory. An evidence-reason must itself be established or proven to exist, if it has to establish something else. Hence, an "unestablished" evidence-reason is a pseudo-evidence or a pseudo-sign. A purported evidence-reason may be countered by a purported counter-evidence showing the opposite possibility. This will be a case of the "counter-balanced." An "untimely" is one where the thesis itself precludes the possibility of adducing some sign as being the evidence-reason by virtue of its incompatibility with the thesis in question. The "untimely" is so-called because as soon as the thesis is stated, the evidence will no longer be an evidence. (For further elaboration, see Matilal, 1985, §1.5).

The Sign and the Signified

All this implicitly spells out a theory of what constitutes an adequate sign. What we have been calling "evidence," "reason," and sometimes "evidence-reason" may just be taken to be an adequate or "logical" sign. The Sanskrit word for it is *liṅga*, a sign or a mark, and what it is a sign for is called *liṅgin*, the signified, the "marked" entity. This is finally tied to their theory of sound inference, that is, inference of the signified from the observation of the logical sign. This is the pre-theoretical notion of the "sign-signified" connection, as explained here. Note that this notion of "sign-signified" relation is different from the "signifier-signified" relation that is mentioned in some modern linguistics, especially Saussure.

A sign is adequate or "logical" if it is not a pseudo-evidence, that is, a pseudo-sign. And the five types of pseudo-sign have already been identified. We have here a negative formulation of the adequacy of the sign. A little later on in the tradition the positive formulation was found. The fully-articulated formulation is found in the writings of the well-known Buddhist logician, Diṅnāga (circa 400–480 AD), in his theory of the "triple-character" reason. We will discuss his contribution briefly below, and in more detail in chapter 4. In fact, an adequate sign is what should be non-deviating, that is, it should not be present in any location when the signified is absent. If it is, it would be "deviating." Thus, the identification of the first pseudo-sign captured this intuition, although it took a long time to get this fully articulated in the tradition. A sign which is adequate in this sense may be called "logical" for it ensures the correctness of the resulting inference. Thus, we have to ask: if the sign is there, can the signified be far behind?

The Triple Nature of the Sign

Diṅnāga formulated the following three conditions, which, he claimed, a logical sign must fulfill:

1. It should be present in the case (object) under consideration.
2. It should be present in a *similar* case or a homologue.
3. It should not be present in any *dissimilar* case, any heterologue.

Three interrelated technical terms are used here. The "case under consideration" is called a *pakṣa*, the "subject-locus." The "similar case" is called a *sapakṣa*, the "homologue." The "dissimilar case" is called a *vipakṣa*, the "heterologue." These three concepts are also defined by the theory. The context is that of inferring a property *A* (the *signified* in our new vocabulary) from the property *B* (the *sign*) in a location *S*. Here the *S* is the *pakṣa*, the subject-locus. The *sapakṣa* is one which already possesses *A*, and is known to do so. And the *vipakṣa* is one which does not possess *A*. The "similarity" between the *pakṣa* and the *sapakṣa* is variously explained. One explanation is that they would share tentatively the signified *A* by sharing the sign *B*. An example would make it clear. Smoke is a sign of fire on a hill, because it is present on that hill, and it is also present in a kitchen which is a locus of fire, and it is absent from any non-locus of fire.

The third condition is easily explained. The sign must not be present where the signified is not present. For otherwise, as we have already noted, the sign will be *deviating*, and would be a "pseudo-sign." Why the second condition? Did Diṅnāga overshoot his mark? Is not the second condition redundant (for the first and the third seem to be sufficient to guarantee adequacy)? These questions were raised in the tradition by both the Naiyāyikas like Uddyotakara (circa 550–625 AD), and the Buddhists like Dharmakīrti (circa 600–660 AD). Some, such as Dharmakīrti, maintained that it was slightly repetitious but not exactly redundant. The second condition states positively what the third, for the sake of emphasis, states negatively. The second is here rephrased as: the sign should be present in all *sapakṣas*. The contraposed version can then be formulated with a little ingenuity as: the sign should be absent from all *vipakṣas*. For *sapakṣa* and *vipakṣa*, along with the *pakṣa*, exhaust the universe of discourse.

Other interpreters try to find additional justification for the second condition to argue against the "redundancy" charge. The interpretation becomes complicated, and we will postpone going into the details until chapter 4. Logically speaking, it seems that the second condition is redundant, but epistemologically speaking, a case of the co-presence of *A* and *B* may be needed to suggest the possibility, at least, that one may be the sign for the other. Perhaps Diṅnāga's concern here was epistemological.

Diṅnāga's Wheel of Reason/Sign

When a sign is identified, there are three possibilities. The sign may be present in all, some, or none of the *sapakṣas*. Likewise, it may be present in all, some or none of the *vipakṣas*. To identify a sign, we have to assume that it is present in the *pakṣa*, however; that is, the first condition is already satisfied. Combining these, Diṅnāga constructed his "wheel of reason" with nine distinct possibilities, which may be tabulated in Figure 1.1.

Of these nine possibilities, Diṅnāga asserted that only two are illustrative of sound inference for only they meet all the three conditions. They are Numbers 2 and 8. Notice that either (– *vipakṣa* and + *sapakṣa*), or (– *vipakṣa* and ± *sapakṣa*) would fulfill the required conditions. Diṅnāga is insistent that at least one *sapakṣa* must have the positive sign. Number 5 is *not* a case of sound inference; this sign is a pseudo-sign. For although it satisfies the two conditions 1 and 3 above, it does not satisfy condition 2. So one can argue that as far as Diṅnāga was concerned all three were necessary conditions. The second row does not satisfy condition 2 and hence none of Numbers 4, 5, and 6 are logical signs; they are pseudo-signs. Numbers 4 and 6 are called "contradictory" pseudo-signs—an improvement upon the old *Nyāyasūtra* definition

FIGURE 1.1
DIṄNĀGA'S WHEEL OF REASON

1 + *vipakṣa* + *sapakṣa*	2 – *vipakṣa* + *sapakṣa*	3 ± *vipakṣa* + *sapakṣa*
4 + *vipakṣa* – *sapakṣa*	5 – *vipakṣa* – *sapakṣa*	6 ± *vipakṣa* – *sapakṣa*
7 + *vipakṣa* ± *sapakṣa*	8 – *vipakṣa* ± *sapakṣa*	9 ± *vipakṣa* ± *sapakṣa*

+ = all, ± = some, – = none.

of contradictory. The middle one, Number 5, is called "uniquely deviating" (*asādhāraṇa*), perhaps for the reason that this sign becomes an unique sign of the *pakṣa* itself, and is not found anywhere else. In Diṅnāga's system, this sign cannot be a sign for anything else, it can only point to itself reflexively or to its own locus. Numbers 1, 3, 7, and 9 are also pseudo-signs. They are called the "deviating" signs, for in each case the sign occurs in some *vipakṣa* or other, although each fulfills the second condition. This shows that at least in Diṅnāga's own view, the second condition (when it is combined with the first) gives only a necessary condition for being an adequate sign, not a sufficient one. In other words, Diṅnāga intended all three conditions jointly to formulate a sufficient condition.

Development of the Wheel by Uddyotakara

Diṅnāga's system of nine reason-types or sign-types was criticized by Uddyotakara, the Naiyāyika, who argued that it was incomplete. We will summarize the main points here; they are discussed in greater detail in §4.10 and chapter 5. Diṅnāga did not consider at least two further alternatives: (a) a situation-type where there is no *sapakṣa*, and (b) a situation-type where there is no *vipakṣa*. The sign's absence from all *sapakṣas* (or all *vipakṣas*) should be distinguished from these two situations. Let us use "0" for the situation-type which lacks any *sapakṣa,* or *vipakṣa,* and "–" for the situation-type where the sign is present in *no sapakṣa* or *vipakṣa* (as before). Hence combining the four possibilities + *sapakṣa*, ± *sapakṣa*, –*sapakṣa*, 0 *sapakṣa* (no *sapakṣa*) with the other four (+, ±, –, 0) *vipakṣa*, we get sixteen portions in our wheel of reason, and the new wheel contains more sound inferences, that is, adequate signs. For example,

> This is nameable, because this is knowable.

Here "knowability" is the sign, which is adequate and logical for showing the nameability of an entity, for (in the Nyāya system) whatever is knowable is also nameable (that is, expressible in language). Now we cannot have a heterologue or *vipakṣa* here, for (again according to the Nyāya system) there is nothing that cannot be named (or expressed in language). Within the Buddhist system, another example of the same argument-type would be:

> This is impermanent because it is a product.

For Buddhists everything is impermanent and a product. Later Naiyāyikas called this type of sign "*kevalānvayin,*" the universal-positive-sign; that is, it is a characteristic of every entity.

Uddyotakara captured another type of adequate reason or logical sign, but he formulated the example of this reasoning (or inference) negatively, that is, in terms of a counterfactual. This was done probably to avoid a doctrinal quandary of the Nyāya school (to which he belonged) in which the explanation of analytic judgements or *a priori* knowledge always presents a problem. His typical example was:

> The living body cannot be without a soul, for if it were it would have been without life.

This is the generalized inference called "universal negative"—*kevalavyatirekin*—in the tradition. The subject *S* which has a unique property *B* cannot be without *A*, for then it would have been without *B*. Since *B* is a unique property of *S*, and since the presence of *A* and *B* mutually imply each other, there is no *sapakṣa*. But it is a correct infezence. Bhāsarvajña (circa 950 AD) did not like the rather roundabout way of formulating the inference-type. He said:

> The living body has a soul, for it has life.

But this would verge on unorthodoxy in Nyāya, for (a) the statement of the thesis includes the sign already, and (b) there seems to be a necessary connection between having life and having a soul. The later Nyāya went back to the negative formulation but got rid of the reflex of the counterfactual that Uddyotakara had. If *A* and *B* are two properties mutually implying each other such that *B* can be the definiens (*lakṣaṇa*) and the class of those possessing *A* can be the definiendum, then the following inference is correct:

> The subject *S* differs from those that are without *A*, for it has *B* (and *A* is defined in terms of *B*.)

This seems to be equivalent to:

> *S* has *A*, for it has *B*.

The verbal statement "*S* has *A* because it has *B*," however, does not expose fully the structure of this type of inference. For one thing, in this version it becomes indistinguishable from any other type of correct inference discussed before. In fact, the special feature of this type of inference is that the inferable property *A* is uniquely present in *S* alone, and nowhere else, and hence our knowledge of the concomitance or pervasion between *A* and *B* cannot be derived from an example (where their co-presence will be instantiated) which will be a different case from the *S*, the case under consideration. In fact, *S* here is a generic term and it will be proper to say: all *Ss* have *A*, for they have *B*, and a supporting example will have to be an *S*, that is, an instance of *S*. To avoid this anomaly, a negative example is cited to cover these cases. Thus we can say, a non-*S* is a case where neither *A* nor *B* are present. This will allow one to infer, for example, absence of *B* from absence of *A* and also (since *A* and *B* are co-present in all cases) absence of *A* from absence of *B*. But the evidence here is *B*. Hence by seeing absence of *B* in all *Ss* we can infer absence of *A*. Such a roundabout formulation was dictated by the peculiar nature of the Diṅnāga-Uddyotakara theory of inference.

Let us try to explain. In this theory, what legitimizes the inference of *A* from the sign *B* is the knowledge that B is a logical sign of *A*. To have that knowledge, we must have another item of knowledge, that *B* has concomitance, an invariable connection, with *A*. The second item of knowledge must be derived empirically, from an example where it is certain that *A* as well as *B* is present. Without such an example, we would not recognize *B* to be a logical sign of *A*. This limitation precluded the possibility of inferring *A* from *B*, where the case is such that all that have *A* are included in *pakṣa*, the subject-locus of the inference. The convention is that the said example cannot be chosen from the members of the *pakṣa*, that is, of the set of *Ss*. Hence the difficulty.

Uddyotakara saw this problem and extended the scope of the theory by saying that in these cases, a negative example, a non-*S* having neither *A* nor *B*, and absence of any counter-example (the sign's absence from all *vipakṣas*), will be enough to legitimize the inference. Udayana (circa 975–1050 AD) later on defended this type of inference as legitimate. For, he said, if we do not admit such inferences as valid, our search for a *defining* property of some concepts could not be justified. Suppose we wish to define cow-hood: what is the unique property of a cow? Now, suppose having a dewlap is a unique property of cow; it exists in all and only cows. What is the purpose of such a "definition," if we can call it a definition (*lakṣaṇa*)? It is that we can differentiate all cows from non-cows. How? We do it by means of the following inference: cows are distinct from non-cows, for cows have dewlaps. Of course, the statement "cows are distinct from non-cows" is equivalent to the statement "cows are cows," but when it is put negatively, the purpose of such inference becomes clearer. This important issue will be elaborated in chapter 5, especially §5.8, §5.9, and §5.11.

Concomitance or Invariable Relation

In the *Pramāṇasamuccaya*, Diṅnāga defined the invariable relation or concomitance of *B* with *A*, which legitimizes the inference of the signified *A* from the sign *B*, as follows:

> When the sign (*liṅga*) occurs, there the signified, that of which it is a sign, has to occur as well. And if the sign has to occur somewhere, it has to occur only where the signified occurs (*liṅge liṅgī bhavaty eva liṅginy evetarat punaḥ*).

This verse has been quoted frequently by Naiyāyikas, Jainas, and other logicians. It actually amounts to saying that all cases of *B* are cases of *A*, and only cases of *A* could be cases of *B*.

Dharmakīrti described the invariable connection in two ways. First, the sign *B* could be the "own-nature" or essential mark of *A*. That amounts to saying that *B* is either an invariable or a necessary sign of *A*. Thus, we infer that something is a tree from the fact that it is a beech tree, for a beech tree cannot be a beech tree without being a tree. This only defines invariability or necessary connection. The second type of sign is one when we infer the "natural" causal factor from the effect, as we infer fire from smoke. It is also the nature or the essence of smoke that it cannot originate without originating from fire. Hence invariable relation means: (i) an essential or necessary property of the class, and (ii) a casually necessary relation between an effect and its invariable cause. Dharmakīrti's contribution is examined in the early sections of chapter 5.

The late Naiyāyikas said that the absence of a counter-example is what is ultimately needed to legitimize the inference-giving relation between *A* and *B*. If *B* is the sign, then *B* would be the logical sign if, and only if, there is no case where *B* occurs but *A* does not occur. If *B* occurs where *A* does not, that would be a counter-example to the tacitly assumed rule of inference, "if *B* then *A*." As we know from the truth-table of the propositional logic, "if *B* then *A*" is falsified only under one condition, when not-*A* is true along with *B*. Thus Gaṅgeśa (f. 1325 A.D.) defines this relation:

> *B's* non-occurrence in any location characterized by absence of *A*.

Alternatively, another definition is given:

> *B's* co-occurrence with such an *A* as is never absent from the location of *B*.

The first is rephrasing of the first definition of *vyāpti* (invariable concomitance) in the *Vyāptipañcaka* of Gaṅgeśa. The second is an abbreviation of what is called his *siddhāntalakṣaṇa,* "accepted definition." These developments, in the analysis of the concept of the invariable concomitance or inference-warranting relation between sign and signified, made by the later Naiyāyikas, will be elaborated in chapter 7 of this book.

On the "Steps" in the Process of Inference: Members of the Syllogism

An essential part of the theory of inference is obviously the knowledge of concomitance or invariance between the inferable property, *A*, and the reason, *B*, the *hetu*. Our knowledge of such invariances is derived, rightly or wrongly, from our observation of such examples illustrating the togetherness of *B* and *A;* we call them *sapakṣas*. The *Nyāyasūtra* author insisted upon the citation of the example to justify or support the reason, to show that there is a relation of concomitance or invariance backing the reason.

A question arises regarding how many steps we need in what is called "*parārthānumana*" or "demonstration to others" of the entire process of inference one makes within oneself. A demonstration is something like the verbal articulation of the process of inference. The Naiyāyikas assert that there should be five steps in this verbal articulation of the inference, where the fifth step would re-state the thesis proven by the reason backed by the required invariance relation. The Buddhist, on the other hand, would need only three steps—statement of the thesis, of the reason, and also of the example. Praśastapāda (circa 450–500 AD) made a very significant comment in his *Padārthadharmasaṃgraha*, while he was explaining the five-step verbal articulation of the Nyāya demonstration. The last step is a re-statement of the thesis and, hence, the opponent obviously points out that it is redundant, for the thesis has already been stated and that it is proven by the adequate reason. The thesis is stated in the first step and the reason in the second step. Hence, says Praśastapāda, if we depend upon what is presented not simply verbally but also by implication as well as the significance of what is presented verbally (compare *arthāt*), then one can only state the first two steps and satisfy the other (opponent) side. We quote (1971: 241):

> Therefore, after stating the thesis, one should verbally articulate only the reason. For intelligent people will be reminded of the invariance based upon prior observation of co-presence and the lack of it (in suitable examples), and therefore they will acknowledge the thesis as established. This verbal articulation should end here (with the statement of the reason).

This was apparently a challenge to the Buddhist to bring down the number of steps in the argument from three to the first two: the thesis and the reason. It is interesting that Dharmakīrti boldly accepted the challenge and said:

> For intelligent people only the reason would be stated (PV II.27).

(There may be a chronological problem here, however. Praśastapāda is considered to be a junior contemporary of Diṅnāga, for he assimilated all the logical developments of Diṅnāga into his re-statement of the Nyāya-Vaiśeṣika system of logic. It is also generally believed that he preceded Dharmakīrti. I accept this chronology, and my above comment is based upon its truth. If, however, it can be shown that Dharmakīrti preceded Praśastapāda, then the above statement has to be modified accordingly. My argument here is not concerned with this issue, however, and the chronological controversy would not upset anything else I have said here about logic. It is significant to note though that Udayana quotes the relevant line of Dharmakīrti while he comments on this particular passage of Praśastapāda.)

1.3 INDIAN LOGIC VERSUS WESTERN LOGIC: DIFFERENCES

If one were to ask at the outset, what is the difference between so-called Indian logic and Western logic, the question would be almost a non-starter. We may put a counter question: "What *is* Western logic?", and thousands of conflicting answers are available from the text books since the time of Aristotle. There is, however, a "modern" conception of logic, and we may try to spell out the difference between Indian conceptions of logic and this. In the broadest terms, one may note briefly the following differences.

First, certain *epistemological* issues are found to be included in the discussion of what we wish to call "Indian logic." The reason is obvious. Indian logic is primarily a study of inference-patterns, and inference is clearly identified as a source of knowledge, a *pramāṇa*. So the study includes general questions regarding the nature of the derivation of knowledge from information supplied by evidence, which evidence may itself be another piece of knowledge. Epistemological questions, however, are deliberately excluded from the domain of modern logic.

Second, to a superficial observer, discussion of the logical theories in India would seem to be heavily burdened with psychologistic and intuitionistic terminology—a feature which, since Frege, logicians in the West have tried carefully to weed out from modern logical discussions. Yet the role of psychology, how one mental event causes another mental event or events and how one is connected with the other, seems to be dominant in the Indian presentation.

The Indians psychologized logic, but perhaps without totally committing the blunder into which an emphasis on psychology may often lead. Thus one may claim that they psychologized logic, without committing the fallacy of psychologism. Alternatively, the claim could be that this was a different conception of logic, where the study of the connections between mental events and the justification of inferentially-acquired knowledge-episodes is not a fault (for a development of this idea, see Matilal 1986, §4.7).

Third, historically, from the time of the Greeks, the mathematical model played an important part in the development of logic in the West. In India, it was grammar, rather than mathematics, that was dominant, and logical theories were influenced by the study of grammar. Why this was so is a question that we cannot answer. This point is to some extent related to the second.

Last but not least, the usual distinction, so well entrenched in the Western tradition, between deduction and induction was not to be found in the same way in the Indian tradition. The argument patterns studied were at best an unconscious mixture of the two processes. Yet it seemed that these mixed patterns were not very far from the way human beings across cultural boundaries would tend in fact to argue or rationally derive conclusions from the available data or evidence or premises.

This last point needs to be emphasized for another reason. Almost all modern treatments of the character of the argument pattern in Indian logic have tended to analyze it as a form of *deductive* reasoning. At best, this might have contributed to an appreciation that forms of rationality in classical India, to the extent they are reflected in the "logical" argument patterns, were not very different from what they are in the West. However, it has also undermined certain unique features of the Indian argument patterns, or at least blocked our clear understanding and appreciation of such features.

One reason for this confusion of modern scholars is that the *inferred* conclusion in the Indian theory was regarded as a piece of knowledge (derived normally from the observation of adequate evidence), and hence it was accorded that certainty which we usually associate with states of knowledge. Inductive conclusions by contrast are, in today's terms, only probable, although they may sometimes have a very high degree of probability. The inductive element of the argument patterns studied by the Indian philosophers has thus often been lost sight of by modern scholars who emphasize the alleged certainty of the inferred conclusion, and then go on to equate the Indian argument patterns invariably with deductive or syllogistic forms.

Let me develop this point further. Since the time of Stcherbatsky, Randle, and others, and even still today, the typical example of the model of inference in Indian logic is reformulated as follows:

A Wherever there is smoke, there is fire.
There is smoke on the yonder hill.
Therefore there is fire there.

A is clearly an example of the form that we call *Barbara* in traditional Aristotelian Logic. In modern first order predicate logic, it would be an example of an inference schema which uses universal instantiation, and would have the form (see Quine, 1961),

$$\{(x)\ (Fx \supset Gx) \cdot Fa\} \supset Ga.$$

A is derived from, and hence regarded as transformationally equivalent to, the following presentation of the argument, which is the one *actually* used in the Indian texts:

B The hill is fire-possessing.
Because it is smoke-possessing (or because of smoke).
For example, the kitchen.

The idea being considered is that whoever asserts *B* means exactly *A*.

The common reconstruction of the Indian argument pattern, *B*, is in fact more often presented, not exactly as *A*, but as

A': Wherever there is smoke there is fire, *as in a kitchen.*
There is smoke on the yonder hill
Therefore there is fire there.

The argument pattern *A* undergoes, however, an often unnoticed but important metamorphosis when it is presented as *A'*. The citation of the example, "kitchen" underscores first of all the fact that unlike the first proposition in *A* (or Aristotle's universal premise) the premise here is unambiguous. For the schema "(x) $(Fx \supset Gx)$" in *A* represents any universal proposition *with or without existential presupposition* (for the problems related to the existential import of the subject term of universal propositions in Aristotle, such as "All *S* is *P*" or "All *F*s are *G*s", one may consult P. F. Strawson, 1966). However, the citation of an example in the first proposition of *A'* shows that it is a universal proposition along with existential import. In other words, the subject term now is definitely non-empty.

In the above *A'*, and in *B*, the insistence on the presence of an example should thus not be lightly dismissed as an inessential detail. For it brings to the fore the inductive nature of the first premise, and thereby exposes the "weakness" of the entire argument pattern from a purely deductive point of view. The Indian philosopher of logic did not generally think of this feature as an indicator of the weakness of their theory of inference (although the skeptics, as well as the Cārvāka or the Lokāyata, who were opponents of the idea that inference is a source of knowledge, severely attacked the theory just on this ground). To counter this attack, the Indian logicians sought some way to accord the conclusion of this type of argument almost the same degree of certainty that is given to the conclusion of a normal deductive argument. However, the point remains that the importance attached to the citation of an example in the Indian schema, *B*, highlights the fact that it cannot be reconstructed as a purely deductive argument, along the lines of *A*.

It is a commonplace in modern logic to distinguish between truth and validity. Roughly, validity has to do with the rules of inference in a given theory. The conclusion may be validly derived from the premises, if and only if the rules of inference are not violated, while it may still be a false judgement. The soundness of the conclusion in deduction depends also upon the adequacy or the truth of the premises. It is now-a-days claimed that a logician's concern is with the validity of inference, not with its soundness, which may depend upon extra-logical factors (the truth of the premises). This is the ideal in formal logic. In India, however, this distinction was not often made, for the philosophers wanted their "logically" derived inferences or their conclusions also to be pieces of knowledge. Thus, validity must be combined with truth. It was allowed that some wild guesses or "invalidly" derived inferences might happen to be true. Such "invalid" derivation, however, would not be a proper route to knowledge. This point will be further clarified when we discuss Diṅnāga in chapter 4.

The point just made is that Indian logic is not formal logic. This does not imply, however, that by introducing some aspects of formal logic in order to interpret the Indian theories we cannot gain any sort of deeper understanding of Indian logic. In fact, we can. Hence, reductions to Aristotelian syllogistic inference along the above lines, and even modified use of Venn diagrams (for example, Chi, 1969), have very often been fruitful in our attempt to understand, analyze and explain the Indian theories, as long as they are taken in context.

Let me develop this point a little further. Since Łukasiewicz, it has been fairly well-known in the West that Aristotle's syllogistic need not be interpreted as resting on an ontology of individuals and the mechanism of quantification. It can be seen instead as involving four operators "A" "E" "I" and "O," treated as primitives, holding upon variables "*u*" and "*v*" which range over non-empty terms (which stand for properties or sorts). This dispenses with the standard logical subject-predicate analysis of sentences, in which the subject identifies an object and the predicate *sorts* (is true of) that object. Modern logic in the Fregean tradition, on the other hand, requires, in its semantics, a domain of individuals, to which are attached properties and relations. Likewise, by subjecting the inference-patterns formulated and studied in the logical texts of India to various different reductions and translations, we might get closer to the nature of Indian logical theories, provided we remain cautious and sensitive to the peculiarities and differences. Venn diagrams, rules of propositional and first order predicate logic, some issues from the logic of classes and relations—all these can be used in our study, if only to underline the differences and uniqueness of Indian logic.

As far as the inductive character of the Indian argument pattern is concerned, it is reminiscent of J. S. Mill's theory of inference and induction. Presently we will see how the general premise is supposed to be supported by a positive as well as a negative example, called the homologue (*sapakṣa*) and heterologue (*vipakṣa*). This invites comparison with Mill's Joint Method of Agreement and Difference, which is regarded as stronger, in its power to generate certainty or high probability, than either the Method of Agreement or that of Difference, when employed independently. Mill, however, obtains certainty by implicitly basing his theory upon a presumed relation of strict and necessary causation between the observed and inferred properties, thereby ruling out accidentally true generalizations. Indian argument patterns too were initially based upon a number of ontological relations, causation, part-and-whole, essential identity and so on, and this feature justified the so-called assumption of certainty or knowledgehood of the inferred conclusions. However, the history of inference unfolded differently in India, for there it took the form of a search for a logical, that is, inference-warranting relation, which was called *vyāpti*—"pervasion" or "concomitance," between the evidence and the conclusion.

We may conclude this section with a quotation of H. N. Randle, who, incidentally, wrote a paper on Indian logic long ago in the journal *Mind* (Randle, 1924). In his book, *Indian Logic in the Early Schools,* published by Oxford University Press in 1930, he said:

> Indian formalism in fact seems to break off abruptly at the point at which western formalism begins, perhaps by a fortunate instinct. (1930: 233, fn. 3)

He was obviously no lover of formal logic, and perhaps would have been surprised by today's development in the area of formal logic in the West. However, he continued:

> But if formal logic is admitted to have a certain methodological value—I think it is as good a mental discipline to turn [Diṅnāga's] wheel of the reasons as to plough the sands of Barbara and Celarent. The study of either logic is almost a necessary introduction to the philosophical literature of either civilization. (ibid.)

The world of philosophy and scholarship has moved a long way since the days of Randle. Still, what he said in the concluding sentence of the above passage is very true even today.

1.4 Some General Characteristics: Subject and Predicate

Any study of logic is intimately connected with the language in which it is conducted. Needless to say, the Indian "logicians" did not use symbols, formulae, or axiomatic constructions in an artificial or formal language. Indian logical theories were discussed primarily in Sanskrit, and the structure of the Sanskrit language figures prominently here. This fact has created some problems of interpretation, for it is extremely difficult, though not impossible, to transfer the philosophical and logical problems from the narrow confines of Sanskrit to the modern philosophical audience in general.

It is commonplace in logic to talk about the analysis of propositions. In the context of logic in Sanskrit, we have to talk about the analysis of Sanskrit propositions. A Sanskrit proposition is what is expressed in a Sanskrit sentence. It will appear that the analysis proposed by the early Sanskrit writers would not be entirely unfamiliar to one accustomed to the usual subject-predicate analysis of modern or traditional Western logic, nor is it unrelated to it. However, the logical as well as grammatical analysis of Sanskrit sentences presents some significant contrasts with the usual subject-predicate analysis. Unless these points of contrast are noted, it will be difficult to appreciate fully some of the concerns of the Sanskrit logicians.

A sentence in Sanskrit is regarded as the expression of a "thought" or what is called a cognitive state (*jñāna*), or, to be precise, a qualificative cognitive state (*viśiṣṭa-jñāna*). A simple qualificative cognitive state is one where the cognizer cognizes something (or some place or some locus, as we will have to call it) as *qualified* by a property or a qualifier. It is claimed by most Sanskrit writers that to say that something or some place is qualified by a qualifier is equivalent to saying that it is a locus of some property or "locatable." As I have discussed elsewhere (Matilal, 1968, 1971), a qualificative cognition is actually to be thought of as a propositional cognition or a judgement. In this and subsequent sections, we will investigate how the Indian analysis of the structure of such states relates to Western analyses of the subject-predicate distinction.

A proposition, in its basic form, is usually explained by Western writers in terms of what we call a *predication*. A simple or atomic proposition is thus better understood as involving the "basic combination" of predication. This expression—"basic combination"—was once used by W. V. Quine (1960: 96). The idea was sharpened by P. F. Strawson (1974). Strawson explains the structure of the so-called basic combination of predication as (1) a combination of (2) a subject and (3) a predicate, and said that it lies at the focal point of our current logic. He has further claimed that:

> [i]f current logic has the significance which we are inclined to attach to it, and which our contemporary style of philosophizing in particular assumes, then it must reflect fundamental features of our thought about the world. (1974: 4)

The claim may be too strong. For all we can say is that the said structure reflects primarily the basic way in which we are accustomed to think about the world. We might be trained and then be accustomed to think about the world in a different way, but in that case our language would not admit a predominantly subject-predicate structure. This is at least conceivable. In Jonathan Swift's *Gulliver's Travels*, three professors of the School of Languages at the Grand Academy of Lagado, were trying to work on a project that would shorten the academic discourse by leaving out, among other things, "verbs and participles, because in reality all things imaginable are but nouns" (p. 219, 1919 edn.). The point is that while a project need not be a radical or outlandish as this one, even a slightly different proposal may appear odd or queer to our readers today who are well-accustomed to modern qualificational logic as well as the subject-predicate analysis of the basic sentences.

The "current" logicians generally agree that the basic predication may best be pictured in the neutral logical schema "*Fa.*" It represents a combination of a singular term or a (proper) name and, to use Quine's terminology, a general term or a *predicate*, a combination which forms a sentence. By "general term" are meant such grammatical terms as substantives, adjectives, and verbs. (Even names or so-called singular terms can be systematically reparsed as *predicates* by following the Russellian trick of representing them as descriptions. However this part of Quine's proposal is controversial and may be ignored for the moment). Verbs, according to Quine, may be regarded as the "fundamental form" of predication, and the adjectivals and the nominals (substantives) may be assimilated into the "verbals." In other words, such phrases as ". . . . is an *F*" and ". . . . is *F*" are mere stylistic varieties of the verb form ". . . . *Fs.*" Predication, then, is illustrated indifferently by "Mama is a Woman," "Mama is big," and "Mama sings" (1960: 96).

Strawson analyses the "basic propositional combination" as a tripartition of function, as I have already noted. This is represented by a simple symbolism "ass *(i c)*," where "*i*" represents a particular, "*c*" the concept specification and "ass *( )*" the propositional combination. The former two underline the duality, that, following Strawson, we may still call the subject and the predicate, while the isolation of the third element is important to capture the function of presenting the particular and the general concept as assigned to each other in such a way as to have a propositional combination. In our "ground level" subject-predicate sentence, the third function is usually associated with the second. Hence the *predicate* is usually a verb or a "verbal phrase," that combines syntactically the concept-specifying element and the indication of propositionality.

This dual role of our ordinary predicate phrases must be recognized, even if we try to maintain Quine's strictures against the predicate-term being accessible to quantifiers or the variables of quantification. Apart from worries about ontological commitment to abstract (in Quine's words, intentional) properties, there does not seem to be any good reason why we cannot quantify over the predicate-properties which are denoted by singular abstract terms such as "sweetness" or "singing."

Now, in the Indian context, the basic combination is not called a proposition. It is a structured whole that is grasped by an atomic cognitive event. We call it an atomic *qualificative* (*viśiṣṭa*) cognition. One element is called the *qualifier* while the other the *qualificand*, and their combination forms the structured whole. It can be represented by:

$Q\ (a\ b)$

where "*a*" represents the qualificand, "*b*" the qualifier, and "*Q*( )" the indication of "qualificativity." I shall be using these symbols for convenience only, as I have done in my earlier writings (especially Matilal, 1968). One can read "*Q (a b)*" as "*a* qualified by *b*." The similarity of this symbolism with Strawson's "ass *(i c)*" may not be only superficial. As far as the separation of the syncategorematic element of a given combination is concerned, both agree. Both leave us open to treat the "predicate" element as a singular (abstract) property. For the cognition of a blue pot can be expressed either as a sentence ("This pot is blue.") or as a phrase ("this blue pot"). Besides, our symbolism admits the following two basic rules:

(1) $Q\ (a\ b) \cdot Q\ (a\ c) \rightarrow Q\ (a\ (b\ c))$
(2) $Q\ (a\ b) \cdot Q\ (b\ c) \rightarrow Q\ (a\ Q\ (b\ c))$.

"*Q (a (b c))*" can be read as "*a* is qualified by both *b* and *c*" and "*Q(a Q (b c)*" as "*a* is qualified by *b*, and *b* in its turn is qualified by *c*."

1.5 Qualifier versus Predicate-Property

A qualifier and a predicate-property may not always be the same, such that we can say that there is only a terminological variation. In fact, an Indianist would like to say that not all predicate-properties are qualifiers nor are all qualifiers predicate-properties. This is not simply because in an expression such as "there lies the blue pot" the qualifier, which is the blue pot, would probably not be called a predicate-property. Even if we concede this, still, in a given situation, a predicate-property, that is, what the Indianist would call a *vidheya-dharma*, may not be the same as the qualifier property (*viśeṣaṇa*). Let me illustrate this point. Suppose I wish to infer a property, *s*, as belonging to a given locus, *p*. Naturally the inferable, for example, the to-be-inferred property (*sādhya*), would be the *vidheya-dharma*, for example, the predicate-property. According to our basic intuition, the subject is what is being talked about and the predicate is what is being talked about it. Sometimes, it has been said to be a distinction between *that* and *what*. Consider now the following two "propositionally equivalent" verbalized expressions, representing two numerically different knowledge-episodes:

(a) Sound (noise) is impermanent (that is, impermanence-possessing).

(b) Impermanence resides in sound (noise).

The qualifier in the first is impermanence, while in the second, it is residence-in-sound. The qualificand in (a) is sound but in (b) impermanence is the qualificand. Thus, the qualifier-qualificand distinction is always related to the structure of some knowledge-episode or qualificative cognition. However both (a) and (b) can alternatively be reached as inferred conclusions, for example, as the resulting knowledge-episodes of a process of inference. In either case, the to-be-inferred property, that is, the predicate-property, remains the same, impermanence. For, it does not matter whether (a) is reached or derived from the knowledge-episode (premise), "sound has product-hood which is pervaded by impermanence" or (b) is reached from "Product-hood which is pervaded by impermanence resides in sound;" in either case, it cannot be denied that impermanence is the property we wish to establish by the inference. This may lead one to believe that the qualifier-qualificand distinction is perhaps closer to a subject-predicate distinction conceived as based upon a grammatical criterion (confer Strawson, 1974), though even this could be misleading.

1.6 A SKELETAL THEORY OF INFERENCE

The last point in §1.5 may appear a bit enigmatic unless we give an account of a skeletal theory of inference in the context of Indian logic. This skeletal theory seems to be presupposed, consciously or unconsciously, in all the representations of inference-patterns in India, although it became more explicitly formulated somewhat later in the history. I shall present it as a theory of substitution, where one property, by virtue of its logical relation with another property, forces the substitution of the latter in its place. That is (taking "*p*" to stand for the locus or *pakṣa* of the inference, "*h*" for the reason-property or *hetu*, and "*s*" for the to-be-inferred property or *sādhya*:

(1) There is *h*-pervaded-by-*s* in *p*

leads to:

(2) There is *s* in *p*.

Alternatively,

(3) *p* has *h* pervaded-by-*s*

leads to:

(4) *p* has *s*.

In an historically earlier version, found in the *Nyāya-sūtra* and other contemporaneous texts, this was formulated as:

(5) There is *h*-connected-with-*s* in *p*

leads to:

(6) There is *s* in *p*.

The spelling out of "connected-with-. . . . " in terms of "pervaded-by. . . . " was how progress in the history of Indian logic was achieved, among other things. We will have occasion to come back to the various ways in which the phrase "connected-with-. . . . " as well as "pervaded-by. . . . " were expanded.

To add flesh to this skeleton, I give an example:

(7) Sound has product-hood-connected-with-impermanence

leads to:

(8) Sound has impermanence.

This is an elaboration, presumably with minimized distortion, of the following:

(9) Sound has impermanence, because of its product-hood.

As we have seen in §1.3, (9) has generally been transformed, by almost all modern interpretaters, into a proto-Barbara:

All products are impermanent.
Sound is a product.
Therefore, Sound is impermanent.

Or, sometimes, it is rendered as:

Whatever is a product is impermanent.
Sound is a product.
Therefore, Sound is impermanent.

This is equivalent in structure to the schema *A* in §1.3. Our "substitution" model, however, follows more closely the actual analysis offered by the Indian logicians. With this skeletal model before us, we can now look more closely at the qualificand-qualifier distinction and its relation to the subject-predicate distinction.

1.7 MASS TERMS

The Sanskrit logicians tried to explain the structure of the "atomic" qualificative knowledge with a model that I have earlier called the "property-location" model. This, in some respect, resembles what Strawson (1959) has described as a "feature-placing" language. In a "feature-placing" language, Strawson notes, the subject-predicate distinction has no place. The model sentence would be something like "ϕ is here" or "there is ϕ here now." One advantage here is that this language gives place-and-time-identifying expressions the status of what are called logical subject-expressions, and spatial and temporal regions take the place of ordinary particulars. There are serious limitations of such a language, as have been discussed by Strawson, although he has pointed out that, in a feature-placing language, "we can find the ultimate propositional level we are seeking (Strawson, 1959: 209)." In the above, we have seen that the Sanskrit logicians concentrated upon a structure of knowledge-episodes that is akin to this form, for the locus, *p*, can be (in fact, has been) interpreted as a spatio-temporal location, where the to-be-inferred property, *s*, is to be located. In one formulation (see Diṅnāga's texts) the word "*atra*" is explicitly used. This means "here" or even "here/now," if the understood verbal element ("*asti*") is in the present tense.

W. V. Quine, while he was discussing the category of "mass terms" (a phrase coined by Otto Jesperson), which resemble the "feature-universals" of Strawson, remarked that these mass terms represent a primitive, archaic survival of a level of thought, the one developmentally where the baby has not apparently learned to identify particulars. Of course, the assumption involving baby-psychology is open to question. However, the point is that our adult language retains a considerable number of *mass* terms. Moreover, the category of mass terms has been the "problem child" of quantification theory, for the referents of these terms do not easily yield to individuation and hence we cannot quantify over them.

The problem of fitting mass terms to quantification, or "feature-words" to sortals, is a genuine one. Quine's proposal has particularly been under attack, for example by T. Parsons (1970), R. Sharvey (1978, 1979), and Helen Cartwright (1970). J. van Heijinoort (1974) has argued that the grammar of the mass-term is "far from being a negligible side-show" (p. 264), for "stuff-talk is an important part of our language, parallel to object talk" (p. 265). It has been noted that in modern physics there has been "the true systematization of stuff-ontology" (p. 266). It has further been noted that abstract terms are also "much-terms," that is, the grammar of abstract terms, such as prettiness and courage, is similar to the grammar of mass terms. Sometimes it has been facetiously remarked that English may not have real "count names" (Sharvey). A. N. Prior once suggested (1976: 183) that "possibly all things are, or can be said to be made of stuff."

Our stuff-talk can be connected with property-talk, for there seems to be an obvious connection between stuff-ontology and property-ontology. Suppose by "property" we mean non-universal, abstract features, or even tropes, for example, the property of being a swimmer or the ability to swim. This will be a non-universal, if we believe, as we probably should, that this ability to swim varies from person to person, for there may not be a single objective property that we can talk about here. This will then be a perfect example of what the Nyāya call an "imposed" property or *upādhi*. The use of the same expression "ability to swim" would then be like the use of the term "water" for water found in different spatio-temporal locations, as the river-water now is different from the water in this glass.

Consider a thought experiment. We may mentally integrate the individually located water stuff in this world into a spatially integrated whole. "Water" then becomes a singular term referring to this whole, which has a spatio-temporal spread. Then to talk about the water in this glass we can delimit the stuff by its spatio-temporal location. We can likewise conceptually integrate all the different abilities to swim that are found in various agents into a "conceptual spread," and to talk about John's ability to swim, we can delimit this abstract feature, the ability to swim, by its spatio-temporal location, in this case, John.

The purpose of this exercise has been to show that the problem of individuation of a stuff like water is similar to that of an abstract feature, or a non-universal property. Thus, consider:

(1) The water in this glass is cold, and

(2) John's ability to swim is poor (from: John is a poor swimmer).

The Sanskrit logicians would see them as equivalent to the following analyses:

(3) Water, which is characterized by being a locatee, where such locatee-hood is conditioned by a location-hood resident in the glass, has coldness (or is cold-ness possessing).

(4) The ability to swim is characterized by being a locatee, where such locatee-hood is conditioned by a location-hood resident in John, has the quality of being poor.

In both cases, we have to add also that the locatee-hood is delimited by the present time. This can be further sharpened to take care of other well-known indexicals.

1.8 PROPERTY: LOCUS AND LOCATEE

I have been suggesting that a "property-location" model best suits the arguments and inference-patterns studied in Sanskrit. What is this model? As we have noted, to some extent it appears to be similar to the imaginary language called the "language without particulars," or "feature-placing" language, which was described by Strawson (1959). He has also pointed out the limitations of such a language. The Sanskrit logicians' language is not exactly the same, there being important differences which will be noted presently. It is not clear, however, whether, in virtue of these differences, the language studied and developed by the Sanskrit logicians would overcome the alleged difficulties faced by feature-placing languages.

First, a terminological problem: using the word "property" as a translation of the Sanskrit word "*dharma*" has rather unfortunate consequences, for the word "*dharma*" has a wider extension than the word "property," and also has many non-logical connotations. But the situation need not be regarded as hopeless. "*Dharma*" sometimes means not only abstract properties or universals but also concrete features, that is, the particular features of some object or locus. "*Dharma*" and "*dharmin*" constitute a pair in Sanskrit that is equivalent to the pair "locatee" (or the locatable) and "locus" (location, which may be a place or a time or even an abstract object). What Strawson called a "feature" would be a locatee on this view.

A particular property is not a "property-particular," but a locatee (or a locatable) can be a particular in the sense of being a unique characteristic of a singular locus: for example, sky-hood belonging to the sky, and the sky only. The particular feature of a person would be her unique *dharma* or a locatee of which she is the locus. However, *dharmas* in Sanskrit include not only qualities like color and shape, attributes like the motion of a moving body, abstract universals like pot-hood or cow-hood, but also the concrete substantial masses like the particular body of water or fire, or even such concrete objects like a post or a rock!

It is the last two groups of *dharma* or locatee that would call for some explanation. It would be very difficult to call them "properties," if we followed the conventions of the English language. That is why I have chosen terms like "locatee" or "the locatable." Consider the following sentences:

(1) There is black ice on the road.

(2) There is fire on the hill.

(3) There is a pot on the ground.

These three would be transformationally equivalent to:

(4) The road has black-ice on it, or, the road is black-ice-possessing.

(5) The hill is fire-possessing.

(6) The ground is pot-possessing.

The expressions (4)–(6) clearly underscore the locus-locatee model by combining two particulars, if we rephrase them as:

(7) Some black-ice is located on the road.

(8) Some (body of) fire is on the hill.

(9) Some (indefinite) pot is on the ground.

Here the left-hand side gives the locatees and the right hand side the loci. This is not a language without particulars, rather a language with particulars only, the universal element being implicitly present only in the relational factor—the combiner of locus and locatee. The Sanskrit linguistic intuition would allow us to call the three elements, black-ice, fire, and a pot, *dharmas* of their respective loci (*dharmins*). But we cannot call them properties, according to the ordinary linguistic intuition of English. For it is counter-intuitive to call a pot a property of the ground on which it is present. Let us see why.

The logical language in Sanskrit was obviously influenced by the grammatical analysis of the Sanskrit language. This is a thesis which scholars like Staal and Faddegon formulated, though they never cited any cogent argument in its favor. Certain grammatical operations are particularly relevant here: namely, use of the location suffixes and the reciprocal use of the possessive suffixes. We can say, "There is a pot on the ground" (= *bhūtale ghaṭaḥ*), which is equivalent to "The ground (is) pot-possessing" (= *ghaṭavad bhūtalam*). This equivalence in Sanskrit is much like the equivalence between passive and active constructions in English. The expression "pot-possessing" is a bit odd, and sounds artificial in English due to the paucity of possessive suffixes in English. One may think of "health" and "healthy" or "wealth" and "wealthy," but these are rare. On the other hand, "*ghaṭavad*" (= pot-possessing) seems as common in Sanskrit as "sweet" or "blue," or other such adjectival expressions.

A predicate expression, in the canonical notation of Quine, is syntactically akin to a verb since it combines the double function of specifying a general concept and a propositional combination. If a predicate expression is taken to be a sortal, then it is syntactically akin to a common noun. The nominal "man" or "pot" specifies a general concept that supplies the principle of individuating the particulars it collects. Analogically, we may speak of the predicate expressions of the Sanskrit logicians as syntactically akin to the adjectivals. Adjectives are usually found without articles or plurals, although there are certain clear cases of adjectives that specify sortal universals, or to use Quine's term, terms which "divide their reference", for example the term "spherical."

Adjectives and mass terms (feature-words) share some grammatical properties. However the received opinion has been that we will be better off by assimilating the adjectives into general terms, whose paradigms are sortal-terms. The grammar of our adult language provides us with the mechanism of deriving an abstract property from each adjectival. This is as much true of a natural language like Sanskrit as it is of English and Latin. Thanks to the predominance of "have" verbs in English or Latin, use of abstract singular terms derived from adjectives or nouns does not sound odd in such languages. Thus "*a* is *f*" or "this mango is sweet" can be easily rephrased as "*a* has *f*-ness" or "this mango has sweetness." In Sanskrit the "have" verb is usually missing, but the use of genitive and locative suffices makes a smooth transition from the adjectival to the abstract singulars possible, for example:

(10) *paṭo nīlaḥ* (= The cloth (is) blue)

(11) *paṭasya nīlimā (asti)* (= The blue color *of* the cloth is there)

(12) *paṭe nīlam (asti)* (= There is blue color *in* the cloth).

Although these are equivalent, (11) seems to particularize the general concept "blue color," that is, the locatee.

The most common form of the substantive suffix in Sanskrit is *-tva* or *-tā* (comparable to English "-ness" or "-hood"). This mechanism of substantivization turns both adjectivals and nominals into words expressing the so-called abstract locatables. And a locatee-word can easily be turned into an adjectival by the use of possessive suffixes, *-vat*, *-mat* and *-in*. Sanskrit logicians use this double mechanism of substantivizing and possessive suffixes to assimilate the usual subject-predicate sentences into their locus-locatee model. Thus:

(13) The mango is sweet

becomes

(14) The mango is sweetness-possessing.

Remember the maneuver from (4)–(6) to (7)–(9). Can we do the same maneuver in (14)? (14) would then be:

(15) (There is) sweetness-possessing-ness in the mango,

or

(16) (There is) sweetness in the mango.

We are back to the locus-locatee model, where here the locus = the mango, and the locatee = sweetness-possessing-ness = sweetness. So far very few would object to the equation—sweet-ness-possessing-ness = sweetness. Can we generalize it? Can we say:

(17) *x*-possessing-ness = *x*?

Sanskrit logicians argue that the two operations—use of possessive suffix and substantivization—are reciprocal to each other. Hence,

(18) $x + vat + tva = x$,

(*tadvattvaṃ tad eva*). If we accept this, then we have to allow such equations as:

(19) Fire-possessing-ness = fire.

(20) Pot-possessing-ness = pot or (a pot?).

This means that as locatees or *dharmas*, it does not make a difference whether we say "fire-possessing-ness" or "fire." On the other hand, ontological worries not withstanding, one may call pot-possessing-ness a property of the ground, but not "pot" or a pot. But as locatees, *dharmas*, there is not much difference! That is, at least, the claim by the Sanskrit logicians. The Sanskrit grammarians who discuss the meaning of the suffixes such as *-tva* and *-vat*, would support such conversions.

The oddity of this claim must be explained further. The expression "pot-possessing" is an adjectival or what Strawson calls a *g*-word. Hence it is on a par with "sweetness-possessing." We may accept "sweetness-possessing-ness" as being conveniently abbreviated as, or equated to, "sweetness," for both denote in some sense, abstract properties. But (19) and (20) do not seem to be acceptable equations because not only is a pot or fire a "concrete" object (as in "a pot is blue" or "fire burns") but even their predicative use ("This is a pot" or "This is fire") introduces a sortal universal, a concept, that applies to an object that the subject term is supposed to identify. The proposal of the Sanskrit logicians seems to be one for a third use of such terms, distinct from "pot" in the subject place or the predicate place. The word in (20) introduces a locatee—a non-particular *potty* feature of some locus. The word "fire" in (19) then introduces a locatee—a fiery feature, or fire-presence. We may recall here that Quine has remarked that the feature-words or the mass terms have the "hybrid air of abstract singular terms." We may substitute "genuine" for "hybrid," for a locatee such as fire may be a quasi-abstract entity. The word "pot" in (20) may then be regarded as indicating a *potty* substance or pot-presence, to bring it closer to fire, a feature as in (19).

We have thus clarified what the Sanskrit logicians meant by *dharma* and *dharmin*, the locatee and the locus. We may translate *dharma* as "property" only out of politeness. But to do justice to such cases as (19) and (20), we may use "locatee" or "the locatable." This category of the locatee seems to include not only general attributes, but also abstract and quasi-abstract entities. If the expression "pot" seems awkward we may make it "pot-presence." In fact, what I shall call (in chapter 7) the presence-range and absence-range of such locatees or *dharmas* would be more useful in the formulation of the rules of inference in this language.

CHAPTER 2

Debates and Directives

2.1 Origins

The Sanskrit word for discussion or debate is *kathā* or *vāda*. There was a long and time-honored tradition in ancient India according to which philosophers, thinkers, or religious teachers used to meet each other in order to debate a controversial issue, about which the two sides held opposite views. In this respect, the situation in India resembled to some extent the Greek situation during the time of Socrates, Plato, and Aristotle. One need not belabor this point of resemblance, for perhaps it was just a historical accident, and we must remember, too, that the subject matter for debate in India differed considerably from that in Greece. While the Greeks were primarily interested in moral and political issues, the Indian interest lay in such metaphysical questions as the distinction of the soul from the body, in the purpose of life and concern for the after-life, and only consequently also in moral issues.

As early as the *Bṛhadāraṇyaka Upsaniṣad* (Chapter IV, *Brāhmaṇa* I), a pre-Buddhist text, it is reported that the philosopher King Janaka used not only to patronize debates between the sages and priests but also to participate in such debates. Women debaters, and by the same token women scholars and philosophers, were not unheard of at that time. It was Gārgī, the woman scholar in Janaka's court, who debated with a certain Yājñavalkya, along with many others, and finally declared the latter to be the best among those scholars of Kurū and Pāñcāla who had assembled in Janaka's court on the occasion in question. Yājñvalkya, it seems, used to come to Janaka's court frequently. On one occasion, Janaka challenged Yājñavalkya with the question: "What is on your mind Yājñavalkya today? Do you want cattle as a gift? Or do you wish to participate in a philosophical discussion about subtle truths?" Yājñavalkya replied, "Both!"

Although debate was popular at the time of the Upaniṣads, we still did not have a theory of the structure and variety of debate. This came along later, in the *śramaṇa* period, with the rise of the Buddha, the Mahāvīra Jina, and other ascetics or religious reformers (*śramaṇas)*. Gradually "good" debates were separated from "bad" ones, much as the notion of a good argument from that of a wrong or an unacceptable one. By the third and second century BC, monks and priests were required to have a training in the art of conducting a successful debate. Several debate manuals were written in different sectarian schools. Instructions for learning the method of debate were also inserted, as separate chapters, in large texts within different schools. Unfortunately, the early debate manuals are not extant in Sanskrit. Part of the picture can be recovered from the Buddhist Chinese sources (see Tucci, 1929a, 1929b) as well as from Pali sources like the *Kathāvatthu*. The *Kathāvatthu*, though written much later, is supposed to be a report of the Buddhist Council, supposedly held around 255 BC but according to the latest research, perhaps as much as one hundred years later. It records various topics for debate which a Buddhist monk may undertake, as well as various types of argument. It also discusses how they are resolved.

In this text we find examples of actual debate, how they were conducted and the strictly defined rules that guided them. From an analysis of such actual cases of debates, we can discover the underlying logical theory on which they were based. It is, therefore, worthwhile dealing with the theory and structure of a debate as it was presented in this and other standard texts. Apart from the *Kathāvatthu* (discussed in §2.3), I will follow mainly the *Caraka-saṃhitā* (§2.4, 2.5) and the *Nyāya-sūtra* (§2.7, 2.8), for there the topic is presented very systematically, and also, fortunately, they have been preserved for us. I will also examine briefly the discussions of debate in Jaina texts (§2.6).

2.2 DEBATE: A PREFERRED FORM OF RATIONALITY

A passage from the *Milinda-pañho* (1962, 2.6), which relates a conversation between the Greek king Menander and the Buddhist monk Nāgasena, is worth quoting in this connection (Menander, incidentally, is supposed to have ruled over the Punjab and the adjoining areas of what used to be called the Indus Valley). At the invitation to debate with the king, the monk Nāgasena supposedly said that he would debate with the king with the proviso that it was a debate for the wise, and not a debate for the king. On being asked to specify this distinction further, Nāgasena said:

> When scholars debate, your Majesty, there is summing up and unravelling of a theory, convincing and conceding, there is also defeat,

> and yet the scholars do not get angry at all.
>
> When the Kings debate, your Majesty, they state their thesis, and if anyone differs from them, they order him punished, saying "Inflict punishment upon him."

Despite the touch of levity, reminiscent of the Queen of Heart's "Off with her head!" in Lewis Carroll's *Alice in Wonderland*, it is significant to note what these lines reveal to us. They reveal a world where scholars used to enter into a debate that was controlled by strictly defined rules and where defeat or victory was decided, and such a decision was reached on the basis of the well-defined principles of argument. J. Bochenski, in his *History of Formal Logic*, commented that the situation was "not unlike that which we meet in Plato" (1961: 421). One may have reservations about this urge to note similarities with the Greek situation, but it is useful to record in detail the rules and categories that define the parameters of the ancient Indian debates, because of the contributions they made to the development of logical thinking in India. Human rationality may not be globally definable, for it takes a contextual character in different traditions, as well as in different contexts of other types. But there seems to be a universal trait that we recognize (even if we are unable to articulate it) in different rational arguments and decisions. By virtue of this trait, we are able to recognize a rational argument as rational. Some say today that, even if rationality is "marginally context-neutral," it is philosophically more interesting to see how far and to what extent it is context-dependent or whether it is totally so. However, though the context-dependence of certain basic ideas such as rationality is worth exploring, their context-transcendent character is equally so. We might end up in a narrow relativistic view of the world, if we ignore completely the context-transcendent aspect of such basic ideas.

Rationality can be used or abused. Clever and disputatious persons can always try to win a debate using clever tricks thereby confounding the audience and the opponent. All debate manuals in India provided an elaborate list of such tricks, to help the programme of training the novices so that they would be able to identify and rebut such tricky arguments when advanced by their opponents. In this way a theory of logical adequacy or acceptability was developed in order to separate the tricky arguments from the good ones.

2.3 DEBATE IN THE BUDDHIST CANONS

There were strictly formulated debates and controlled deductions in the early Buddhist canonical literature, the *Abhidhamma*. The *Abhidhamma* is a later elaboration of Buddhist philosophy out of the *Matika*, "matrix of the system" propounded in broad outlines in the *Nikāyas*. Our concern here is with one particular text, the *Kathāvatthu*, which belongs probably to the second century BC. It takes up more than two hundred disputed points and then argues each in turn, following a structured form of debate. The general procedure is this. The opponent is made to state a thesis, and it is then refuted by the Theravādin Buddhist, the proponent, following the logical rules of implication. The entire debate is rather prolonged and cumbersome, being divided into a primary debate and a varying number of secondary discussions, that simply check the meanings of the terms used in the original debate.

The primary debate, called *vādayutti,* consists of eight refutations, in fact four pairs, each pair being divided into an affirmation and a negation. Thus, the primary debate is called *aṭṭhamukha* "having eight openings." Of the four pairs, the first forms a complete debate. The other three pairs are deviations of the first, derived by the addition of three such logical expressions as "everywhere," "always," and "in everything." Thus, (1) "Is *a b*?" is qualified as

(2) "Is *a b* everywhere?"

(3) "Is *a b* always?"

or

(4) "Is *a b* in everything?"

It is significant to note that there was here an early awareness of what counted as a logical expression: "everywhere," "always," and "in everything." Obviously, the options were secondary, being applied where appropriate. They introduced universality and omnitemporality in the proposition under consideration.

The debate used to be conducted in question-and-answer form. The question is asked: "Is *a b* ?", and the answer is given, either "yes" or "no." If the answer is "yes," it is asserted that *a* is *b*, or we may say that the statement "*a* is *b*" has truth value True. And if it is "no," then it is denied that *a* is *b*, or, we will say, "*a* is *b*" has truth value False. The structure of each debate is divided into pentads (*pañcaka*) and tetrads (*catukka*), one having five steps and the other four steps. However this distinction is arbitrary, for both use the same principle of reasoning. The idea is first to obtain one truth (one "yes") and one falsity (one "no") by question and answer, and then formulate a conditional: If *p* then *q*. At the next stage, it is shown inconsistent to hold the antecedent true and the consequent false, and then the conclusion is stated as the refutation of the consequent implying the refutation of the antecedent, which was the original thesis, "*a* is *b*," which the other side started with. Thus, formally the debate would be won by refutation. This applies indiscriminately to both the proponent and the opponent. The conditional is formed by substituting the predicate-term in "*a* is *b*" by its true synonyms or by equivocation (or by quibbling or by sophistry) or by something implied by it. Thus, it is obvious that, when the opponent to the Theravādin formulates a conditional by equivocation, he still wins, for the formal validity of his argument is not impaired thereby. Those modern scholars who have remarked that the notion of formal validity did not at all enter into the minds of ancient Indian logicians, should ponder over this point. Strictly defined rules guided the discussion, and hence to win the Theravādin had to expose the equivocation or other tricks used by the opponent. I shall illustrate the point below.

Two disputants start a debate and in two stages they interchange their positions, one asking questions while the other answering. The first stage is called *anuloma* "the way forward," while the second is called *pratiloma* "the way back." He who asks a question first sums up the argument by refuting the other. Here is an example from *Kathāvatthu*:

I. *The Way Forward (anuloma)*
Theravādin: Is the soul known as a real and ultimate fact?
Puggalavādin: Yes.
Theravādin: Is the soul known in the same way as a real and ultimate fact is known?
Puggalavādin: No, that cannot be truly said.
Theravādin: Acknowledge your refutation:

(1) If the soul be known as a real and ultimate fact, then indeed, good sir, you should also say, the soul is known in the same way as any other real and ultimate is known.
(2) That which you say here is false, namely, (a) that we s*hould say*, "the soul is known as a real and ultimate fact," but (b) *we should not say*, "the soul is known in the same way as any other real and ultimate fact is known."
(3) If the later statement (b) cannot be admitted, then indeed the former statement (a) should not be admitted either.
(4) In affirming the former (a), while
(5) denying the latter (b), you are wrong.

II. *The Way Back (pratiloma)*
Puggalavādin: Is the soul not known as a real and ultimate fact?
Theravādin: No, it is not known.

Puggalavādin: Is it not known in the same way as any real and ultimate fact is known?
Theravādin: No, that cannot be truly said.
Puggalavādin: Acknowledge the rejoinder:

(1) If the soul is not known as a real and ultimate fact, then indeed, good sir, you should also say: it is not known in the same way as any other real and ultimate fact is known.
(2) That which you say is false, namely, that (a) we *should say* "the soul is not known as a real and ultimate fact," and (b) we *should not say* "it is not known in the same way as any other real and ultimate fact is known."
(3) If the latter statement (b) cannot be admitted, then indeed the former statement (a) should not be admitted either.
(4) In affirming (b) while
(5) denying (a), you are wrong.

The logic on which the summing up is based is virtually the same in either case. Hence both are credited with formal validity. Both are exploiting a well-known definition of implication, according to which "if *p* then *q*" means "not both *p* and not *q*." It is true, of course, that the propositions or terms are not represented here by symbolic letters, *p*, *q*, and so on. However, the stoic logicians, we may note in this connection, did not use such symbolism, although Aristotle did. The stoics identified the propositions by referring to them by "*the first*" "*the second*" (see Kneale and Kneale, 1964: 159). A similar procedure is followed here. There is another noteworthy point (due to A. K. Warder). Two expressions in Māgadhī forms, *vattabbe* and *no ca vattabbe* ("should be said" and "should not be said"), are invariably used, and they take the place of modern brackets around the sentence or proposition which follows.

For our purpose, we may transcribe the argument as follows:

I. *The Way Forward*
(1) If *A* is *B*, then *A* is *C*;
–therefore—
(2) not both: (*A* is *B*) and not (*A* is *C*);
–therefore–
(3) if not (*A* is *C*), then not (*A* is *B*).

II. *The Way Back*
(1) If *A* is not *B*, then *A* is not *C*;
—therefore—
(2) not both: (*A* is not *B*) and not (*A* is not *C*);
—therefore—
(3) if not (*A* is not *C*), then not (*A* is not *B*).

This is how the argument was represented first by S. Z. Aung in the *Prefatory Notes*, to the *Kathāvatthu* (Aung, 1915: xlviii-l). I. Bochenski (1961) gave an improved version of the same.

Note that the argument thus formulated is term-logical, that is, the variables ("*A*," "*B*," and so on) range over terms not propositions. St. Schayer (1933), and following him A. K. Warder (1963; 1971), thought, however, that there had been "anticipations of propositional logic" in the *Kathāvatthu*, for one could represent the arguments as substitution instances of the following *propositional* schemata:

I. *The Way Forward*
(1) If *p*, then *q*;
—therefore—
(2) not: *p* and not *q*;
—therefore—
(3) if not *q*, then not *p*.

II. *The Way Back*
(1) If not *p*, then not *q*
—therefore—
(2) not: not *p* and not not *q*
—therefore—
(3) if *q*, then *p*.

What are the structures of the schemata, so represented? We might be tempted to take the last two steps as together constituting a *modus tollendo tollens* ("if *p* then *q*, and, not *q*; therefore, not *p*"). In such a formulation, the conclusion, "not *p*," is reached from two premises, "if *p* then *q*" and "not *q*." This is inaccurate, however. What we really have is a conditional, stated in step (1), with the meaning of the conditional is defined in step (2), while the last step, step (3), is reached by the implicit use of the law of contraposition. If the conditional (1) is understood as (2) then the contraposed version, (3), follows. The conclusion, "not *p*," is then reached, not by *modus tollens*, but by *modus ponens* ("if not *q*, then not *p*, and, not *q*; therefore not *p*").

Bochenski disputes Schayer's claim about there being "anticipations of propositional logic" by the disputants in *Kathāvattu*. It is true that the term-logical versions given above fit well the Indian formulations, as Aung and Bochenski contend. Since in most cases substitution of terms are called for, one would be happy with the term-logical versions. However, the principle of inference that is involved here, contraposition and *modus ponens*, seems to be neutral on the issue. It is of course easy to follow the underlying arguments most of the time, especially if they are put into their propositional versions.

2.4 GOOD VERSUS BAD DEBATE IN CARAKA

Socrates (*Meno* 7.5 c–d) referred to the debate by "the clever, disputatious and quarrelsome" person, which he denounced, and contrasted it with the debate by "friendly people," which was by far preferable. There seems to be an echo of this Socratic wisdom in Caraka's (circa 100 AD) two-fold classification of philosophical debate in the *Caraka-saṃhitā* (III.8.27 ff.). The first kind is called by Caraka *sandhāya sambhāṣa*, "amicable debate" or discussion which used to be held between fellow scholars who were friends. The second kind is called *vigṛhya sambhāṣa*, a "hostile debate" which used to be held between disputatious philosophers. This was not very different from a verbal wrangling. The former was in a spirit of "co-operation" (confer *sandhāya*) while the latter was in a spirit of opposition (compare *vigṛhya*).

The "amicable" debate should be held, according to Caraka, with a person who is learned, and endowed with admirable qualities, such as modesty, generosity, power to speak clearly and convincingly, and lack of selfishness or self-glorification. One need not be afraid of defeat in such a debate for one may learn the truth about the subject matter under discussion. Besides, in such a debate, if one defeats the other, one need not take pride or feel overjoyed. One should not speak ill of the other, nor should one stupidly stick to a view which is decidedly one-sided (*ekānta*). In such a debate one should not speak about something one does not know well. And above all, one should respect the opponent.

The "hostile" debate is however very different. One may indulge in it, says Caraka, provided one can gain something or further one's cause. But before one enters into such a debate, one should carefully examine the good and bad points of the opponent as well as one's own. The good points of a debater are learning, knowledge, memory, talent or imaginative power, and power to deliver a speech. The bad points are anger, lack of equanimity, fear, lack of memory, and inattention. Caraka warns that these good and bad points of the proponent, as well as of the opponent, should be carefully weighed before one commits oneself to debate in the hostile manner.

Not only the attributes of the opponent but also of the assembly before which this debate will take place must be examined carefully. Opponents, says Caraka, are of three kinds: one of superior intelligence, one of inferior intelligence and one of equal intelligence—equal, that is, with the debater. The assembly is usually of two kinds: an intelligent assembly and one that is not so. The assembly, from another point of view, can be divided into three kinds: friendly, hostile, and indifferent. Caraka says that, faced with a hostile assembly, even if it consists of people who are learned, knowledgeable, and intelligent, one should not enter into a "hostile" debate. The same is true of a hostile assembly comprised of unintelligent or stupid (*mūḍha*) people.

However, if the assembly is friendly or even indifferent, and at the same time unintelligent, then one may enter into a "hostile" debate with an opponent who is not famous and not liked by great people. Such an opponent can be defeated even without much skill in the art of the question-and-answer process in a debate. In other words, the debater may use different tricks, physical and verbal, to carry the assembly with him and declare that the opponent is defeated because he lacks both knowledge and practice.

According to some, one may debate in a hostile manner with an opponent of superior intelligence. But the considered advice, according to Caraka, is not to enter into such a debate with a person of superior intelligence. With the inferior or the equal, one may debate before a friendly assembly. In an indifferent, but intelligent (and learned), assembly, the debater should carefully examine the merits and shortcomings of the opponent, and then, avoiding the areas where the knowledge of the opponent is deemed superior, he should quickly move to the area where the opponent lacks knowledge or expertise and defeat him there. After stating this strategy, Caraka lists some of the ways by which an "inferior" opponent can be vanquished. For example, if the opponent lacks learning, he can be defeated by the utterance of a long quotation from a well-known text; if he lacks knowledge, then by uttering sentences with difficult words in them; if he lacks talent, then by means of words with multiple meaning; if he is afraid or nervous, then by frightening him further, and so on.

All this may not be thought to have much to do with logic as such, but, as the history of logical thinking in India is partly to be traced in the history of the debate tradition, we can see some relevance here. Caraka's classification of debate generates fourteen varieties in all, which can be summarized in Figure 2.1.

Having classified debate in the above manner, Caraka goes on to describe the categories or concepts that should be known by anybody entering into a debate. This list is rather elaborate (consisting of 44 items) and not very systematically ordered. It includes such concepts as that of the "defeat situation" or clincher of the issue in a debate, which is called a *nigrahasthāna,* and along with it several of its sub-varieties as well. A more systematic account of the categories related to the concept of debate is to be found in the *Nyāyasūtras* (circa 150 AD), which appears to be a crystallized version of what we find in Caraka. This, however, may or may not settle the problem of chronological priority between the two texts in favor of Caraka. For, although most of the terms are the same, and their descriptions similar, Caraka's *Caraka-saṃhitā*, being primarily a medical text, might have recorded an earlier stratum in the development of the "science of debate" (*vivāda-śāstra*). I shall discuss only what is relevant for our purpose from the *Caraka-saṃhitā*, and then go into the discussion of the *Nyāyasūtra*.

FIGURE 2.1
CARAKA'S CLASSIFICATION OF DEBATE

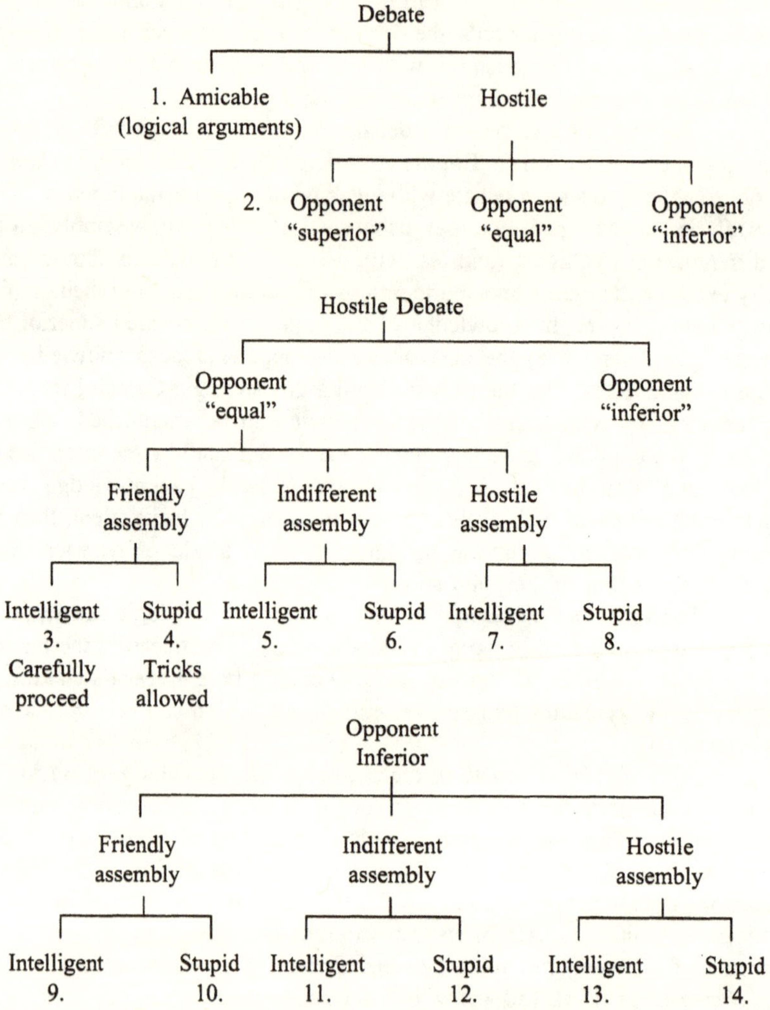

The "hostile" debate, which has been subdivided into thirteen or fourteen types above, is taken up again by Caraka, who now divides it into two main types, *jalpa* and *vitaṇḍā*. As these two terms are too technical to be straight-forwardly translated into English, I shall call the first the "j-type" hostile debate and the second the "v-type" hostile debate. The *Nyāyasūtra* also uses the same two terms, and Caraka's characterization of these two agrees with that of the *Nyāyasūtra,* as we will see presently. For Caraka, the j-type is a debate where two theses are explicitly stated (such as one saying "There is after-life" while the other saying "There is no after-life"), and defended by citing reasons along with the refutation by each of the other with the help of some further independent reasons. The v-type is said to be a special variety of the j-type where only the refutation of the opponent is achieved, but no establishment of one's own position is attempted. The *Nyāyasūtra*, as we will see, gives a more refined definition of these two, systematically connecting them with other technical concepts, in terms of which the entire theory of debate has been articulated there.

2.5 CARAKA'S ACCOUNT OF GOOD DEBATE

Instead of giving an account of Caraka's rather long chapter on debate or *vāda-śāstra*, I shall select only what is more relevant for our purpose, that is, more significant as far as theories of logic are concerned. Thematization of the debate, as well as organization of various concepts and categories that both constitute and differentiate good debates from bad ones, is itself an indication of the advance made in intellectual horizons and of the sophistication reached in logical abstraction. It is significant to note that Caraka distinguishes between the statement or articulation of the thesis, that is, a (pro)position which is to be proved or established such as "the soul is eternal," and the establishment or proving of (1) that thesis with the help of (2) the reason, (3) an example, (4) showing the relevance of these two (reason and example) to the present thesis, and (5) re-stating the thesis now as a proven conclusion. In Caraka's terminology this is called *sthāpana*, its nearest analogue in the West, in the context of logic, would be "demonstration." The thesis is called the *pratijñā* (the same term is used in the *Nyāyasūtra*) and it is defined as the (verbal) statement of what is to be proven. The "demonstration" includes five articulated steps, called figuratively its "limbs" (*avayava*) in the *Nyāyasūtra*. Having thus distinguished "demonstration" from "articulation of the thesis," Caraka developed the concept of "counter-demonstration" (*prati-sthāpana*), which likewise includes five steps (the same five as in a demonstration), but now used to establish a contradictory thesis, such as "the soul is not eternal." The idea is that if proving "A is B" involves articulation of the five steps (which is very much like a proof-procedure in its primitive form), then disproving it would amount to repeating the procedure with the contradictory thesis "A is not B."

Caraka makes a significant comment in explaining the concept of "reason" as part of the demonstration. The "reason" is what causes the apprehension or recognition of the object or the fact to be proven. Thus, it is the evidence on the basis of which something, some truth, is recognized or "established as proven." This shows the ambiguity in the earlier writings of two terms *pramāṇa* and *hetu*. They were sometimes interchangeable. The former is, etymologically speaking, that by which something is *known*, while the latter is that by which something is established or demonstrated to be so. The means of establishing something to be so can also be a means for knowing something to be so. Hence the two may, on occasion, coincide. But gradually they came to be separated, as it was realized that the former is connected with epistemology, that is with evidence and the acquisition of knowledge, and hence has a broader role to play, while the later can be restricted to "logic," for example, to the context of an argument based upon an inference or of the "demonstration" of such an argument to convince the others. This separation, apparently reflecting an advance in logical studies, was partially realized in the *Nyāyasūtra*, where two interrelated categories, *pramāṇa* "means of knowledge" and *prameya* "objects of knowledge" (the knowables), were put at the top of a list of sixteen categories. The rest, for example, the fourteen other categories, were concerned exclusively with method, or philosophical methodology as it is sometimes called now-a-days. In fact in the *Nyāyasūtra*, there was a two-fold transformation: partial establishment of the *pramāṇa-vidyā*, the study of knowledge and its evidence-cum-instrument; and transformation of the early debate categories into a more pervasive and acceptable philosophical methodology. Diṅnāga took his cue from Akṣapāda, and while criticizing Vātsyāyana he established a full-fledged *śāstra* called *pramāṇa-śāstra*, the study of knowledge and its evidence-cum-instrument that was roughly equivalent to epistemology in the West. More on this later.

In a different place (*Sūtrasthāna*, chapter 11), Caraka says that all concepts can be divided into two, real and unreal, and there are four ways by which we can "examine" them: verbal testimony, perception, inference, and causal inquiry (*yukti*). This fourfold method of "examination" (*parīkṣā*) is endorsed in the context of establishing whether the concept of *ātman* or the self is real or unreal. Testimony is explained as the statements of reliable persons, those who are learned and devoid of any fault in their character. Perception is the cognition of the present, which arises out of a fourfold contact between the self, the mind, the senses, and the objects. Inference is preceded by perception and is related to any object, past, present, or future. Causal inquiry (*yukti*) is that cognition by which different causal factors leading to a particular effect, such as the harvest or building a fire, are determined.

In the same context, Caraka calls these four also "*pramāṇas*" (instruments of knowledge). The definition of perception is similar to that found in the *Vaiśeṣika-sūtra*. That of inference is reminiscent of *Nyāyasūtra* 1.1.5. The distinction between inference and *yukti* is not very clear. Caraka simply implies that knowledge of the causal factors is given by this instrument of *yukti* (induction?), so that people may produce the intended effect by bringing together (*yoga*) these relevant causal factors. It is significant to note that in the chapter on debate, when the instruments of knowledge are again listed, we have five: testimony, perception, inference, tradition, and analogy. Here *yukti* is conspicuous by its absence. Tradition is explained as the traditional authority or the scriptures, from which we derive knowledge. Analogy is self-explanatory. From a logical point of view, however, the examples of inference are the most interesting (compare Warder, 1971: 136–7).

2.6 THE ACCOUNT OF DEBATE IN THE JAINA CANONS

In Jaina canonical literature, we have not only a number of kinds of technical vocabulary connected with logic and debate but also an interesting classification of *hetu* or logical reason. The ambiguity of the term *hetu* is already foreshadowed in the *Sthānāṅga sūtra* 338 (circa 100 BC?). Here the term *hetu,* "reason," is used in three alternative senses, and in each sense it is classified into four types. First, it is identified as meaning the "reason" used by a debater. The four different types of "reason" in debate give us four different types of rejoinder:

(1) *Yāpaka* is a rejoinder (mostly an improper one) put forward to "kill time." The debater is trying to think of a proper answer but, as it takes time to find a good reason, he tries to stall the opponent with an improper rejoinder which the opponent will have to take some time to figure out.
(2) *Sthāpaka* is a proper rejoinder which establishes the position. The debater now hits upon the right reason, the right reply.
(3) *Vyaṃsaka* is quibbling in a debate. The debater does not know the right rejoinder and hence picks out a word in the thesis of the opponent and quibbles. "He has (a) new (= *nava*) book," says one. "He does not have *nava* (= nine) books, only one," says the other. Since the word *nava* is a homonym and may mean either "new" or "nine" depending upon the context, the debater starts quibbling.
(4) *Luṣaka* is a rejoinder where the debater "calls the bluff" of the opponent who is quibbling in the above manner.

Second, the term *hetu*, "reason," is used in the sense of being epistemic evidence by which the thesis may be established. This is again of four kinds: perception, inference, analogy, and testimony. Recall our previous reference to the early conflation of the notion of *pramāṇa* "evidence" with *hetu* "reason," which can be seen again here.

Third, the *hetu* "reason" may be classified in the following four formal ways:

(1) This is, because that is
(2) This is not, because that is
(3) This is, because that is not
(4) This is not, because that is not.

The above four forms of argument are given here in their exact translation from Prakrit. A point to note here is that "not" is consciously separated as a logical word, and four varieties are reached by the use of such a logical word either in the premise (evidence) or in the conclusion. In other words, a positive evidence (a presence) may yield a positive conclusion or even a negative conclusion. Similarly a negative evidence (absence of something) may yield a positive or a negative conclusion. We will see such patterns again in other texts. Another important point to note is that this is perhaps the first time such argument patterns are given using pronouns which are surrogates for modern variables. The argument pattern in India was usually given in terms of concrete examples, viz, "there is smoke, therefore there is fire" (the hackneyed example of the Indian logicians). This feature, which was nothing more than a stylistic device, had misled some Indologists and modern writers in Indian logic to surmise that the Indian logicians were not consciously aware of the underlying forms of the argument or their generalization in logic. They were, according to this view, concerned with particular examples and at most regarded them as types. Although the Indians did not use symbols, I believe it would be wrong to construe that they were unaware of the formal side or the concept of generalization in logic. The above is a counter-example to such a view, where variables, that is, pronouns, are consciously used.

2.7 *NYĀYASŪTRA*: THE METHOD OF GOOD DEBATE

There is a close affinity between Caraka's section on debate and the *Nyāyasūtra* version of the same. There are also certain post-canonical Buddhist debate-manuals available to us from the Chinese sources (see Tucci, 1929a, 1929b) which reflect similar theories and style. It is difficult to determine which are earlier strata and which are later. For not only is their authorship still in doubt but also it was the practice of the compilers to copy verbatim earlier fragments or texts. In any case, the *Nyāyasūtra* presents a more systematic and perhaps an improved version, and a discussion of it will be fruitful from the point of view of our study of logical theories.

The term for philosophical debate in the Nyāya school was *kathā* (literally "speech" or "discourse"). Vātsyāyana uses the term in the beginning of his commentary on *Nyāyasūtra* 1.2.1. The *Nyāyasūtra* mentions three kinds of debate: *vāda*, *jalpa,* and *vitaṇḍā*. Uddyotakara (Vātsyāyana's commentator) explains that this threefold classification is dependent upon the nature of the disputants. The first variety is between a proponent and his teacher or somebody with a similar status. The other two are between those who want victory. Thus by implication the goal of the first is establishment of truth or an accepted doctrine, that of the other two is victory. The first corresponds to Caraka's friendly or congenial debate, and the other two to his hostile debate.

Nyāyasūtra 1.2.1 states that *vāda*, the good or honest debate, is constituted by the following characteristics:

(1) Establishment (of the thesis) and refutation (of the counter-thesis) should be based upon adequate evidence or means for knowledge (*pramāṇa*) as well as upon (proper) "hypothetical" or "indirect" reasoning (*tarka*).
(2) The conclusion should not entail contradiction with any tenet or accepted doctrine (*siddhānta*).
(3) Each side should use the well-known five steps of the demonstration of an argument explicitly.
(4) They should clearly recognize a thesis to be defended and a counter thesis to be refuted.

The last characteristic is logically very interesting. For it led to the formulation of the rule for contradiction. Vātsyāyana explains that when the mutually-incompatible attributes are ascribed to an identical subject-locus, and they are ascribed with reference to the same point of time, and when neither of them are deemed certain or established, then and then only a contradiction arises. Uddyotakara illustrates the point of such a rule of contradiction by citing some examples *not* counter to it:

(1) "The soul is permanent and the cognitive event is impermanent." No contradiction, for permanence and impermanence are not attributed to the same subject-event.
(2) "This substance (a chariot) moves now, and it was not moving a little while ago." No contradiction, for motion and rest are not attributed to the substance at the same time.

The five-step argument-schema has already been referred to in §1.2, and in connection with Caraka. The second characteristic here ensures that well-known and accepted doctrines are not upset or rejected by this type of debate where we try to discover truth. The very first characteristic underlines the commitment of this type of debate to rational procedure. Both *pramāṇa* and *tarka* are technical terms elaborately explained elsewhere in the *Nyāya* system. Four well-known *pramāṇas* or means of knowledge are recognized there: Perception, Inference, Comparison, and Testimony.

Tarka, which I have tentatively translated as "indirect reasoning," has been rather ambiguously explained in *Nyāyasūtra* 1.1.40. From the elaborate comments of Vātsyāyana and Uddyotakara, it transpires, as I have explained elsewhere (Matilal 1986: 79), that it is a reasoning based only upon some *a priori* principle, or what comes closest in the Indian tradition to something *a priori.* For it is repeatedly warned by both the above authors that this reasoning cannot deliver a conclusion that would constitute a piece of empirical knowledge. In their technical vocabulary, the claim is that *tarka* is not a *pramāṇa*, but it lends essential support to a *pramāṇa*. Later logicians formulate the *tarka* as a *reductio*:

> If *A* were not *B* then *A* would not have been *C*. But it is *absurd* to conceive *A* as not-*C* (for it is *inconsistent* with our standard beliefs or rational activity). Hence, *A* is *B*.

Here we have the same interplay in the conditional as before: we deny the antecedent by denying the consequent. On the other hand, *tarka* had a close affinity also with the so-called *prasaṅga* type of argument which Nāgārjuna championed in the Buddhist parlance, and after which a sub-school of the Mādhyamika Buddhists, *Prāsaṅgika,* was named. The later Naiyāyikas, such as Udayana, used such arguments to lend support to the inductive generalization employed in the kind of inferential reasoning sketched in chapter 1. According to Udayana, a lingering and nagging doubt about the truth of a general statement can be set at rest with the help of such an hypothetical reasoning (see Bagchi, 1953).

One question arose in connection with this good debate (*vāda*). Since here no party is looking to humiliate the opponent, would there be any clincher or defeat-situation (*nigrahasthāna*)? We may recall, however, what Nāgasena told King Milinda: in a good debate there could be defeat or censure or clincher but no animosity. For a debate should technically always end in a clincher. The solution to this is easily given. *Nyāyasūtra* 5.2.32 informs us that in this type of debate the detection of faulty reason or pseudo-reason (*hetvābhāsa*) would be the proper clincher. Thus, faith in logical argument is re-asserted here. Nobody should win using a pseudo-reason.

Besides, technically two or three other clinchers or censures can be relevant in the *vāda* debate. Since it is required that the five-step argument be used, two kinds of censure may occur: (1) *hīna*, "insufficient," if less than five steps be used, and (2) *ādhika*, "redundant," if more than five steps were used. Uddyotakara says that even *apasiddhānta*, "accepting of a false tenet or doctrine," may arise in this debate as a clincher, for one of the four characteristics mentioned above emphasizes that there should not be any contradiction of an accepted tenet. The debater cannot without censure embrace any false doctrine. The Nyāya list of clinchers in debate will be further elaborated below and in §3.5.

We may note that, in the Buddhist tradition, Vasubandhu, in a manual for debate, defined the *vāda* debate as a discourse (*vacana*) which is conducted for the sake of establishing one's own thesis and refuting (disestablishing) the opponent's (contrary) thesis. Vasubandhu's text is not available to us. However, Uddyotakara (1915: 150–151) quotes him and tries to find fault with his definition in every possible way. Uddyotakara excels in such policies, although his discussion of this point is not philosophically interesting. Hence we will omit it here.

2.8 *Nyāyasūtra:* The Method of Bad Debate

Jalpa, the second type of debate, is defined in *Nyāyasūtra* 1.2.2 as a debate where, among the stated characteristics of the first type of debate, only such characteristics as would seem appropriate would be applicable, and in addition, the debater can use, for the establishment of his own position and for the refutation of the opponent's thesis, such means as (1) quibbling (*chala*), (2) illegitimate rejoinders (*jāti*) and (3) any kind of clincher (*nigrahasthāna*). Three kinds of quibbling are listed, twenty-four kinds of illegitimate rejoinders and twenty-two kinds of clinchers (compare *Nyāyasūtra* 1.2.11–14, 5.1.1–39, 5.2.1–25). The full lists will be examined in the next chapter; here follows a brief description of how they are used in bad debate.

It has been indicated that this debate has victory as its goal. Hence the debater may indulge in all sorts of tricks to outwit the opponent. However, he runs the risk of being censured and defeated by clinchers if the opponent can catch him at his own game. Quibbling is based upon equivocation. One kind (*vāk-chala*) is illustrated by the use of a homonym:

One says: The boy has a *nava* (= new) blanket.
The quibbler says: No, the boy does not have *nava* (= nine) blankets, only one.

The word "*nava*" in Sanskrit has two meanings: (1) new, and (2) nine. Obviously the quibbler's reply can be refuted. As Vātsyāyana says, either the quibbler does not understand the proper meaning of the uttered sentence, in which case he is defeated because of lack of comprehension, or he understands it, in which case he does not refute the thesis. For "*x* is not *B*" is not a refutation of "*x* is *A*."

The second type of quibbling (*sāmānya-chala*) is by stretching the meaning of a word in its very general sense while actually it has been used in a particular or specific sense:

One says: He is a brahmin, possessed of scriptural knowledge.
Reply: No. For some (fallen) brahmins do not possess scriptural knowledge.

Here the opponent wrongly construes the first statement as asserting brahminhood as the ground for possession of scriptural knowledge and hence refutes it by citing the cases of fallen brahmins. The debater uses the word "brahmin" to refer to a particular brahmin where the connection between brahminhood and scriptural knowledge holds good. The opponent quibbles and protests that the connection is not universally valid, for there are counter examples, for example, *vrātyas* or fallen brahmins.

The third type of quibbling (*upacāra-chala*) is based upon the conflation of an ordinary use of a word with its metaphorical use:

One says: The cradle cries.
The quibbler says: No. The cradle cannot cry, for it is an inanimate object.

Here, according to the Sanskrit idiom, the word "cradle" can be metaphorically used to refer to the baby in the cradle. Similarly, the word "*mañca,*" which means a platform, can metaphorically refer to the people or speakers on the platform. The opponent obviously takes it literally in order to quibble. He can easily be defeated as explained above.

Nyāyasūtras 1.2.15–16 raise an objection based upon the apparent lack of distinction between the first and the third type. For in both cases, unlike the second type, one object is the intended meaning ("new" and "the baby") while another object ("nine" and "the cradle") is imputed as its meaning. The answer is right given by pointing out an essential difference between the two. In the first, the properties are considered as the subject of refutation (newness versus the property of being nine) while in the third, the subject-locations *dharmin* are so considered (the cradle versus the baby). Hence it is argued here that this is not a distinction without a difference.

An illegitimate rejoinder (*jāti*) is based upon what we may call false parity of reasoning. The rejoinder is made usually with the help of a false analogy, based upon superficial similarity. A logically sound argument is one which illustrates an inference of a property (*s*) from the presence of another (*h*) in a particular subject-locus (*p*). However, the Indian logicians invariably demand that a relevant example must be cited to show that the logical connection between what we infer (*s*) and that by which we infer (*h*) is a genuine, not a superficial one. The example and the subject-locus of inference both are said to have shared characteristics, for example, to resemble each other in respect of containing the property, *h*, by which we infer the presence of what is inferred, *s*, in that locus. Here the possibility was open for a number of illegitimate rejoinders, where the disputant cites a spurious example in support of his counter-thesis—an example that has only superficial resemblance with the subject-locus in illustrating only an accidental connection between what we infer, *s*, and that by which we infer, *h*. Identification of several types of such accidental connection (which do not legitimatize inference, or victory in debate) led to the search for the exact nature of the logical, by which I mean simply "inference-warranting," connection. This "inference-warranting" connection was called *vyāpti*, *pratibandha,* or *niyama*, terms which have been translated as "pervasion," "concomitance," or "invariance" in modern writings. The study of the futile rejoinders in debate thus led to a gradual unfolding the nature of this logical connection.

One example of a futile rejoinder will make the above point clear:

The proponent says: Sound is impermanent because it is a product, such as a pot.
The opponent rejoins: If by sharing one property of the pot, product-hood, sound shares impermanence, another property of the pot, then by sharing one property of the sky (or space), for example, invisibility—(*a-mūrtatva* = "to be something that we can neither see nor touch"), sound would share permanence, another property of the sky (or space).

Nyāyasūtra 5.1.2 describes this rejoinder, and the next *sūtra*, 5.1.3, exposes its futility as a proper rejoinder to the argument:

> Just as cowhood (as a reason) establishes the cow, that (impermanence of sound) is also established (by the universality of the connection of impermanence with product-hood).

This translation (and interpretation) of *Nyāyasūtra* 5.1.3 leaves no doubt about the awareness of the need for the universality of the relation between what we infer (*s*) and by which we infer (*h*). Although the word for "universality" is not found in the *sūtra*, the example of *cowhood* makes it clear that the logical or inference-warranting relation must be a universal one. Just as all cows have cowhood, all cases of producthood have impermanence. Hence rejoinders based upon mere (non-universal) analogy are bound to be wrong. This refutes, in my view, the rather pervasive opinion of modern writers on Indian logic that awareness of the need for a universal relation for making a correct or sound inference was not present at the time of the compilation of the *Nyāyasūtra* but appeared only later, with Diṅnāga. Diṅnāga was no doubt one of the finest logicians of India, and we owe to him a great deal as far as formulation of the universal concomitance relation and other logical theories is concerned. However, the pre-Diṅnāga writers had enough sense to understand and underline what constituted a sound inference.

The third items in a bad debate are called the clinchers or "checks" in a debate situation. One type of clincher (the complete list will be supplied in §3.5) is *contradicting the thesis* (*Nyāyasūtra* 5.2.4). It is defined as a case where the reason adduced contradicts the thesis. Uddyotakara exemplifies it thus:

> The substance is distinct from its quality for the two are *not* apprehended as distinct.

Vācaspati Miśra rephrases:

> The substance is distinct from its quality for they are non-distinct.

Uddyotakara says that there are other varieties of this clincher. For example, it will arise when the predicate contradicts the subject: "She who is a nun is also pregnant." The idea is that the meaning of "nun" includes complete abstinence from sexual intercourse, and pregnancy will be contradictory to somebody's being a nun.

In a bad debate one pertinent question is often raised as follows: why should a debater resort to such means as quibbling and illegitimate rejoinder? For if he finds that the opponent's reason is flawed, he should presumably uncover the flaw itself, supposedly by identifying it as a pseudo-reason. If, however, the opponent's reason is flawless, the debater would not gain anything by using a futile rejoinder. By using such illegitimate means he only makes himself vulnerable to defeat. Thus no debater in their right mind would make use of such false means. The question is as old as the *Nyāyasūtra* itself. *Sūtra* 4.2.50 answers it in a cryptic manner:

> *Jalpa* and *vitaṇḍā* (the two types of bad debate) are meant for preserving the true view (truth), just as the thorns and branches are used for the protection of the (tender) sprout of the seed.

The idea is that a novice may not yet be properly skilled in debate. If he enters into a debate, he may not remember the proper reason at the right time to support his thesis. In such a crisis, he may get away with such tricky debate. In any case, if the opponent is not quick witted, the (novice) debater may gain some time to think of the proper reason. Thus, he may even win the debate and the sprout of his knowledge would be protected.

However, this was not altogether acceptable, and Uddyotakara found a better answer to the quandary. Why should people who care for establishing truth waste time in learning these tricks to outwit the opponent? Uddyotakara says, in the beginning of his commentary on chapter 5 of the *Nyāyasūtra*, that it is always useful to learn about these bad tricks, for at least one should try to avoid them in one's own debate and identify them in the opponent's presentation in order to defeat him. Besides, when faced with sure defeat, one may use a trick, and if the opponent by chance is confused by the trick, the debater will at least have the satisfaction of creating a doubt instead of courting sure defeat. This last point, was, however, a very weak defence, as Dharmakīrti elaborately pointed out in his book on debate, the *Vādanyāya* (Dharmakīrti, 1972).

2.9 THE THIRD TYPE OF DEBATE AND THE SCEPTICS

The third debate mentioned in the *Nyāyasūtra* is called *vitaṇḍā*, which has sometimes been translated as wrangling. This may not always be a fair translation. *Nyāyasūtra* 1.2.3 defines it as a debate where no counter-thesis is established. In other words, the debater here tries to ensure victory simply by refuting the thesis put forward by the other side. Elsewhere, I have called it "refutation only" debate (1985, §1.2). It is sometimes claimed to be a type of bad debate, for the only goal is victory, as in the second type, and the use of such trickery as quibbling and illegitimate rejoinder is allowed.

Philosophers from Vātsyāyana onwards argued that this third type of debate is not only unfair but also that it is impossible to conduct rationally. For the debater cannot simply get away with his destructive strategy and not defend, or even formulate his own position. For, as Vātsyāyana insists, the debater, by refuting the opponent's thesis, *p*, must be forced to accept the opposite thesis, *not-p*, and should then be asked to defend it by citing a reason. If he concedes, he gives up his original stance as a "refutative debater" (= *vaitāṇḍika*). If he does not concede *not-p*, his rationality is to be called in question, and the debate can be brought to a close without allowing victory to the "refutative debater."

The above position is arguably sound, for one could interpret destructive debate in this way. There were skeptics in every tradition, and Vātsyāyana's argument can be interpreted as exposing the irrationality of skepticism. There was indeed a skeptical tradition in India, as I have argued elsewhere (Matilal, 1986). Jayarāśi, and perhaps Sañjaya in earlier days, were its principal exponents. Of course, thousands of texts were lost, and many opponents of the established schools survive only in name and often in anonymous citations. Skepticism was not a well-defined theory, though the sceptical method was used unabashedly by other philosophers who held a non-dual view of reality.

Skepticism, in order to be a sustainable philosophical position, needs (1) to be combined with a notion of refutation which is non-committal, that is, does not imply affirmation of the opposite thesis, and (2) a plausible answer to the charge of irrationality or inconsistency. A commitment-less refutation is possible, I would argue, if it is held to be something close to the notion of illocutionary negation, as developed by J. Searle in his "speech-act" theory. Thus the debater can stick to his "refutation only" of the opponent's thesis, *p*, without conceding, even by implication, the counter thesis, *not-p*.

An illocutionary negation usually negates the act or the illocutionary force, whereas a propositional negation would leave the illocutionary force unchanged, for the result would be another proposition, a negative one, which is asserted just as was the affirmative one. For example, Sañjaya, being asked about after-life, said: "I do not say there is an after-life." We may represent this (in the manner of Searle, 1969: 32–3) as:

$$\sim \vdash (\exists x)\ (x \text{ is } F),$$

(read: "it is not a theorem that there is an F," or "it is not asserted that there is an F"). The propositional negation of the positive thesis is, by contrast, "There is no after-life," which can be represented as:

$$\vdash \sim (\exists x)\ (x \text{ is } F),$$

("it is asserted that there is no F"). Sañjaya said in the same breath both:

(a) I do not say there is an after-life, and
(b) I do not say there is no after-life,

and the charge was that he contradicted himself. However, Sañjaya claimed that he did not contradict himself but only wanted simply to avoid making a false knowledge-claim. He did not want to say that he knew while he did not. Note that the two claims are not in fact contradictory, as the following symbolic representation shows:

(a) $\sim \vdash (\exists x)\ (x \text{ is } F)$
(b) $\sim \vdash \sim (\exists x)\ (x \text{ is } F)$

The notion of illocutionary negation in speech-act theory fits well here with the context of debate.

We may note here that the fourfold (*catuṣkoṭi*) negation of another "skeptic/*vaitāṇḍika,*" the Buddhist Mādhyamika, Nāgārjuna (circa 100 AD), can be explained in the same way, to show that it too does not violate the law of contradiction. It is best to start with the first verse of *Madhyamaka-kārikā*, where the Nāgārjuna says "no" to four interrelated questions, and then ask ourselves whether the joint refutation of these four propositions or theses landed Nāgārjuna into a blatant logical contradiction. The four questions are:

A. Does a thing or being come out itself? No.
B. Does it come out of the other? No.
C. Does it come out of both, itself and the other? No.
D. Does it come out of neither? No.

Using ". . . . causes—" as a two-place predicate to stand for ". . . comes out of—", we may re-write the question, together with its rejection, thus:

A' $\sim \vdash (\exists x)\ (x \text{ causes } x)$
B' $\sim \vdash (\exists x)\ (\exists y)\ (y \text{ causes } x \cdot x \neq y)$
C' $\sim \vdash (\exists x)\ (\exists y)\ \{x \text{ causes } x \cdot (y \text{ causes } x \cdot x \neq y)\}$
D' $\sim \vdash (\exists x)\ \{(\sim x \text{ causes } x) \cdot (\sim (\exists y)\ (y \text{ causes } x \cdot x \neq y)\}$[1]

Alternatively, we may write them as follows. Let "S" = "I say that," and "*Cxy*" = "*x* causes *y*." Then we have the new formulations:

A' $\sim S\ (Caa)$,
B' $\sim S\ (Cba \cdot b \neq a)$
C' $\sim S\ (Caa \cdot (Cba \cdot b \neq a))$
D' $\sim S\ (\sim Caa \cdot \sim (Cba \cdot b \neq a))$

1. The manuscript here reads: "D': $\sim \vdash \sim (\exists x)\ (\exists y)\ \{x \text{ causes } x \cdot (y \text{ causes } x \cdot x \neq y)\}$, or $\sim \vdash (x)\ (y) \sim \{x \text{ causes } x \cdot (y \text{ causes } x \cdot x \neq y)\}$." However, such a formulation takes D as the negation of C, as saying "Is it the case that it does not come out of both itself and the other?", rather than as "Does it come out of neither itself nor the other?". That the formulation we have substituted is the correct one is confirmed by the fact that it is equivalent to "$\sim \vdash (\exists x)(\forall y)\ (\sim y \text{ causes } x)$", that is, "Does it have no cause at all? No," which is exactly the reading assigned to it by Matilal in the paragraph following the formulations.

This formulation shows clearly that A and B are not contradictories, for it is possible for something to be caused partly by itself and partly by another. Hence C is a possibility. However if we reject all three A, B and C, have we exhausted all possibilities concerning the causal origin of a thing? If we have, D is then to be construed as the rejection of production or causation itself. For "Does it come out of neither?" can be rephrased as "Does it not come out at all?" or "Is it not produced at all?". Nāgārjuna, however, says that he rejects this too, that is, says "no" to D also.

2.10 Refutation versus Negation

This leads us to the crux of the matter. The opponent may now justifiably ask the debater who indulges into this type of "refutation only" debate, "What are you talking about?" If the refutation of the refutation of causation amounts to causation (as it should if refutation is construed as ordinary negation such that negation of negation of *p* amounts to *p*), then we are back in the game where the three alternatives A, B, and C, will again arise. But they have been refuted already. Now, before we jump to conclusions and accuse Nāgārjuna of an irrationalism leading to illogical oriental mysticism, we may pause to consider the possibility that the refutation of refutation may not amount to affirmation of any position (causation or anything else).

The rejection or refutation of a position may not always amount to the assertion of a counter-position. This point is brought home to us by the joint refutation of a position and its counter-position. One may say that the debater refuses to presuppose certain things which the assertion of both the thesis and the counter-thesis would necessarily presuppose. Thus, the debater (in this case the Mādhyamika or the Vedāntin) may refuse to admit that he has or has not stopped beating his wife. For the question is loaded.

Besides the above, we may note that the school book version of the law of contradiction (and it is violation of this law that is often branded as a sure mark of irrationalism) tells us that *p* and ~*p* cannot be true together, which leaves open their both being false together. Add to this the fact that the so-called law of excluded middle says something different than the law of contradiction (either *p* or ~*p* must be true and hence both of them cannot be false) and is sometimes not regarded as fundamental. The intelligibility of the fourfold refutation of the Mādhyamika debater has been explained and defended in this way, and the charge of irrationality has been answered, by some modern scholars (notably Staal, 1962). I have accepted this move (rejecting the law of the excluded middle) in earlier writings (Matilal, 1977b), although I now believe that it may not be essential in a defence of Nāgārjuna (see also Matilal, 1990: 154–5).

It has been argued already that a refutation may be distinguished from an ordinary negation (as an illocutionary negation is distinguished from a propositional negation), so that refutation of the refutation of a thesis may be non-committal. If this argument is sound then I believe it is quite feasible for a debater (or a skeptic) to conduct an honest (non-tricky) form of debate consisting only in refutation. Such a debate may be called *vāda-vitaṇḍā*, a sub-variety of the third "destructive" debate, which can be undertaken by a genuine seeker after truth. Such a person may be a skeptic, for a skeptic, too, may be described as a seeker after truth—one who questions all our knowledge-claims, and has not found any alleged basis for such claims satisfactory.

That this was the case, that is, the "destructive" third variety of debate had two sub-varieties—one good and the other disreputable—is proven by a citation by Udayana of the view of a Gauḍa Naiyāyika, called Sānātani:

> According to view of the old Gauḍa Naiyāyika, there are four types of debate (*vāda*, *jalpa*, *vāda-vitaṇḍā* and *jalpa-vitaṇḍā*). (Udayana, 1911: 620).

We may put the classification as in Figure 2.2.

Figure 2.2
Sānātani's Classification of Debate

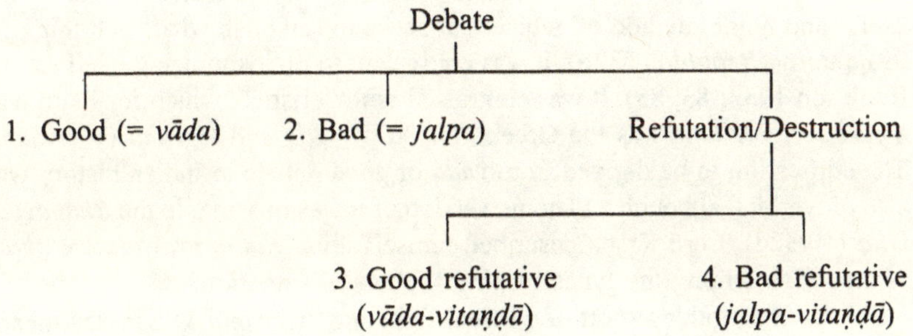

In other words, one "refutative" debate follows the *vāda* model—where logical reasons are adduced and anything which merely masquerades as a good reason (that is, a *hetvābhāsa*) is detected—and nobody is really defeated but truth may be established. The other "refutative" debate follows the *jalpa* model, that is, it is the old tricky debate which most people would try to avoid.

Udayana however, argued that a good refutative debate would not be possible (see Udayana 1911: 620; Matilal 1985: 19). For determination of truth depends upon some positive evidence. Simply by refutation we cannot establish any truth. However, this issue was taken up by Srīharṣa who elaborately refuted Udayana's point (Srīharṣa 1970, introductory section; also Granoff 1978 and Matilal 1977b). Truth may be self-evident or it may be ever elusive (as a sceptic would have it). Hence a positive evidence may not be needed to establish it. It should be noted, however, that Dharmakīrti, who probably followed Vasubandha and Diṅnāga in this respect, clearly rejected in his *Vādanyāya* any form of debate other than *vāda* (Dharmakīrti, 1972: 69-71).

2.11 VĀDA AND "DIALECTICS" IN GREEK THOUGHT

The classification of debates in India, into good and bad, constructive and destructive, has its parallel in early Greek thought. Plato apparently contrasted what he called "dialectic" with "eristic." Eristic is, roughly speaking, the art of arguing or quarrelling with someone. The Greek word *dialegomoi* means "conducting a conversation, an argument." Socrates regarded it as the art of getting at the truth by exposing the latent contradiction in the opponent's thesis. Plato, it has been argued by scholars, elevated the notion of dialectic to the supreme art of conducting a philosophical debate in question-and-answer form for the sake of unfolding the truth. A Socratic *elenchus* was initially a sort of destructive argument. However in the middle and later dialogues, this argumentative tool was unconsciously transformed into a very useful and noble method of debate that seeks to establish what each thing is, its *quiddity* (*Republic,* 533b). It was equivalent to philosophizing itself (cf. R. Robinson 1953: 83, 85). It was contrasted with "eristic", which for Plato was a *verbal fight.* This was the Greek version of *vāda* and *vigraha* (= *vivāda*). The edification to be derived from *vāda* or good debate in Indian history was also proverbial, although a Platonic version of it was missing. In the *Bhagavad-Gīta* (10/32d), Lord Kṛṣṇa described himself thus: *vādaḥ pravadatām aham* "I am *Vāda* among the types of philosophical disputation."

Jalpa is nothing short of a verbal fight and "*vigraha*" in Sanskrit means a fight. The debate that Socrates refers to in *Meno* 75 c–d as "clever, disputatious and quarrelsome" or the dialogue that is illustrated in *Euthedemus* is certainly reminiscent of the *jalpa* or *vigṛhya kathā*. As R. Robinson has noted, an *elenchus,* in a narrower sense, means a form of cross-examination. In a wider sense, it stands for a type of refutation where the opponent under the pressure of incisive questioning may come to feel that he could agree to a position that entails the falsehood of his original assertion. It has, in some of its available descriptions, the unmistakable resonances of the *vitaṇḍā* type of debate of the Indians. *Vitaṇḍā*, as we have seen, is exclusively refutative, whereas *jalpa*, which is also a fight, involves both refutation of the counter-position and establishment of the proposed position. Although Plato used this tool, perhaps unconsciously (Robinson, p. 83) or even confusedly (Kneale and Kneale, p. 9), for constructive purposes as a means for arriving at truths or science, it would not resemble *jalpa*. *Jalpa* was explicitly for victory (compare *vijaya*), not always for truths (compare *tattvanirṇaya*).

In Plato's hand, dialectic becomes hardly distinguishable from the very intellectual type of philosophic activity that rejects the manifold changing appearances, the mundane things of this world, and searches for the changeless essences or forms. Methodology, in this way, comes closer to metaphysics. A dialectician is, for Plato, an inspired philosopher. The method of such Platonic dialectic has its distinct resonance in Vātsyāyana's account of the methodology of a *śāstra*, which is characterized by first naming the concepts, second, defining or characterizing them, and then examining such definitions. Sometimes, it has been said by modern scholars that a philosopher like Nāgārjuna or Srīharṣa should be described as "a great dialectician." The description will perhaps be justified if we keep to this Platonic notion of dialectic.

Aristotle clipped the wings of the Platonic dialectic and turned it into a technique again. The *Topics* of Aristotle was very close to a handbook of dialectics that became a dubious game of debate, an exercise for the muscles of the intellect. In this and its probable appendix, *De Sophistici Elenchi*, we get the nearest analogue of the *vivāda-śāstras* of ancient India. However, the contrasts here would be more useful to note than the similarities.

In the *Analytics*, Aristotle dealt with syllogism, which is sometimes distinguished from dialectic. The latter was, unlike syllogism, an argument from non-evident premises or opinions. Under syllogism, Aristotle studied mainly inferences based upon class-inclusion. However, in a broader sense, a syllogism, even for Aristotle, was any argument in which, after certain truths or views have been assumed, there results necessarily a proposition other than the assumptions but because of the assumptions. Aristotle (*Topics* I, 12), having such a general notion of syllogism in mind, said that every dialectical argument was either a syllogism or an epagoge. An epagoge had several varieties, but its general characterization was that it approached the universal from the particular. Later on in the history similar arguments were called induction. Certain characteristics of the epagoge would seem relevant when we study certain features of the Indian theory of inference and its demonstration. In *De Sophistici Elenchi*, 165b, Aristotle noted that the debater would have to admit an epagoge supported by instances, unless a negative instance could be produced to counter it. Absence of a counter-example, combined with the citation of a supporting example became the all-important element in the Indian theory of inference. And, of course, in a debate situation if the opponent is unable to find a counter-example, he will have to accept the proponent's thesis.

The *Topics* gave us rules for conducting a disputatious debate, and *De Sophistici Elenchi* the rules for detecting invalid arguments. Hence their similarity with the Indian *vāda* manuals is too obvious to be missed. However, it might be a mistake to push this point too far. Some modern scholars (J.D.G. Evans, 1977: 50) have argued, against the predominant opinion of others, that it would be a mistake to regard the *Topics* simply as a manual of instruction on how to win a debate at all costs. Evans' own reading of the *Topics* is that here Aristotle elected to treat such concepts as intelligibility in their full complexity. It was *sui generis*; not to be regarded as a first draft on the *Analytics*.

It may be argued on similar grounds that the *Nyāyasūtra* treatment of the debate categories should not be described simply as a handbook of instructions for conducting debate. The prevailing opinion among the Indological scholars has been that the first and the fifth chapters of the *Nyāyasūtra* should be taken together and viewed as a *vāda* manual. There were of course books such as the *Upāyahṛdāya* and *Tarkaśāstra* (whose contents we will discuss in chapter 3), and it may be that their exclusive concern *was* with instruction, although even this may be debatable. The *Nyāyasūtra* was, however, a different type of text. In spite of the discussion of the debate categories, here the author (and also the compiler) was primarily concerned with the acceptable and sound method for philosophical discourse. He put the discussion of the debate categories in its natural home, in the context of the discussion of the *pramāṇas*, means of knowledge, as well as *prameyas*, the object of knowledge. It was concerned especially with the *pramāṇa* called *anumāna*, literally "after-knowledge." In other words, this tells us what else we know (or what truths can be derived) when we know certain things already. The idea was, in effect, an unconscious search after the nature of rationality as it was understood in the Indian context. The categories and sub-categories of "sophistries" and "checks" were separated from the main argument of the work, the first chapter, and put in the last (fifth) chapter so as not to deflect us from the principal theme of the book. The principle theme of *nyāya* (with a small "n") was to discover what sort of argument-structure would be intelligible and acceptable as generating, or leading us to, knowledge. There are numerous (in fact innumerable, as the commentators note) "misfires" (which *were* "sophistries"), and only a few are likely to hit the mark of truth or knowledgehood. Through the discussion of such misfires and false starts, a picture of the right and acceptable method of arguing emerged. An enquiry into the *Nyāyasūtra* along such lines will prove to be very fruitful. The precise way in which a theory of logically-acceptable argument was derived, in the *Nyāyasūtra*, via a discussion of debating categories, and the nature of the relation between the *Nyāyasūtra* and supposedly pure debating manuals like the *Upāyahṛdāya* and the *Tarkaśāstra,* are the topics that comprise the subject-matter of chapter 3.

CHAPTER 3

Tricks and Checks in Debate

3.1 Tricks

While discussing the bad types of debate, *jalpa* or *vitaṇḍā*, in §2.8, we introduced the notions of "quibbling" (*chala*) and "false rejoinder" (*jāti*). These are the tricks used by the debater in a debate aimed at winning, that is, destroying the opponent. Quibbling has been exhaustively discussed in the previous chapter. Here we shall discuss the detailed lists of different types of "false rejoinder." Different compilations of this list are available in the Nyāya, Buddhist, and Jaina traditions. I shall first discuss the list supplied by the *Nyāyasūtra*, and then supplement it by the other additional types recognized by the Buddhists (§3.3) and the Jainas (§3.4). In the last two sections (§3.5 and 3.6), I will examine the Nyāya and Buddhist lists of "clinchers" or defeat situations (*nigrahasthāna*) in debate.[1]

3.2 Sophistical Rejoinders—Nyāya Style

Nyāyasūtra 1.2.10 defines a false rejoinder or sophistical refutation (*jāti*) as a counter-argument based upon superficial similarity or dissimilarity. In other words it is an argument based upon a false analogy, and the opponent who uses it tries, futilely, to refute the thesis put forward by the proponent

1. Others to have discussed the lists of rejoinders and defeat situations in Nyāya and Buddhist debate manuals include Vidyabhusana (1921), Tucci (1929b), Randle (1930), and Solomon (1976).

by proving the opposite thesis. A logical argument, if it is sound, cannot, however, be based upon superficial analogy. Hence this type of counter-argument is identified as merely sophistical refutation.

All the sophistical refutations are invalid as arguments, since they are based on false analogies. The notion of the validity of an argument is thus an essential part of this theory. A valid argument according to this theory cannot be based upon superficial similarities or false analogies. It must be based upon an essential similarity, a true analogy. What is a true analogy or essential similarity? To begin with, similarity means sharing a property or properties. Essential similarity means, therefore, sharing an essential property. In a sound inference, therefore, the subject or *pakṣa* shares an essential property with the example—which property is necessarily connected with another property, that is, the property to be inferred.

The problem here is formulated from the point of view of an inductive logic. You see an example, a pot, and you see that a pot is an impermanent object as well as that it is something that has been produced or manufactured. But now you see that the object under consideration, for example, a case of sound or noise, is also produced. And hence it shares a common property with the pot. On the basis of this, you infer that the sound too is impermanent. If the argument is formulated in this way then in a debate it can be rejoined in various ways. The *Nyāyasūtra* identifies twenty-four ways of rejoining this type of argument, all are supposedly false or futile, in that they would not stand scrutiny. Different manuals of debate give different lists. For example, the Buddhist *Tarkaśāstra* has a list of sixteen. The *Upāyahṛdaya* has one of twenty-two. Table 3.1 is a comparison of the three lists, derived from Tucci, (1929a: xxi).[2] (For details and accounts of other manuals, see Tucci, 1929a, 1929b.)

I shall now discuss the *Nyāyasūtra* list.

1. Similarity-Based Rejoinder

Although all the types of rejoinder that we call *jāti* are fundamentally similarity-based, the first type is specifically so. Let us see how.

The proponent: A sound is impermanent for it is a product, just as the case of a pot.

---

2. The manuscript simply reproduces Tucci's rather confusing chart. We have adapted it in line with the subsequent discussion and numbered the false rejoinders in the order they appear in the respective texts.

TABLE 3.1
FALSE REJOINDERS

Nyāyasūtra	*Upāyahṛdaya*	*Tarkaśāstra*
1 *sādharmyasama*		1 *sādharmya*
2 *vaidharmyasama*		2 *vaidharmya*
3 *utkarṣasama*	1 *utkarṣasama*	
4 *apakarṣasama*	2 *apakarṣasama*	
5 *varṇyasama*		
6 *avarṇyasama*		
7 *vikalpasama*		3 *vikalpa*
8 *sādhyasama*		
9 *prāptisama*	11 *prāptisama*	} 5 *prāptyaprāpti*
10 *aprāptisama*	12 *aprāptisama*	
11 *prasaṅgasama*		11 *prasaṅga*
12 *pratidṛṣṭāntasama*	17 *pratidṛṣṭāntasama*	?13 *pratidṛṣṭānta*
13 *anutpattisama*	20 *anutpattisama*	14 *anutpatti*
14 *saṃśayasama*	15 *saṃśayasama*	
15 *prakaraṇasama*		
16 *ahetusama*	10 *ahetusama*	6 *ahetu*
17 *arthāpattisama*		12 *arthāpatti*
18 *aviśeṣasama*		4 *aviśeṣa*
19 *upapattisama*		
20 *upalabdhisama*		7 *upalabdhi*
21 *anupalabdhisama*		
22 *nityasama*		15 *nitya*
23 *anityasama*		
24 *kāryasama*	7 *kāryasama*	8 *saṃśayasama*
	3 *bhedābheda*	
	4 *praśnabāhulyam, uttarālpatā*	
	5 *praśnālpatā, uttarabāhulyam*	
	6 *hetusama*	
	8 *vyāptisama*	
	9 *avyāptisama*	
	13 *viruddha*	
	14 *aviruddha*	
	16 *asaṃśaya*	
	18 *śrutisama*	
	19 *śrutibhinna*	
		9 *anirukti*
		10 *kāryabheda*
		16 *svārthaviruddha*

The rejoinder: Sound is permanent, for it is incorporeal (or intangible), just as the case of the sky.

The rejoinder claims that if sound is argued to be impermanent on the basis of its sharing a particular property (producthood) with an object known to be impermanent, a pot, then by parity of reasoning, it can be argued to be permanent on the basis of its sharing another property (incorporeality) with a known permanent object, the sky. NS 5.1.3 resolves the problem in a way that reveals the structure of the logical theory as understood at that point in the history by the Nyāya school. But first the second type must be explained.

2. Dissimilarity-Based Rejoinder

Proponent: Sound is impermanent because it does not share a property with the permanent object, the sky, for example, the property of being produced.

Rejoinder : Sound is permanent because it does not share a property with the impermanent object, a pot, for example, the property of being intangible.

The solution (NS 5.1.3): sharing, or not sharing, just any property at random does not constitute a sound ground for inference. A generic connection is aimed at, just as something becomes a cow because of its connection with cowhood—a genuine universal property. The impermanence of sound (*śabda* = sound, noise, words) can be established if it can be shown to be a product. For the connection between these two properties, impermanence and producthood, is general, just as the connection between a cow and cowhood is general or universal. Thus, Vātsyāyana comments:

> If one proceeds to establish the required inferable property on the basis simply of similarity or dissimilarity then there will be lack of any regularity (*a-vyavasthā* = randomness). Irregularity does not arise with respect to some special property. For something is a cow because of its similarity with another cow—which similarity is actually cowhood, not the cow's having the dewlap etc.

It is interesting to observe that at this early stage, the notion of a universal property is appealed to, in order to bring out or explain the notion of a universal, that is, invariable, connection. It is the latter that became crucial in their theory of logic. Here the conception of a universal connection is being hinted at on the analogy of a universal property.

Later on, this connection came to be designated by such terms as *vyāpti*, *niyama,* and *pratibandha*. It would be wrong to conclude, along with most other Indological scholars, that because the early writers on logic used more often than not such terms as *sādharmya* (similarity) and *vaidharmya* (dissimilarity), there was therefore no conception of a general, logical, that is, inference-warranting, connection. In other words, it is wrong to think that inference is regarded, at this stage, as being mostly analogical rather than logical. The earlier terms were *vyavasthā*, *pratibandha,* and so on. The almost general opinion is that the idea of the universality of the inference-warranting connection originated with Diṅnāga, and the earlier logicians based their theory of inference on naive analogy. Nothing is farther from the truth, as will be evident to anybody reading seriously and critically these early writers. If, for example, it was impossible for them to look beyond analogy as the basis of inference, they would not have developed a theory of pseudo-reasons or logically unsound reasons (*hetvābhāsa*) as well as a theory of sophistical (futile) rejoinders based upon the notion of whimsical or inessential similarity. In this regard, I agree with the contention of K. Chakrabarti (1977:45 ff.) that Gotama and Vātsyāyana had a notion of universal concomitance, although, I must add, I do not think that Chakrabarti's rather strained and often far-fetched philological interpretations of such terms as *sādharmya* or *vaidharmya* (as "universal concomitance" and "universal exclusion" (1977:54)) are correct or even necessary to prove this point.

In the above, I have selected suitable examples of two types of false rejoinders from Vātsyāyana's commentator, Uddyotakara. Vātsyāyana's own examples, however, were not totally free from fault. In fact, he said that the soul may be inferred as having action/motion (or lacking it) on the basis of its similarity with such a substance as a block of stone (or on the basis of its dissimilarity with such a middle-sized substance as a piece of stone). And the rejoinder will prove the soul to be motionless on the basis of its similarity with a ubiquitous substance such as the sky. This was a very clumsy way of exemplifying the two types of rejoinder. Besides, Vātsyāyana's mistake was to illustrate the case of a false rejoinder to an incorrectly-formulated sound argument with an example that could be (and perhaps is) a correct rejoinder. Thus:

Proponent: The soul has motion by virtue of its similarity with a substance like a block of stone, which can move.

Rejoinder: The soul is motionless by virtue of its similarity with a ubiquitous substance like the sky, which is also motionless.

Here the rejoinder is not false in so far as it is admitted by Nyāya that the soul, like the sky, is both ubiquitous and motionless. However we may learn a lesson from Vātsyāyana's example, namely that the structure of the argument called a false rejoinder is the same as that given here. The opponent's conclusion is a correct one although the formulation of his rejoinder (argument) was incorrect. Although the ubiquity of a substance is the right reason for its being motionless, we cannot formulate the argument in the way given above. Similarity with a ubiquitous substance such as the sky is not what warrants the inference, but rather the generalization "whatever is ubiquitous is also motionless." Hence the opponent's argument, we may say, is a false rejoinder although its conclusion happens to be true.

We may note here further that this first pair of rejoinders, if they had been valid, could have been construed as demonstrating that the proponent's original reason was in fact a type of faulty or pseudo-reason, the one called the counter-balanced (*sat-pratipakṣa*), where the original inference is stopped by a counter inference with an equally plausible reason (cf. §1.2). However, as Uddyotakara notes, these are in fact only *false* rejoinders and hence cases of a *pseudo*-counter-balanced reason.

The next six rejoinders can be grouped together, for they are all false for the same reason.

3. Rejoinder by the Addition of a Property, and 4. Rejoinder by Subtracting a Property

Proponent (as before): Sound is impermanent for it is a product, just as the case of a pot.

Rejoinder: Sound could be visible (coloured) because it is (as you say) similar to a visible substance, a pot.

This is the false rejoinder by adding a property. Since sound cannot be visible, the opponent can now argue that the proponent's argument based on similarity with a pot is wrong. The rejoinder by substracting a property is:

Rejoinder: Sound could be inaudible since, as you say, it is similar to a pot which is audible.

Here the opponent shows that there follows the undesirable consequence of the sound's lacking a genuine property, audibility, and thereby wishes to refute the proponent.

5. Uncertainty-Based Rejoinder, and 6. Certainty-Based Rejoinder

Inference on the Indian theory requires that prior to the actual inference there should not be certainty about the inferable property's being present in the given place or the subject. Its presence or absence there should be in doubt. If this lack of certainty is extended to the example, making it doubtful whether the inferable property is present there or not, we have a case of 5, an uncertainty-based rejoinder. Similarly, the Indian theory requires that as far as the example is concerned, it should be certain that the inferable property is present there. If this certainty (or lack of uncertainty) is extended to the subject or the locus (*pakṣa*), then we have a rejoinder based upon certainty. An example of the uncertainty-based rejoinder is:

Proponent (as before): Sound is impermanent for it is a product, just as the case of a pot.

Rejoinder: If it is doubtful whether impermanence characterizes sound or not, it might as well be doubtful whether impermanence characterizes the pot, the example. (And if the example is dubious, the proponent's argument would be refuted). An example of the certainty-based rejoinder:

Proponent (as before): Sound is impermanent for it is a product, just as the case of a pot.

Rejoinder: If it is certain that the pot, the example, is characterized by impermanence then the subject, sound, because of its similarity with the example, is also for certain characterized by impermanence. (And if it is certain that the inferable property is present in sound, then the inference of the proponent is useless).

7. Rejoinder by Alternation

The reason is present in the subject, as well as is in the example, but there may be another property present in the subject, which is absent from the example. Hence the inferable property may be present in the example while it may likewise be absent from the subject. An example is:

Rejoinder: Sound is a product as the pot is, but sound is (sometimes) generated by the separation or breaking of physical bodies, and this property of being so generated is absent from the pot. Hence impermanence may be absent from sound, while it is present in the pot.

8. Rejoinder by Casting Doubt upon the Example

The proponent claims that it is certain that the inferable property is present in the example, but doubtful whether it is present in the subject. If this doubt is extended to include the example, we have a case of this type of rejoinder. An example:

Rejoinder: If it is doubtful whether sound is impermanent or not, and if the pot is like the sound, then it may be doubtful whether the pot is impermanent or not. (The proponent loses, for the supporting example loses its point.)

In NS 5.1.5, an answer to all these six rejoinders (that is 3 to 8) is given. It is pointed out that the example and the subject need to share only one particular property, the reason (that is, producthood), which warrants the inference, but it would be wrong to suppose that they must share many other (or all) properties. All these six rejoinders are based upon such a wrong construal, and hence must be rejected. Uddyotakara in this context says that what constitutes a proper example is a case where both the reason and the property to be inferred are seen to be present without any obstacle. Nothing more is required.

9. Connection-Based Rejoinder, and 10. Disconnection-Based Rejoinder

If the reason *h* establishes the inferable property *s*, it must be connected with the latter. Since connection means in some sense togetherness then perhaps the latter can even establish the former. And if *h* establishes *s* without such connectedness, then anything else can do so too. In both cases, the reason loses its reasonhood. Example:

Rejoinder 9: Either producthood cannot establish impermanence, for the essential distinction between them (one as the ground for the other) is lost,

Rejoinder 10: or producthood is similar to any other property being disconnected from impermanence and hence cannot establish impermanence.

To give the refutation of this rejoinder, it is said (NS 5.1.8) that connection does not mean identity, nor does disconnection mean complete independence. The two pot-halves are connected to produce a pot, but the cause (the pot-halves) and the effect (the pot) are distinct. Similarly a magic (*abhicāra*) ritual may be responsible for the death of the intended victim, although the two are not seen to be connected physically.

11. "Reason for the Reason"-Rejoinder, and
12. Counter-Example-Based Rejoinder

If the reason which must be recognized to be present in the example, is challenged, and a further reason for such a recognition is demanded, we have a case of a "reason for the reason" rejoinder. If another example is cited which is characterized not by *s* but by its opposite (*not-s*), then we have a case of the counter-example-based rejoinder. Examples:

Rejoinder 11: If the pot is a product, what makes it a product? Or, what is the reason for its being a product?

Rejoinder 12: The example of 12 is not very clear. Uddyotakara accepts Vātsyāyana's example. I believe it consists in the citation of any counter example. Vātsyāyana offers:

Proponent: Sound has motion for it has qualities that generate motion and action, just as a piece of stone.

Rejoinder: Sound is motionless, just as the sky, which is motionless although it has qualities that may generate action and motion.

How may the sky have such qualities? Vātsyāyana says that its connection with wind makes it possible for its having such qualities.

The answer to this rejoinder is given (NS 5.1.10) by saying that the reason for the reason is not required, just a lamp only is required to show other objects, but no further lamp is required to show the lamp itself. And a counter-example does not have any bite unless it contains also the reason unambiguously (NS 5.1.11).

13. Non-Origination-Based Rejoinder

The reason (*h*) can reside in the subject or *pakṣa* (*p*) when and only when the latter has come into existence. When the latter has not come into existence, the reason cannot reside there, nor can the inferable property (*s*). Example:

Proponent: Sound is impermanent for it is a product, just as the case of a pot.

Rejoinder: Producthood resides in a sound only after the sound has been produced. Before this time, there will be no producthood in the non-originated sound, and so producthood cannot always establish impermanence.

The reply here is simple. Sound comes into being only after its production and then has all the required properties. Before that time, sound is non-existent, and hence nothing can be shown with regard to such a non-existent entity.

14. Doubt-Based Rejoinder

The example of this rejoinder is:

Proponent: Sound is impermanent for it is a product, just as the case of a pot.

Rejoinder: If sound, by virtue of its sharing the property producthood with the example, the pot, has to share impermanence, why can it not, by sharing the property perceptibility-through-the-senses, with a real universal like cowhood, also be permanent like a universal?

Here we must note two peculiarities of the Nyāya school. According to this school, (a) universals such as cowhood are real, objective entities, and (b) some of them are perceptible. The reply (NS 5.1.15) to this rejoinder is: mere sharing of a property cannot sustain doubt, for the distinctive property, when it is recognized, would settle it. If doubt is still maintained when both common and distinct properties are recognized, then this is an over-pronounced, neurotic (hyperbolic) doubt, which is absurd.

15. Counterpoise-Based Rejoinder

This actually seems to be genuine rejoinder, although it can become a false one in certain circumstances. A thesis is adduced with a reason and an example. Then a counter-thesis is adduced by the opponent with another reason and a different example. If the second reason is adequate, that is, backed by a genuine universal relation between *h* and *s*, then the rejoinder is valid. However, if such adequacy is not found, it will be a false rejoinder. Example:

Proponent: Sound is impermanent, for it is produced by effort, for example, a pot.

Opponent: Sound is permanent, for it is audible, for example, soundhood.

The opponent exploits the Nyāya theory of sound and soundhood. According to Nyāya, those universals which are perceptible are perceived by the same sense as grasps their loci. Hence if sound is grasped by the faculty of hearing, soundhood is also grasped by the same faculty. Thus, soundhood is audible.

There is a genuine problem here in the Indian theory of inference in general. If the universal connection (invariance) between producthood and impermanence is proven by such examples as a pot, then a universal connection between audibility and the permanence can be shown by such an example as soundhood. Diṅnāga noted this point, and it constrained his theory of inference. He said (see chapter 4) that in any inference there should be just one reason which must fulfill three specified conditions, and, in the given case, the proponent's reason fulfills these conditions, but the opponent's reason is only a pseudo-reason, the one called the "uniquely inconclusive" (compare *asādhāraṇa*), for it characterizes the subject, sound, and sound only. In Buddhism, in any case, soundhood is not a real entity, and hence the question of its perceptibility does not arise. For Nyāya, the only available answer is that in one of the two inferences, the invariable relation between the reason and the inferred property does not obtain.

16. Rejoinder by Rejecting the Reason

The reason becomes a reason by establishing the inferable property, *s*. However, is it a reason before the property *s* is established, or after, or simultaneously? The answer to each of these three dialectical questions is *no*. For, if the first, the reason cannot establish a non-existent *s*. If the second, the reason does not exist. And if the third, which one will establish and what will be established by it?

The answer (NS 5.1.19) is that the reason establishes the *s* by letting us know about *s*, which is a knowable, not by causing *s* to come into existence Hence the above alternative questions are immaterial.

17. Presumption-Based Rejoinder

Presumption (*arthāpatti*) is an inference based on negative evidence—the conclusion is presumed because no other alternative explanation is available. This rejoinder is based upon such a presumption. Example:

Rejoinder: If by sharing a property with a non-permanent entity, a pot, sound is to be impermanent, then by sharing another property with a permanent entity, the sky, when this property is intangibility, sound may be judged permanent. For otherwise how else can we explain its similarity with the sky, a permanent entity?

The reply (NS 5.1.22) is simple, for it states that such presumptive judgement cannot prove anything conclusively and mere similarity is not the issue here.

18. Non-Differentiation-Based Rejoinder

If similarity, that is, sharing one common property (*h*) is the basis for sharing another common property (*s*), then all things may share one common property, thinghood, or existence. Thus, any one thing can be non-different from any other thing.

The reply (NS 5.1.29) states that *h* establishes another *s* on the basis of its invariance with the latter, and thinghood is not going to establish any property other than one invariant with it.

19. Evidence-Based Rejoinder

If there is evidence or a ground for the presence of the inferable property as well as evidence for its absence in the same subject, we have a case of rejoinder 19. Example:

> Both producthood and intangibility are present in sound and while the former is a ground for showing its impermanence, the latter would be a ground for showing the lack of impermanence.

In the Counterpoise-Based Rejoinder, both arguments are fully developed, while in the Evidence-Based Rejoinder, the two sides are only indicated to form a rejoinder. The reply is simply restatement of the previously made point.

20. Apprehension-Based Rejoinder

If the inferable property *s* is apprehended in a place where the assigned reason *h* is absent, we have a case of rejoinder 20. This is supposed to show that the invariance or concomitance of the reason *h* with the inferable *s* is falsified (violated) by the case in question. However it is a false rejoinder, for the properly falsifying case would be a place where *h* is present and *s* is absent, and not one when *s* is present but *h* is absent. Example:

Proponent: Sound (or word) is impermanent, for it is invariably connected with human effort.

Rejoinder: If by "sound" we take any noise, then there is the case of noise produced by the branch of a tree broken by wind—here human effort is absent but impermanence is present.

The reply to this has already been given. Vātsyāyana refers to the doctrine of plurality of causes to account for such cases.

21. Non-Apprehension-Based Rejoinder

Example:

Proponent: A word is non-existent before it is uttered.

Rejoinder: No. A word is not apprehended before its utterance because there are obstacles to such apprehension. We cannot see water underground for the ground conceals it.

Proponent: No. In the case of words, no such obstacle is apprehended.

Rejoinder: No. Such non-apprehension of the obstacles is due to the non-apprehension of the obstacles to these obstacles, not due to their non-existence.

The reply is as follows. If the object or obstacle exists, it can be apprehended. Non-apprehension of obstacles should establish their non-existence.

22. Impermanence-Based Rejoinder

If mere similarity with a pot establishes the impermanence of sound, then, since there is a similarity between a pot and everything else (for everything shares one common property, existence), everything would be impermanent.

The reply (NS 5.1.33–34), as expounded by Vātsyāyana, is that mere similarity or mere dissimilarity is not the factor that warrants an inference. A particular kind of property-sharing warrants inference, because a property becomes a reason *h* by being invariably connected with the inferable, *s*, and then prompts us to infer. The reply given to rejoinder 18 should also be remembered. Here a good criterion of a logical reason is given (NS 5.1.34). A special property, which is recognized in the example as having the force of warranting an inference, is what is called a reason.

23. Permanence-Based Rejoinder

Impermanence, or any other inferable property, may be disputed by such counter-questions as: is impermanence a permanent attribute of sound or, is it an impermanent attribute? If the former, sound becomes permanent, while if the latter, sound also becomes permanent.

This has the flavor of a paradox. In fact it can very well be transformed into a dialectical tool in the hand of the dialecticians. Many well-known philosophers in India (such as Candrakīrti, Jayarāśi, Srīharṣa) used this tool. However, it could be a futile rejoinder too.

The reply then would be this: we cannot treat the property of impermanence as a distinct locatee which is contained in the container, sound. For then we need separate relations to connect them. In fact such dialectical questions are pointless, for impermanence simply means that an entity can and does go out of existence. It is not like a visible property, having a particular color or shape. Besides, even the denial of a property (in the rejoinder) can be subjected to such dialectical inquiry. Thus no thesis, positive or negative, can be established, if we give in to such pointless questions (see further Matilal 1971, pp. 159–61).

24. Effect-Based Rejoinder

There are, apparently, two possibilities. A thing may be caused to come into existence by certain causal factors, or, being existent all the time, it may be manifested by the so-called factors. Hence sound may be permanent, for it may be manifested by causal factors that destroy the obstacles to its manifestation. Example:

Proponent: A word is non-existent before it is uttered.

Rejoinder: What you call coming into existence is actually manifestation.

The reply is given by emphasizing the same point as made in 21. We do not recognize any obstacles to the apprehension of sound before it appears, and it is futile to imagine such obstacles and then argue that by destroying such obstacles we make sound manifest.

Uddyotakara notes that this rejoinder is distinct from doubt-based rejoinder (number 14 above) for, in the latter, doubt arises due to similarity with both the subject and the example. Here (in 24) there is a genuine doubt: is non-apprehension due to non-existence or due to obstacles to manifestation? It is also distinct from the similarity-based rejoinder (number 1), for the reason adduced here is transformed or modified: "being produced" is transformed into "being manifested."

3.3 Sophistical Rejoinders—Buddhist Style

In this section, we consider the lists of sophistical rejoinders found in two Buddhist texts, the *Upāya-hṛdaya,* and the *Tarkaśāstra.* The pre-Diṅnāga text on Buddhist logic called *Upāya-hṛdaya* (or, as E. Frauwallner suggests, *Prayogasāra*) was received from Chinese sources by Tucci (1929b). Among other things, this text supplies in its fourth chapter a list of twenty varieties of refutation (*duṣaṇa*), all based upon similarity and dissimilarity. Thus these refutations were virtually varieties of *jāti* or futile rejoinder. Almost half of the names on the list were common to the list given in the *Nyāyasūtra*. It will be worthwhile to note the additional varieties here. The numbering is as in the chart above.

(3) Rejoinder Based on Difference-Cum-Non-Difference. The opponent attacks by asking whether the example is different or non-different from the subject *(pakṣa)*. Example:

Proponent: The soul is eternal, for it is imperceptible by the senses, just as the sky is.

Rejoinder: A dilemma: if the sky is not different from the soul, then it violates the principle that the example is not to be identical with the subject locus; and if the sky is different from the soul, then they cannot share a property, especially the reason-property "imperceptibility by the senses."

This rejoinder can be easily answered. However the point to note is that the proponent's inference would not be acceptable to a Buddhist. Hence the rejoinder may not be futile on this interpretation. To wit: both the sky and the soul would be fictitious entities, if the doctrine of momentariness is accepted, and as fictitious entities they will be extensionally equivalent. Thus, the rejoinder's point, that we cannot use one as the example and the other as the subject locus, may stand.

(4) Rejoinder by Showing that the Answer Is Outweighed by the Question.

Proponent: Same as before.

Rejoinder: Since whatever is imperceptible by the senses is not necessarily eternal, how can you establish the proposition? The question is under-determined by the answer. In other words, the evidence falls short of what is being proven.

Our comment is that the rejoinder may again not be futile. For without establishing the necessary connection (of invariance) between the reason and the inferable property (for example, eternality) we cannot proceed to prove thesis of the proponent.

(5) Rejoinder by Showing the Question Is Outweighed by the Answer.

Proponent: Same as before.

Rejoinder: There are two types of things that are imperceptible: things like atoms (which are non-eternal, according the Buddhists) and things like the sky (which are eternal). Thus how can you prove eternality of the soul by virtue of such imperceptibility?

Here the rejoinder as the answer outweighs the question. The rejoinder is again not shown to be wrong but only disproportionate, and hence inadequate to the question. These two rejoinders are no doubt peculiar, for they might be logically flawless. Their weakness lies probably in their overstating or understating the point at issue. The text without any commentary does not throw much light on their significance. Solomon (1976: 187) makes an interesting comment: "Can they mean reading less than what is meant or reading more than what is meant?"

(6) Rejoinder of Parity of Reason.

Proponent: Same as before.

Rejoinder: Since the sky and the soul are two different things, they cannot share a same property. For the feature of imperceptibility attached to the sky would be distinct from the feature of imperceptibility attached to the soul. Thus we cannot have a reason here, that is, a property of the soul that must be the same as one attached to the sky, the example.

This again may be a valid rejoinder since the requirement is, for a valid inference, that the same property is shared by both the subject-locus and the example. For one may insist that the feature described by "not perceptible by the senses" may be different as the locus of such a feature varies.

(8) Pervasion-Based Rejoinder.

Proponent: The sky is eternal because it is imperceptible.

Rejoinder: The sky is all-pervading. Since it pervades everything, should everything by the same token be imperceptible?

This exploits the ambiguity of the word "pervading." The sky pervades all in one sense but the inference-warranting relation, pervasion, which is admittedly transitive, is a different type of relation.

(9). Non-Pervasion-Based Rejoinder.

Proponent: As in 5.

Rejoinder: Atoms are imperceptible but non-pervasive (spatially, that is, atoms are at the opposite end of the spectrum from the all-pervasive sky). Hence, how could the soul, being imperceptible, be eternal?

Again, a misuse of the word "pervaded" based upon equivocation.

(13) Contrary Rejoinder.

Proponent: The soul is eternal, but everything else is non-eternal. For the soul is not included in everything.

Rejoinder: If everything is non-eternal, the soul must be so. For if a blanket is burnt for the most part, it is odd to call it an "unburnt" blanket. Its more proper to call it a burnt blanket.

Solomon (1976: 188) finds this example puzzling, while Tucci thinks that this is a *pratijñā-virodha*, something contrary to the original thesis, and refers to a similar example in Diṅnāga's *Nyāyamukha*. I believe, however, that it is not especially puzzling. The idea is that if everything is *F* or almost everything is so, then it is futile to find something non-*F*.

(14) Non-Contrary Rejoinder.

Proponent: The soul is imperceptible, just as the sky is.

Rejoinder: The sky does not have consciousness, hence the soul would also be unconscious. Or, if the soul is conscious, the sky would have to be conscious.

This is a good example of a futile rejoinder based upon a false notion of similarity. Solomon unnecessarily thinks that this corresponds to number 18 of the Nyāya school (see above), the non-differentiation-based rejoinder. I believe, however, that they are different.

(16) Rejoinder Based on Non-Doubt.

Proponent: The soul exists, for it is imperceptible.

Rejoinder: Imperceptibility of an existent is always due to the presence of some obstacle. However if no obstacle can be found in the case of the soul, then the soul does not exist.

This seems to be a worthwhile rejoinder despite the touch of sophistry. Doubt about the unperceived object is removed when its non-perception is causally explained as being due to the presence of an obstacle of some sort. If no explanation is forthcoming, even a doubt about whether such a thing exists, has to be given up.

(18) Testimony-Based Rejoinder.

Proponent: The soul is eternal but imperceptible—so says our *Śruti* (the scriptures).

Rejoinder: Another (Buddhist) scripture says that the soul does not exist. And the scripture of the Jainas says, "The soul is non-eternal." This disparity among the scriptures cannot be explained.

(19) Rejoinder Based on the Difference of Scriptures.

Proponent: As in 10.

Rejoinder: Another scripture says that the soul is non-eternal. Thus, if you accept one scripture, why not the other? If you accept both, there is a contradiction.

Both 10 and 11 rejoin that acceptance of the authority of the scriptures would be inconclusive. Both rejoinders seem to be legitimate.

In the *Upāyahṛdaya* list, there is another futile rejoinder (number 10) called *kālasama*, which seems to be identical with number 16 of the *Nyāyasūtra* list, called by a different name, *ahetusama*, rejoinder based on the rejection of the reason. It has been already noted that not all the rejoinders listed in the *Upāyahṛdaya* would be futile. On some acceptable interpretation they may constitute sound objections to faulty arguments. A couple on the Nyāya list can also be interpreted in this way.

We will now turn to the *Tarkaśāstra,* whose list of sixteen is a quite different kettle of fish. According to G. Tucci (Tucci, 1929a), it probably antedated Diṅnāga, and an earlier redaction of it might have been present even before Vātsyāyana. Vasubandhu might have followed this text. The list of sixteen is subdivided into three groups, ten based on being contrary to the fact, three on false statements, and another three involving contradiction. Except for two, each of them matches with some name or other on the Nyāya list. Those two are explained below.

(9) Rejoinder Based on Non-Utterance.

Proponent: Word is impermanent because it is produced by effort.

Rejoinder: The utterance of the reason "produced by effort" creates the impermanence of the word. However, when such an utterance is not made, the word would be permanent. And once it is made permanent, it cannot be impermanent.

The equivocation in the rejoinder is too obvious to merit refutation. The utterance of the reason establishes, but does not create, any property of the subject-locus.

(10) Rejoinder Based on Difference of Products.

Proponent: The word is impermanent, like a jar.

Rejoinder: They (the word and the jar) cannot both be the same, that is, impermanent, for they produce different results. (Hence they cannot share the same property, impermanence, for they are very different as their respective products show).

This can be easily answered. Other examples of this type are noted, but I wish to skip them.

It should be mentioned here that the Rejoinder Based on Doubt, noted in the *Tarkaśāstra,* is different from number 14 on the Nyāya list, The Doubt-Based Rejoinder. It corresponds rather to the last one, number 24, on the Nyāya list, The Effect-based Rejoinder. Number 13 on the *Tarkaśāstra* list may not be the same as one on the Nyāya list, number 12, although they have the same name Counter-Example-Based Rejoinder. Number 16 on the *Tarkaśāstra* list is conceivably a new variety, which is explained as follows:

(16) Rejoinder Based on Contradicting One's Own Thesis. This seems to be a convoluted refutation which includes at least three of those found in the above Nyāya list (9, 10, and 16).

Proponent: The word is impermanent for it is produced.

Rejoinder: If *h* is connected and hence "united" with *s*, then it loses its force or power to prove *s*. If it is disconnected and hence is quite distinct from *s*, then also it cannot prove *s* (lack of connection disqualifies *h* from being the ground for inferring *s*).

Proponent (again): If your refutation is connected, and hence "united" with my thesis, then it cannot refute for the same reason. And if it is disconnected and hence "disunited" with the thesis, then also it cannot refute.

Rejoinder (again): If *h* comes before the statement of the thesis, then *h* cannot be a reason without there being a thesis for which it is a reason. And if the thesis is stated before *h*, then *h* becomes useless, for the thesis is already established.

Proponent (in final reply): I can say the same thing about your refutation vis-a-vis my position.

This seems to be reminiscent of Nāgārjuna in the early part of his *Vigrahavyāvartanī*, and is also a precursor to the elaborate argument of Srīharṣa in the introductory section to his *Khaṇḍanakhaṇḍakhādya*. Use of equivocation with regard to expressions like "connection" or "disconnection" (*prāpti*, *a-prāpti*) is obvious in the first part of the rejoinder, and hence this can be connected with numbers 9 and 10 on the Nyāya list. Obviously "connection" does not mean sameness in every respect nor does "disconnection" mean lack of influence in every respect. The rejoinder is based upon such assumption.

The second part is a reflex of number 16 on the Nyāya list. The reply of the proponent exploits the same point used by the rejoinder. This seems to be the general pattern of the destructive "refutation only" (*vitaṇḍā*) debate. And, I have argued above, it can of course be made respectable within limits.

A note on the last item on the Nyāya list, number 24, The Effect-Based Rejoinder, may be in order here. This seems to be connected with the Rejoinder Based on Doubt, number 8, on the *Tarkaśāstra* list, as noted above. Vācaspati (1936: 1151, under NS 5.1.37), comments that in the Buddhist tradition the Effect-Based Rejoinder is differently interpreted:

Proponent: Sound is impermanent because it is a product.

Rejoinder: A pot is a product from clay, and so on, while sound is a product from the striking of two material objects or the activity of the vocal organ, and so on. Since these two effects (products) are distinct from each other, such effecthood (producthood) cannot establish impermanence of the sound.

Vācaspati quotes from both Diṅnāga and Dharmakīrti in this context.

A certain lack of interest in formulating examples of futile rejoinders was in evidence in the later Buddhist school. Vasubandhu was not reluctant to talk about them (confer his *Vādavidhi*), but Diṅnāga in his *Nyāya-mukha* did not attach much importance to the subject of rejoinder (*jāti*) as a special topic for study. He claims that all wrong or futile rejoinders can be assimilated into some pseudo-reason (*hetvābhāsa*) or other. Diṅnāga developed a new logical theory in his *Hetucakraḍamaru* and successive works. This new way of analyzing arguments and inferences dominated the scene for about 700 or 800 years thereafter. In the *Nyāya-mukha,* Diṅnāga said, "refutation shows that the inference or the formulation of the argument is defective. *Jātis* (futile rejoinders) are those that expose the defect of such refutation." They are futile because they do not follow the rules for the sound inference (logic). They can be tackled in two ways. The proponent may not notice the defect of the refutation, in which case it would be a "clincher" or "check" called "overlooking the fault that should be pointed out" (*paryanuyojyopekṣaṇa*), number 19 on the *Nyāyasūtra* list of clinchers. Alternatively, the proponent may notice and point out the defect, in which case it would be a legitimate exposure of a fault. Diṅnāga also adds, "there can be an infinite variety of such rejoinders; therefore, I have no interest in enunciating them all" (compare Tucci's translation, 1930: 71).

Dharmakīrti followed the lead of Diṅnāga and summed up his view in the *Nyāyabindu* thus: "The futile counterpart rejoinders are the exposure of non-existing defects in the proponent's argument."

3.4 SOPHISTICAL REJOINDERS—JAINA STYLE

The Jainas for the most part accept the Nyāya conception of futile rejoinders. *Nyāyasūtra* 1.2.18 is discussed and referred to in the Jaina literature. However, Akalaṅka defined a futile rejoinder cryptically as a "wrong answer" (*mithyottaraṃ jātiḥ*). Akalaṅka's definition is quoted in the later texts and defended as giving the right analysis of a futile rejoinder.

It is however argued by the Jaina logicians that although the Naiyāyikas were right to thematize and classify the concept of *jāti* or sophistical rejoinder, they were wrong in their insistence on the use of such sophistry in a tricky debate for the purpose of victory (*vijaya*). Sophistry can of course confound the opponent in a debate, if he is one of lesser intelligence. Otherwise, an opponent may be confounded only for the time being. An intelligent debater can easily call the proponent's bluff and win the debate. Thus, in using sophistry the debater digs his own grave and makes himself easily vulnerable to defeat. In this respect, the Jaina logicians were on the same side as the Buddhist. Repeating Diṅnāga's view, the Jainas said that there may be infinite number of ways by which such false refutations may be formulated. Hence it may not always be worthwhile to enumerate or classify them exhaustively.

The Jaina doctrine of non-onesidedness (*anekānta*) was open to many refutations, some of which may well be sophistical (see below, chapter 6). Non-onesidedness means, roughly speaking, that things are not entirely different from each other nor are they totally identical. In other words, the relationship between one thing and another is one of difference-cum-nondifference (*bhedābheda*).

The opponent may now stand up and say: since a camel on this view is also non-different from yoghurt, one being asked to eat yoghurt may rush after a camel! This example is from Akalaṅka. It is reminiscent of the Connection-Based (futile) Rejoinder in the Nyāya list. It is said that the Buddha was born (previously) as an animal, and an animal can be a Buddha too. But still one should not forget the difference. For the Buddha is undoubtedly worthy of respect while animals are considered fit to be eaten (Akalaṅka, *Nyāyaviniścaya*, II, verses 273–74; in Akalaṅka, 1939).

Hemacandra commented that resolution of all the false rejoinders lies in explaining and examining the characteristic of a sound reason, which is, according to the Jainas, "not being otherwise possible." The reason, *h*, must be connected with *s*, by the relation of not being otherwise possible without *s* (cf. Matilal, 1982: 142–144). When this is emphasized, false rejoinders would be exposed and nullified.

3.5 CHECKS: THE NYĀYA SCHOOL

In the Nyāya School, a debate was like a game of chess, in that the opponent and the proponent make their moves and at the end there is a clincher, when one side will be checkmated. The various conditions under which one could be checkmated in debate were technically called *nigrahasthāna*. *Nigraha* means "defeat" or "censure;" hence this can be translated as a situation for defeat, or a ground for censure. We shall again follow the *Nyāyasūtra* list, which has twenty-two types of "defeat-situations."

1. Loss of the Proposed Thesis. This, and the following four on the list, can be described as tampering with the central elements in the argument schema, the thesis and the reason. The proper thesis is lost if it can be shown that the main characteristic of the counter-thesis is conceded in one's own thesis. We will follow Uddyotakara's interpretation, as Vātsyāyana's interpretation has certain problems. Example:

A: Sound is impermanent, for it is perceptible.
B: Objection: The universal, cowhood, is perceptible but permanent.
A: If cowhood is permanent, although perceptible, sound may be so.

This rather stupid reply by "A" invites the clincher that "A" has abandoned the original thesis. In Vātsyāyana's example, "A" replies to "B" by conceding that his own example, a pot say, may also be permanent because it is perceptible like cowhood. This is actually either a case of a deviating pseudo-reason, or else a case of an unestablished example. Vātsyāyana was apparently criticized by Vasubandhu and Diṅnāga (Uddyotakara referred to them as "*eke*" = some). Hence Uddyotakara gave the better example cited above, and argued that this type of censure depends upon the particular way the debater answers the opponent, and not whether something is essentially wrong with the argument.

Dharmakīrti repeated Diṅnāga's criticism in his *Vādanyāya*. Udayana sought a compromise. Naturally, in any clincher of this kind, some pseudo-reason or other may lie at the root. However, this type of clincher comes prior to the discovery of such a pseudo-reason. Udayana said that both examples, the one of Vātsyāyana and that of Uddyotakara, could be called "loss of the proposed thesis." In fact, the scope of this clincher was widened by Udayana. According to him, if the debater concedes, under pressure from the opponent, loss of the thesis, or the reason, or the cited example, or any qualifying adjective thereof, he is open to this type of defeat. Later logicians called it *uktahāni* "loss of what has been said," that is, giving up of any part of the originally-stated argument.

2. Changing the Thesis. This, as the name indicates, arises when the original thesis is changed or modified under pressure. Example:

A: Sound is impermanent, for it is perceptible, like a pot.
B: How about the objective universal, cowhood, which is both perceptible and permanent?
A: But cowhood is a pervasive entity while a pot is a non-pervasive, middle-sized (material) object.

Here "A" loses if "B" points out that this is a different issue. It may be that "A" is trying to distinguish between two types of perceptibles, the material objects and the abstract-universals as a preliminary to a further argument to support this thesis. But this silly way of putting the matter clinches the issue against him.

3. Contradicting the Thesis. This arises if the adduced reason contradicts the thesis. Example:

A: A substance is distinct from its qualities for we cannot perceive the substance without its color.

Here the adduced reason is in conflict with what the thesis states. Uddyotakara notes seven varieties of this clincher. In fact, any kind of lack of consistency in the debater's formulation of the argument is included here. For example, "the female ascetic is pregnant" is a thesis where the predicate contradicts the subject.

4. Denying the Stated Thesis. This arises if the debater is forced to deny in some way or other what he originally stated as his thesis. Being opposed by the retort that sound cannot be non-eternal because of its perceptibility, for cowhood too is perceptible and also eternal, the debater may say, "I did not mean to say that . . . " or "I was saying what somebody else holds," or "Who says that sound is non-eternal?" and so on.

In Loss of the Proposed Thesis (number 1), the denial is implicit, while here the debater explicitly denies something he has stated before.

5. Changing the Reason. This is something like shifting one's ground, in which, when one reason is found inadequate, the debater tries to cite another reason or qualify his previously adduced reason. Vātsyāyana's example is too elaborate and complicated. I cite the following as an example.

A: Everything that arises is destroyed.
B: No. Destruction arises but there is no destruction of destruction.
A: I mean: Everything that arises as a positive entity is destroyed.

"A" first uses "arising of any entity" as the reason, and then qualifies it as "arising of any positive entity," which is a different reason.

Some later logicians are not inclined to differentiate 3 from 5. Udayana says that in a full-fledged statement of an argument there are two formally-distinguishable parts: one that is stated to be proven or part of such a part, the other that is intended to prove it. Number 3 is a denial of the former, whereas 5 is a denial of the latter.

Checks 1–5 are all dependent upon the "wrong comprehension" of the nature of a logical argument or its "syllogistic" or proper verbal form. The next four checks, 6–9 depend upon the lack of linguistic comprehension.

6. Irrelevant Speech. This arises when the debater, finding no good and relevant reply, talks irrelevantly.

A: Sound is non-eternal, for it is a product.
B: But "product" is a noun, it is derived from the verb "produce," and so on.

"B" loses for the reply obviously has no relevance to the argument at hand.

7. Meaningless Sound-Utterance. This arises when the debater uses meaningless sounds to avoid any good reply.

A: As in 6.
B: No sound is eternal, for ka-ca-ta-ta-pa-etc., like ja-jha-etc.

It is like arguing *s* is *p* because *abracadabra.*

8. Incomprehensible Speech. To avoid the issue, the debater may indulge in incomprehensible speech and will be censured for the same. Udayana says that this may arise from the use of (1) highly technical expressions, (2) too ornate and roundabout expressions, or (3) highly ambiguous expressions. Neither the opponent nor the assembly would be able to understand the meaning even when the speech has been repeated thrice. Including this as a clincher avoids the use of riddles and such like in debate.

9. Incoherent Speech. Again, to avoid the issue, the debater uses a syntactically-disconnected word sequence, and he is censured for doing so. The example given is of the use of such expressions as: "Ten pomegranates, two cakes, this deer-skin, her father old." We might think of "Colorless sleep furiously green." Veṅkaṭanātha in his *Nyāyapariśuddhi* (Veṅkaṭanātha, 1901) calls it *ananvita* "lack of syntactic connection among the words."

Note that in 7, mere sounds (= letters) are uttered, which do not form any word at all. In 9, however, words are uttered, but they do not constitute any sentence giving any connected meaning or thought.

The next four Checks, 10–13, concern the wrong presentation of the well-recognized steps of the argument schema. As noted in chapter 1, according to the Nyāya school, the full-fledged presentation of the argument is given in five steps with a definite and fixed order.

10. Reversal of the Usual (Fixed) Order. If one states the reason first and then the thesis (or violates the usual order in some other way), he is open censure for his lack of knowledge of the fixed order. Obviously this gave rise to a controversy about what should be accepted as the standard fixed order and why. Different schools might choose a different order. However the debaters must acknowledge prior to the debate what order they will be following.

11. Omission of One or More Steps. This, obviously, is self-explanatory. One cannot simply state the reason without stating the thesis or the example.

Of course, this is itself debatable, for if the other side understands the debater, he may get away with a cryptically expressed argument. However, this is a technical fault, and can be used as a censure if the opponent pretends or actually feels that he does not understand the argument because it is not fully stated.

12. Adding Unnecessary Steps. If one reason or one example is sufficient, mention of a superfluous reason or example will be censured. This is also a technical fault.

13. Repetition. If without being asked to repeat, the debater re-states any words or ideas, he is liable to be censured for the same. For example:

A: Sound is eternal and letters are permanent.

Here, the second part repeats the first.

The next four, checks 14–17, arise from the illegitimate avoidance of the issue by the debater.

14. Silence. Even when the argument has been repeated thrice by the opponent or the assembly, the debater may fail to restate or answer and remain silent. The Buddhist and the Jainas, however, refuse to call this a clincher, for since silence does not prove anything, one way or another, it cannot show that the debater is bewildered. One may remain silent when one is faced with an improperly-formulated question (a position of proto-Wittgensteinian vintage).

15. Ignorance. The debater may fail to comprehend the stated argument even when it has been stated three times by the opponent or the assembly. He expresses or acknowledges his lack of comprehension and thereby is censured. Notice that while in 8, the utterance by the opponent is itself incomprehensible and recognized to be so by the assembly, here in 15, the utterance is comprehensible and recognized to be so by the assembly, but the debater fails to comprehend it.

16. Lack of Intellect. The debater here fails to comprehend, not the argument, but what would constitute a good reply to such an argument. He might betray his lack of intelligence by reciting a stray verse or smoothing his hair, or rubbing his palms one against the other (as Vācaspati says).

17. Evasion. The debater, being unable to give an adequate reply, tries to break off the debate by saying, "I am busy now," or "I am called by nature," or "I have another appointment," or "I am tired," and so on.

The next four, 18–21, are somewhat more serious than the previous ones. And the last one, 22, is the most serious one, which is universally accepted as a ground for defeat or censure.

18. Sharing the Fault. This arises when the debater, instead of refuting the opponent's reply with logical reason, replies by saying, "If this is the fault in my position, your position suffers from the same fault." This does not resolve the issue. Whoever resorts to this reply, concedes that his position is also faulty.

19. Overlooking the Opportunity to Censure. This is self-explanatory. The debater may be stupid enough to overlook a fault in the opponent's argument and fail to censure him. Then he will be censured himself in return by the opponent or by the assembly.

20. Censuring the Uncensurable. This is the opposite of 19. The debater may from stupidity attempt to censure the opponent when his argument has not been followed at all. Finding a flaw where it does not exist becomes a ground for censure. This is the wrong-footed censure.

21. Conceding a Wrong Theory. A debater usually accepts certain standard views as true. A debater belonging to the Sāṃkhya school would be committed, for example, to the theory that an effect pre-exists in its cause. In the course of the argument, if he says something that goes against this well-accepted tenet of the Sāṃkhya school, he can be censured on this account.

22. Citing a Pseudo-Reason. Any of the five cases of pseudo-reason can be used to censure any argument. The reason adduced may be either (1) a deviating reason, or (2) a contradictory reason, or (3) an unestablished reason or (4) a counter-poised reason, or (5) a mis-timed reason (cf. §1.2).

It is clear that the last five are more serious and logically relevant ways of faulting an argument of the opponent and thereby defeating him in the debate.

3.6. CHECKS: THE BUDDHIST SCHOOL

We may safely ignore the earlier Buddhist sources, such as *Upāyahṛdaya* and *Tarkaśāstra* and even the *Yogācāra-bhūmiśāstra*, because of the unsystematic nature of their discussion of the checks. Besides, they add very little to what we can gather from the Nyāya school. On the other hand, Diṅnāga explicity argued against the usefulness of supplying a list of clinchers or checks in the above manner and omitted such a section from his discussion in the *Nyāyamukha* (compare Tucci, 1930: 71).

For a more creative reshuffling of this topic, as well as for a constructive criticism of the Nyāya classification, we have to go to Dharmakīrti. He took a first look at the issue in his *Vādanyāya* and had a considerable influence upon his successors in both Buddhist and non-Buddhist traditions. He said that we need to recognize only two varieties of clinchers or defeat-situations (checks): one pertaining to the proponent while the other to the opponent. The first (by the proponent) is the statement of what is not an essential part of the proof or the argument; alternatively this may be also the non-statement of what is an essential part of the proof. (This dual interpretation is due to an ingenious compounding of words with negative particles which Dharmakīrti himself explained). The second (by the opponent) is an attempted exposure of a non-existent fault, or alternatively, the non-exposure of a real (existing) fault (again, the dual interpretation).

Dharmakīrti convincingly argued that all the twenty-two types of clinchers of the *Nyāyasūtra* can either be rejected or ultimately be reduced to one of the above two, or rather four, varieties. It is obvious that numbers 19 and 20 of the Nyāya were in an indirect way the precursor of Dharmakīrti's more systematic and sophisticated formulation of the types of clinchers.

This concludes our examination of the theory of debate in ancient India. We will now see how some of the ideas about logic which emerged from such debating theory were refined and systematized by later authors, beginning with Diṅnāga.

CHAPTER 4

Diṅnāga: A New Era in Logical Thinking

4.1 Diṅnāga's Theory of Inference

The creative period in what we may call "Buddhist Logic" starts with Diṅnāga (circa 400–480). Although there were some so-called logical texts written by the Buddhists in the pre-Diṅnāga period (see G. Tucci, 1929a, 1929b, and the preceding chapter), we must recognize that the Buddhist contribution to the development of logic in India actually began with Diṅnāga. Diṅnāga was perhaps the most creative logician in medieval (400–1100) India. He developed and systematized a theory of inference, as well as a theory of the concept of a logical reason or adequate inferential sign (*hetu*, *liṅga*), which became most influential among the logicians of all colors—Buddha, Hindu and Jaina—and was at the center of discussion and criticism in all the writings on logical theories for several centuries to come.

Diṅnāga wrote a couple of manuals specifically on logic, the *Hetucakraḍamaru,* summarized in §1.2, and the *Nyāyamukha*. However, in his *magnum opus,* the *Pramāṇasamuccaya,* he put his theory of logic in the broader context of his view on epistemology, that is to say, in the context of his *pramāṇa* theory. A *pramāṇa* is an instrumental cause for generating *pramā* or knowledge. Thus, in short, "*pramāṇa*" is a source or a means of knowledge. In this chapter, we will discuss Diṅnāga's theory of inference, the extent to which it is influenced by his epistemological doctrines, and its relations with his philosophy of language.

4.2 Knowledge in What Sense?: Ensuring Certainty

To explain the Buddhist view of knowledge, we have to mention two kinds of knowledge or knowing episode. Both are claimed to be cases of cognitive awareness that arise as episodes. There is no ownership of such episodes (for there is no person distinct from the "aggregate" of such episodes and much else besides) but each such episode is a discrete member of some awareness-series or other. Hence, we can say that each awareness-episode belongs to a particular awareness-series (an awareness-series is only a continuous sequence of distinct awareness-episodes that are connected casually in some relevant sense—the relevant sense being such that the latter is dependent upon the former for its "origination"). Hence, only in figurative language can we say that an awareness arises in a "person," or that a "person" owns the awareness.

In order to be a knowledge-episode, a cognitive awareness must be certain. This element of certainty is shared by both kinds of knowledge under discussion here. But there are two ways of ensuring this certainty, the *direct* way and the *indirect* way. "Ensuring certainty" implies removing doubt, that is, all possibilities of error. It is agreed that error creeps in as we let our mind, our fancy (imagination = *vikalpa*) take over. Hence, the *direct* way to ensure certainty is to prevent the play of fancy before it sets in. Prevention is much better than cure. This is possible only when the pure sensory awareness presents the datum (we call it the "percept") untainted by any imaginative construction (or any play of fancy). This is, therefore, the first kind of knowledge, according to Diṅnāga: sensation or sense-perception. Each such sense-perception perceives also itself. Therefore, each perceptual event, according to Diṅnāga, has the following structure: [percept-perception (percept)-(self-) perception]. Each percept is a unique particular. Perception is knowledge because the unique particular shines here in its own glory, uncolored by any play of fancy, any operation of the mind. This is the much-coveted epistemologist's foundation. For Diṅnāga, it is not simply a foundation; more importantly, it is knowledge *par excellence.*

There is also an *indirect* way of ensuring certainty, according to Diṅnāga. This is not a preventive measure as before, but a curative measure. The play of fancy is allowed to set in, but possibilities of error are gradually removed. A doubt is transformed into a certainty, for, the grounds of doubt are all removed or destroyed. This can happen either through the employment of an inferential mark called the "indicator" reason (*liṅga*), or through a proper linguistic expression, a word (*śabda*). In both cases we deal with a general notion of *sign*. It is through the route of a sign that we are led to the object, finally the particular. Since we are not directly confronted with the object, we cannot take the direct route. We cannot prevent the operation of the mind before it sets in. We, in fact, let our fancy play, and then use it to reach the required certainty.

How does a sign lead to the knowledge of the object? It would be highly uninteresting if we say that there will be a particular sign for each particular object, so that seeing the sign, we would know that the object is there. Seeing my friend's car parked outside, I know that my friend is in. But it is more interesting and non-trivial when we can talk about a general sign for a number of particular objects. In the previous case, we have to see not only the sign, but also, at least once, both the sign and the object together in order to learn that it is the sign of that object. In the latter case, we connect a general sign with a general concept under which several particular objects fall. In fact, the general aspect of the sign is connected with the general aspect of the objects concerned. Seeing, or obtaining, a particular sign, we consider its general aspect and from the general aspect of the sign we are led to the general aspect of the object. Our mind, our "imaginative" (constructive) faculty, will take us that far. But if the connection between the general aspects is the right one (in the manner to be described below), the general aspect will remove all rival possibilities or opportunities for all errors to lead us to the certainty that there is a particular object there, an object that falls under that general concept.

4.3 The Concept of a Sign

What is a sign? Diṅnāga said that any property can be the sign for a second property, provided (1) it has been observed to be with the second property at least once, and (2) no example of the "contrary possibility" has been observed or cited. A contrary possibility would be a case where an instance of the sign is present but not the property signified by it. The first condition could be called suggestion of the possibility, while the second, exclusion of the contrary possibility. Our knowledge of the sign will lead to knowledge of the property, provided certainty is reached through this dual procedure: the possibility is suggested begetting an uncertain awareness and contrary possibilities are excluded yielding certainty.

Diṅnāga used the above theory of sign and object to show how, apart from sensory perception, inference and linguistic utterance yield knowledge in the *indirect* way. A body of smoke is observed with a body of fire suggesting the possibility of one being the sign for the other. This means that sighting of a fire or a body of smoke may lead to a doubt: perhaps, there is also smoke (or fire, as the case may be) there. In such cases, only two conditions of the triple-conditioned (*trairūpya*) inferential mark or *hetu* are fulfilled, according to Diṅnāga, and hence, only a dubious awareness can be generated as a result. For certainty, we need the third condition called *vipakṣa-vyāvṛtti* or, in our language, "exclusion of other possibilities." This needs awareness about the absence of any example ("counter-example")—a case where the sign is present but the object is not. Now, this also determines which one of the two, fire or smoke, in the previous example, could be the sign or the inferential mark or indicator, and which one would be the object, the inferable object. Examples of fire without smoke are easily available, but none of smoke without fire. Hence, our sighting of a body of smoke suggesting the possibility of fire makes it certain by excluding any contrary possibility, viz., that of there being smoke somewhere even when no fire is there.

The above way of putting matters, as far as inference is concerned, would raise problems for logicians; but with Diṅnāga, the epistemologist, this would be unproblematic. For the logicians, inference of fire from smoke would arise from the relation that we have pinpointed as "exclusion of the contrary possibilities" (or "absence of a counter-example"). But, some would argue, the above way of putting matters would be psychologizing logic. For logic, it does not really matter how a person argues or arrives at the inferential conclusion (for example, by first noticing the suggestion of the possibility and thereby entertaining a doubt and then arriving at a certainty). It would be enough to say that *A* is a logical sign of *B*, provided *A* is such that no case of *A* is a case of non-*B*, or, what comes to the same thing, that every *A* is *B*. The only assumption needed here would be that there are *A*s and *B*s. In this way, it will be argued, logic can be freed from the fault of the psychologism.

While I fully approve of the way logic is to be done, or is being done today without reference to psychological or epistemological implication, I would like to maintain that the above way of psychologizing logic is not a totally censured procedure. For, we are not interested here in the particular way a person infers or derives his conclusions, but rather in the general "impersonal" conditions or factors that give rise to knowledge-episodes and other awareness-episodes. Besides, each knowledge-episode is identified by virtue of what is "contained" in it or "grasped" by it, and not by virtue of its ownership. And what is contained in such knowledge is derived from what is expressed or expressible by a corresponding utterance or linguistic expression. Logic, which seems to avoid psychologism, deals, nevertheless, with sentences, utterances, statements, or propositions. To be sure, utterances are no better than episodes (similar to our knowledge-episodes), and propositions are no worse than abstract entities.

Conceding in this way the charge of psychologizing logic (psychologism is not always a crime), we may return to Diṅnāga, the epistemologist. One of the traditional problems, that survived for a long time in the history of Indian logic, one that has at the same time been a puzzle for modern researchers in Indian logic, is the following. According to Diṅnāga's celebrated theory, the *hetu*, indicator-reason must have these three characteristics:

1. It must be present in a location where the property characterizing the locus would be also present.

2. It must also be present in a *similar* location.
3. It must not be present in any *dissimilar* location.

The triple condition mentioned in 1, 2, and 3 above is nothing but the articulation of a particular relation between the property to be inferred, technically called the *sādhya*, on the one hand, and the reason, or *hetu*, on the other. The notion of a "similar location" and "dissimilar location" (*sa-pakṣa* and *vi-pakṣa*) are two technically defined concepts in the system. A similar location is one where the likes of the inferred object would be present. A dissimilar location is a place where the likes of the inferred object will never be present. An example will make it clear. Suppose we are trying to infer whether sound is impermanent on the basis of its being a product. In this case, producthood would be the basis for the inference and technically called the "reason" (*hetu*), and the characteristic of being impermanent is the property to be inferred. A similar location would be any place where impermanence is present, for example, a pot. A dissimilar location would be any permanent entity such as the sky or the atoms. Thus, the triple condition would be satisfied if (1) not only the location of the locus's property is also the locus of producthood, the *hetu*, but also the following two conditions hold: (2) there is a location, for example, a pot, where producthood is present as well as impermanence, inferred property, and (3) there is no place where impermanence is absent but producthood is present. Condition 3 in effect says that impermanence must be connected with producthood in such a way that if producthood is present, impermanence cannot be absent therefrom.

The problem with this theory is that it seems that not all the three are jointly necessary. Even if (2) is not interpreted as "it is to be present in *all* cases where the object to be inferred is present," it seems clear that (l) and (3) together would be sufficient to make the indicator-reason adequate to generate a sound inference. This apparently falsifies Diṅnāga's insistence upon the necessity of (2) along with (1) and (3) as constituting the required sufficient condition of the indicator-reason.

It is difficult to say categorically what Diṅnāga actually intended. For there are passages in Diṅnāga that indicate that he wanted both conditions to be necessary, however, there are other passages where it seems that he conceded the charge of redundancy. Among the modern interpreters, Kitagawa (1965) cites philological evidence to demonstrate that Diṅnāga did not intend the second condition, that the reason is present in some locus or other where the property to be inferred is also present, to be a contraposed version of the third condition. The second condition was necessary, according to Kitagawa, in order to avoid confusion between two types of pseudo-reason (*hetvābhāsa*), inconclusive (*anaikāntika*) and incompatible (*viruddha*). Kitagawa pointed out one strong argument in favor of his interpretation of Diṅnāga. While

Diṅnāga was illustrating the pseudo-reason at *Pramāṇasamuccayavṛtti* II 6c, d and 7, he cited cases where the indicator-reason would satisfy the second condition but not the third and vice versa. Now, it would have been impossible for such cases to be recognized if the two conditions were logically equivalent according to Diṅnāga. S. Katsura (1983), however, has recently convincingly argued that Kitagawa's interpretation was on the wrong track, for there is unmistakable evidence that Diṅnāga in several places of his *Pramāṇasamuccayavṛtti* recognized that the second condition states positively what is stated in the contraposed version of the third condition. This was how later Buddhists such as Dharmakīrti interpreted Diṅnāga. In the history of logic it is not unusual to find such anomalies of interpretation. The history of Indian logic was no exception to the general state of affairs. Hence it is not unusual to see such ambiguities in the writings of a great logician like Diṅnāga.

I have already said that part of the problem arises as soon as we switch from epistemology to logic. In epistemology, our problem is to find how certainty is to be attached to an awareness-episode, when the said direct route to certainty, disallowing the mind or the play of fancy to operate, is not available. It is to be observed that an awareness-episode may very well be true or fact-corresponding, even when it lacks the required psychological certainty. For it lacks certainty when, and only when, proper evidence or argument cannot be given. But this does not affect the fact of its being true. The epistemological enterprise is to supply the required evidence or argument, so that we may not attach psychological certainty to a false awareness (because very often we feel sure even of our false awareness.) Thus, if the proper evidence or argument can be adduced, we can eliminate false psychological certainty, and arrive at what we may now call logical certainty. Psychological certainty is simply subjective, while logical certainty is supported by an evidence or reason.

In inference, an awareness of *A* (the indicator-reason) with regard to a particular case or a set of particular cases (called *pakṣa*) leads to an awareness of *B* (the inferable object property). First, we have to grant that the awareness of *A* with regard to the particular place or places must be certain, if it has to yield certainty in our awareness of *B* with regard to the same place. The situation is this: certainty of *A* with regard to the particular place coupled with some additional information will yield certainty of *B* occurring in the same place (*pakṣa*). This additional information comes from our previous knowledge. An assumption is made, namely, if a rule or pattern emerges from previous knowledge we may hold it true also for the case under consideration. Therefore, if previous knowledge yields that contrary possibilities (possibilities of there being *A* without there being *B*) are absent, we may hold the same to be true in the case or cases under consideration. In this way, the indicator-reason *A* will fulfill the third and the first condition of a proper sign and thus we may reach the required certainty. But Diṅnāga insisted that something more is needed as the additional information from previous knowledge in order to lead us to the required certainty: condition 2. In other words, exclusion of contrary possibilities is not enough, information about an actual case of co-occurrence of *A* and *B* in a place is to be supplied from previous knowledge in order to ensure the required certainty. Why? Is it not enough to know that there cannot be absence of *B* in the present place, for example, the case under consideration, for there is *A*? What, in other words, did Diṅnāga have in mind when he insisted upon the second condition as being necessary?

4.4 CONDITION 2 VERSUS CONDITION 3: EPISTEMOLOGIZING LOGIC

One answer to the above question is the following. We find it easier to collect from previous knowledge some information about a co-occurrence of *A* with *B* than that about the exclusion of the contrary possibilities. Hence, we can imagine that the citation of a case of co-occurrence would bring us nearer to certainty. For example, a doubt whether there is *B* or not would be brought within the range of possibility. Next, the exclusion of contrary possibilities would assign the required certainty.

This answer seems plausible if we regard Diṅnāga as being concerned here only with the psychology of inference, and not with logic. But I would now argue that this answer is wrong, for Diṅnāga cited definite examples where such gradual steps, viz., doubt—possibility—certainty, have not been marked separately. This leads us to the consideration of those particular examples where contrary possibilities are eliminated, but it is not possible to obtain examples of co-occurrence from previous knowledge, for *A* is such that it could be and is present only in the given places, for example, the cases under consideration. In other words, *A* is a unique mark or character of the *pakṣa*, the case (or cases) under consideration. For example,

> P1: Sound has impermanence, for it has sound-hood (or audibility).

It does not seem counter-intuitive to say that sound-hood or being a sound (or a noise) cannot be the logical mark or basis for inferring impermanence. If, however, we reformulate the argument as given below, as is the practice with most modern writers of the history of Indian logic, it seems logically impeccable.

> P2: Whatever is a sound or is audible is impermanent. This is audible (a sound). Ergo, this is impermanent.

I submit that P2 cannot be a proper reformulation of P1. For P1 does not want to show, as P2 wrongly assumes, that a particular case is a case of sound (an audible object) and, therefore, it is impermanent. Rather it tries to show that all cases of sound are impermanent, for they are simply the cases of sound. I shall, therefore, dismiss P2 as a reformulation of P1, and consider only P1 instead. It should also be noted, in the light of my previous comments, that the proposition "sound is impermanent" may very well be true or the awareness that sound is impermanent may be fact-corresponding, but Diṅnāga's claim here is simply that it lacks the required logical certainty (in the sense defined earlier).

We can now face the question of justifying this claim. If the contrary possibility of something being a sound and not impermanent has been excluded by the information available from previous knowledge (that is, by the available information), why can't we decide that sound (all cases of sound) is impermanent? Here we reach the crux of the matter. We have to remember that all cases of sound are not (at least, in principle) part of the available information. They lie outside the domain that is constituted by available information. We are only certain of one more thing: sounds are sounds, or have sound-hood (or have audibility). This is an *a priori* certainty. But this does not guarantee that cases (instances) of sound are the kind of things of which impermanence or permanence is predicable. It could be that sounds are neither. Such a guarantee is available only if we could cite a case, independently of the present situation, where both the indicator-reason and the inferable object exist together, and show that the present case is similar to such a case. This is, therefore, part of the justification for Diṅnāga not being totally satisfied with the exclusion of contrary possibilities (*vipakṣāsattva*), and thereby insisting upon citation of a similar case or a case in point (*sapakṣasattva* = *sādharmyadṛṣṭānta*). P1 is, accordingly, declared as inconclusive or uncertain. Hence, it is not a deductively valid argument as is P2. It is being declared as uncertain, because it is quite a different sort of argument whose certainty is not determinable.

The above discussion raises many fundamental philosophical and logical issues—issues connected with the meaning of negation, logical negation and contraposition, contradictories and contraries, possibility and certainty. While I do not wish to enter into such issues in the present context, I would claim that all these issues are relevant here. Briefly, I would note a couple of points. First, the above justification assumes that lack of togetherness of *A* with non-*B* does not necessarily imply togetherness of *A* with *B*. As Richard Hayes (1986) has rightly stated, while "every *A* is *B*" may presuppose (as it does in the interpretation of the Aristotelian syllogistic) that there are *A*s, "no *A* is non-*B*" may not, under this theory, presuppose that there is at least one *A* which is *B* also. For, as I have already argued, all *A*s may be such things with regard to which the question of their being either *B* or non-*B* does not arise. Hence, "an *A* is neither *B* nor non-*B*" is a further possibility that is not eliminated by the exclusion of the contrary possibilities. And since such a further possibility is not eliminated, the required certainty that the case under consideration is *B* is not reached. Citation of a "positive" example with *A* and *B* together eliminates the said third possibility, and thereby leads us to the required certainty.

From what has been stated so far, it follows that "not non-*B*" is not always equivalent to "*B*," for sometimes it could mean something with regard to which the question of being either *B* or non-*B* does not arise. Further, *B* and non-*B* are not contradictories, in this way of looking at things, since they can only be contraries in the sense that they both may fail to apply to some cases (which are neither *B* or non-*B*).

4.5 A JUSTIFICATION OF DIṄNĀGA'S HESITATION ABOUT CONTRAPOSITION

It may be noted here that part of the problem is connected with the confirmation of induction. For, Diṅnāga insisted (in the account of the second type of inference noted in his *Hetucakra*) that to confirm that all products are perishable or impermanent we need not only a perishable product, such as a pot, as a positively-supporting example, but also a nonperishable non-product, such as the sky, as a negatively-supporting example (compare *vaidharmya-dṛṣṭānta*). The puzzle here is reminiscent of C. G. Hempel's puzzle in a similar context, viz., confirmation of an induction. Just as each black raven tends to confirm that all ravens are black so each green leaf, being a non-black non-raven, should confirm that all non-black things are non-ravens (which is equivalent to saying that all ravens are black).

For Diṅnāga, however, one can propose the following resolution of the puzzle. Taking some liberty with the notion of negation and contraposition, one may say that for Diṅnāga while "all ravens are black" implies "all non-black things are non-ravens," it is not equivalent to the latter. In other words, the latter may not imply the former. For, suppose all black ravens are destroyed from the face of the earth. It will still be true that all non-black things are non-ravens, for there will be green leaves, and so on, to certify it, but "All ravens are black" need not be held true at least under one interpretation of such a universal proposition (for there are no ravens to confirm it!). This also means that in Diṅnāga's system we will have to assume that only universal affirmative propositions carry existential presupposition.

If we view matters in this way, we can find an explanation why Diṅnāga insisted that both a positive and a negative example are needed to confirm the required inference: sound is perishable because it is a product. It seems to explain also why in the above example, P1, it is claimed that because of the lack of a positive example to confirm that each audible fact is perishable, the inference (certainty of the conclusion) is not decidable. We may notice that Diṅnāga did supply the so-called negative example in each of the three cases in his *Hetucakra* to confirm the assertion "No non-*B* is *A*."

But why this stricture upon "All audibles are perishable"? Why can it not be implied by "All nonperishable things are nonaudible"? One may think that we need to be sure that there are audible things before we can assert that all audibles are perishable. But this will not do. For if we admit the first character of the "triple-character" of the reason we have to allow that there are audible things, for we have admitted that sounds or noises are audible. Hence the previous consideration for disallowing equivalence between "all audibles are perishable" and "all nonperishable things are nonaudible" does not arise in the context of the given inference. Then, why this insistence? An answer to this puzzle is not easily forthcoming from the tradition of the Buddhist logicians after Diṅnāga.

A tentative suggestion may be given. Suppose that "audible" and "perishable" have only their contraries in such formulations as "inaudible" and "nonperishable." This means that there may be things that are neither audible nor inaudible. The "audible-inaudible" predication applies to the domain of only percepts: color and shape, sound, smell, taste, and touch. Further suppose that the domain of perishable-imperishable things may not lie wholly within the domain of audible-inaudible things. In this case it would be possible that some imperishable things (or even a perishable thing) could be neither audible nor inaudible! It is not always counterintuitive to say that nonperishable things such as the sky or the soul are very different sorts of things to which neither audibility nor inaudibility will apply. In this case it may be trivially true (allowing some ambiguity in the notion of negation) that no nonperishable things are audible. But confirmation of this trivial truth will not remove the said doubt whether an audible thing is perishable or not. For it may be neither! Such a dubious possibility is removed only if we can cite an example that is both audible and perishable (or imperishable, as the case may be). If we believe that a particular instance of sound is both audible and perishable then citing such a supporting example we can decide that sound is perishable. This way of citing an example from the domain of the *pakṣa* (which should ideally remain in the twilight zone of doubt until the inference is concluded) to support the *vyāpti* relation is called the *antarvyāpti-samarthana*. This was a later development in the post-Diṅnāga period.

The above defense of Diṅnāga is admittedly very weak. But Diṅnāga the epistemologist, was concerned with both the certainty over all possible doubt and the confirmation of induction. Since he claims that the "negative" example is not enough and a "positive" example is needed for the required certainty, he must deny that "all ravens are black" is in any way implied by "all non-black things are non-ravens." This denial forces us to search for a possible situation that may not have been eliminated. Suppose "non-black" in my dictionary means white. It will still be true that all non-black things are non-ravens, which may be confirmed by a white crane. Further suppose that I have never seen a raven and that I imagine that they are neither black nor white, they are grey. Only an actual black raven can remove my doubt in this case. The oddity implicit in such a consideration is not any more serious than the oddity in assuming that a green leaf confirms the rule "all ravens are black," or even in claiming that certain predicates are projectible in the sense of N. Goodman, while the complements of such predicates need not be so.

I have tried to show that there is a deep philosophical problem that is implied by a rather odd claim by Diṅnāga: a "positive example" is still necessary even when there is a negatively-supporting example. It is obvious from Diṅnāga's writing that he was never comfortable with such a so-called "negative" example (where no "positive" example is available for citation). What I have stated here is, I think, compatible with what S. Katsura (1983) has recently argued. Katsura cites two passages from Diṅnāga (PSV (K) 149b3–5, 150b5) where it is clearly said that a "negative" example may be unnecessary if the *vyāpti* "invariance" relation is supported by a "positive" example, and if the two examples are "well-known" either would be sufficient for they imply each other. I interpret that these comments of Diṅnāga are concerned with the cases that are called *anvaya-vyatirekin* (in Nyāya), for example, cases where both (a "positive" and a "negative") examples are available (*prasiddha* "well-known") but not both of them may be cited in the argument-schema. In other words, these comments do not concern the "limiting" cases where a "negative" example is cited simply because no positive example is even available (confer, *vyatirekin* or *kevala-vyatirekin* and the *asādhāraṇa* in the *Hetucakra*). The *asādhāraṇa* or "uniquely inconclusive" evidence (number 5 in the *Hetucakra*) is such a limiting case. For Diṅnāga, both the *asādhāraṇa* and the *vyatirekin* (which is claimed to be correct by Nyāya) are equally inconclusive for similar reasons (absence of a citable positive example to support the induction).

4.6 THE TRIPLE-CONDITION AND KNOWLEDGE FROM WORDS

In the above, I have been mainly concerned with the exact significance of the so-called second character of the "triple-character" of the indicator-reason or the inferential sign. Many post-Diṅnāga writers found this to be redundant from a logical point of view, and it was generally admitted that the first character (which transpires as *pakṣadharmatā* in the Nyāya system) along with the third (which becomes another description of the *vyāpti* relation) would be sufficient to yield correct inferential knowledge. In this section, I shall concentrate upon the third character in order to show how Diṅnāga extended his theory of inference to include also his theory about how to derive knowledge from language or words giving rise to the celebrated Buddhist doctrine of *apoha*, or exclusion of rival possibilities, as an explication for universals. The general sign, whether inferential or linguistic, leads us to the knowledge of the signifiable object provided it is (empirically) established that the former is excluded from whatever excludes the latter, the signifiable object.

Perception yields knowledge of the particulars. Knowledge from the sign, that is, from inference and language, is always about the general. We cannot know the particulars in this way. From my knowledge of the inferential sign, a body of smoke, there arises my knowledge of fire in that place (the *pakṣa*), that is, my knowledge that the place excludes connection with non-fire. Our non-perceptual knowledge based upon the sign cannot be more definite than this sort of general connection. We cannot, for example, know what particular fire-body is there in the place from simply seeing the smoke that is there, but we can only ascertain that the hill (the place) is, at least, not without fire (that is, it is not the case that the hill lacks fire; confer *ayoga-vyavaccheda*). Similarly from the word "fire" (that is, the utterance of the word "fire") the hearer has a knowledge of the object referred to only in some general way. The hearer becomes aware that the object referred to is not something that is non-fire. The sign "fire" (the word) certifies simply the lack of connection of the intended object with non-fire. Just as the knowledge of smoke (the inferential sign) leads to our knowing that the hill lacks the lack of connection with some fire-body, knowledge of the word "fire" leads to our knowing the object of reference as excluded from non-fire. Just as from smoke we cannot know what particular fire-body is there, from the word "fire" too we cannot know a particular fire-body but only that something excludes non-fire. If by the meaning (*artha*) of a word we understand what the hearer knows from hearing the utterance of it, then "fire" can be said to mean "exclusion of non-fire" or "what excludes non-fire."

After underlining the similarity between both the ways an inferential sign and a linguistic sign yield knowledge of the signified, Diṅnāga argued that this would be a reasonable course to take in order to dispense with the objective universals of the Naiyāyikas (or at least a large number of such universals) as ontological entities, distinct from the particulars. It is easy, for example, to assume that because common names, that is, kind-names and material-names, are applied to different and distinct particulars, we must posit some common or shared character, shared by the group of particulars to which they are applied. Realists like the Naiyāyikas regard these shared characters (kind-properties or fundamental class-properties), at least some of them, to be not only real but also distinct from the individuals that instantiate them. This has traditionally been understood as the problem of universals. For if we assume, as the Naiyāyikas do, that a shared character such as "cowhood" or "firehood" is a distinct reality locatable or manifested in a particular then we are further required to assume a suitable relation that would make the manifestation of one reality in another possible. In other words, there should be a relation that will make it possible for one reality, cowhood, to be located in another, a cow. The Naiyāyikas' answer is that there is such a relation, *samavāya*, which we translate, in the absence of a better word in English, as "inherence." This relation combines real universals with particulars. This raises many intricate questions. For example, how can a real entity be shared by many real and distinct entities, and still be one and the same? How can one and the same entity be present in many disconnected and different spatio-temporal locations? What happens to such an entity if and when all its particular manifestations are extinct? Whenever a new set of similar entities (artefacts) are manufactured, do we thereby create new (objective) universals? And so on and so forth.

In simple language, the familiar problems of universals arises in this way. We would generally say that there are cows, and pots, there is water, fire, gold, and so on. In effect this means that there are distinct (identifiable) individuals (in this world) to which we apply the term "cow" or "fire." We need a philosophical explanation to answer the obvious question: what warrants us (that is, becomes the *nimitta* for us) to apply such terms the way we do apply such terms, to different individuals? Words, to use the modern style, either denote or designate objects, yes. But is there any basis, causal or otherwise, that we can call the *nimitta*, for such designation or denotation? What accounts for the use of the same term to designate different particulars? For, if there is none, language-learning would be for the most part an unexplained mystery.

4.7 KNOWLEDGE OF WORD-MEANING AND *APOHA*

Some philosophers would like to treat the above question as only a rhetorical question, the answer to which is obvious. It will be claimed that there is some unity among the disparate entities denoted by a term, the unity that provides the *nimitta*, that is, that accounts for the application of the term in question. This unity may not be regarded as an ontologically real entity distinct from each individual that has it. If such *nimittas* or "bases," that is, the purported unities, are observable criteria (as happens in most cases), then the problem is easily resolved. King Daśaratha had three wives, and, hence, these three individuals shared the feature, being married to Daśaratha, by which we may only refer back to the three observable events of marriage. But, for most of our basic terms such a device is not at all available. To sustain the claim that the purported unities in such cases are distinct realities has been one of the hardest problems in philosophy. And yet one has nagging doubt as to whether the full-fledged nominalistic program can succeed. In fact, it seems preferable if one can maintain that the so-called abstract universals, those unities, are neither full-blown realities, as the Naiyāyikas and some other realists would like to have them, nor totally dispensable concepts. In this matter, the Buddhist of the Diṅnāga-Dharmakīrti school seems to suggest a way out. This is called the *apoha* doctrine. It is regarded as an epistemological resolution of an ontological problem. The point is the following. We need not accept universals as real and distinct entities merely on the basis of the familiar argument that has been sketched here, unless of course there are other compelling reasons to believe in such entities. Our ability to use the same term to denote different individuals presupposes our knowledge or awareness of sameness or similarity or some shared feature in those individuals. This shared feature may simply be our agreement about what these individuals are not, or what kinds of terms cannot be applied to them. "This is a cow" denies simply such predicates as cannot be predicated of the object in question. True, we cannot talk here in terms of a broader indefinite class on each occasion. The cow is said to be excluded from the class of non-cows, and the white lotus from both the class of non-white and that of non-lotus. But such classes (the so-called complement classes) are constructible each time with the help of the particular linguistic sign (the word) we use on each occasion. They are arguably less substantial and less objective than the positive class of lotuses or the class of blue things. For, in the latter cases, there is a tendency in us to believe further that there are objective class-properties shared by, and locatable in, the numbers of such classes. If these objective class-properties are explained in terms of some other realities that we do concede, well and good. In our previous example, "being married to king Daśaratha" did not present any problem. Similarly we can, for example, say that the university studentship is only a convenient way of talking about a bundle of particular facts, admission of each person in university as a student. But in some cases the so-called objective property tends to be a unitary abstract property, a full-blown real universal, and thereby invites all the other problems that go along with it. In the case of a constructed class of non-cows, the search for a common property as an objective class-property is less demanding, for it is clear from the beginning that we cannot find any objective property (except the trivial one, non-cowness) to be shared equally by horses, cats, and tables. The program for finding such a common property is, so to say, "shot" from the beginning. We may note that the trivial property, the lack of non-cowness or denotability by "cow," is constructible on each occasion and hence it is a "conditional" or conceptual property.

If the above argument is sound then we have captured at least part of the Buddhists' philosophical motivation for developing the *apoha* doctrine as a viable alternative to the doctrine of real universals. It is also true that in constructing the so-called "negative" classes, we implicitly depend upon the notion of some "positive" class-property. For how can one talk about the class of non-cows without having the notion of the class of cows? (In modern terminology we call the class of non-cows the "complement" class in order to underline this dependence upon the initial class of cows.) This is, in substance, part of the criticism of Kumārila and Uddyotakara against the Buddhists.

A tentative answer is the following. We can formulate or construct the class of non-cows as the class of those entities where the term "cow" is not applicable. True, the word "cow" itself is a universal. But we do not have to accept any objective universal such as cowhood over and above the word "cow." (This coincides with the nominalist's intuition that words are the only universals that we may have to concede. This is also partly Bhartṛhari's intuition about universals when he talks about word-universal (*śabda-jāti*) and object-universal (*artha-jāti*) and makes the latter only a projection of the former. But this will take us beyond the scope of this introductory work.) We can actually define our "negative" class as one constructible on the occasion of the use of each substantial word in terms of the word itself. Once this is done, a search for the common unitary class property (a real one) is not warranted any more, unless for some other compelling reason. This is not pure nominalism, for word-universals are admitted.

There may be an alternative answer, which may not amount to a very different sort of consideration. Each non-perceptual awareness of a cow (which follows, and is inextricably confused with the pure sensory perception of a cow-particular) has a common "cow-appearance" (*go-pratibhāsa*). We may treat this as the shared feature of all the distinct events of our non-perceptual awareness of cows. This would be similar to a type of which each awareness-event (of a cow) would be a token. Now the class of non-cows can be redefined as the class of non-cow-appearance, which may then be explained as the class of items that are not connected with the awareness-events having cow-appearance. Now the origin of this cow-appearance or appearance of the cow-form (distinct from the appearance of the object, the particular, in the perceptual awareness) belonging to the nonperceptual awareness, can be traced to our desire to conceptualize and verbalize, that is, to sort out distinct awareness-events and make them communicable. This becomes possible due to the availability of the concept "cow" and the word "cow." In this consideration, we also move closer to the Bhartṛhari thesis about language, according to which words and concepts are implicitly and inextricably mixed up so much so that a concept is nothing but an implicit speech-potential, a not-yet-spoken word.

This cow-appearance or cow-form is no part of the objective reality that we sensorily perceive but it is supposed or imagined to be there. Hence it is less substantial than such an objective universal as cowhood, which it is meant to replace. This suggested paraphrase of "cowhood" by "denial of or exclusion of non-cow predication" may be regarded as philosophic reparsing. (We can take this paraphrase to be somewhat like the "paraphrasis" in Jeremy Bentham's theory of fiction. As W. V. Quine has noted, this is a method that enables a philosopher, when he is confronted with some term that is convenient but ontologically embarrassing, to continue to enjoy the services of the term while disclaiming its denotation.) Diṅnāga's motivation in explaining cowhood as exclusion of non-cows was not very far behind. Indeed, Dharmakīrti found the real universals of Nyāya ontologically embarrassing and suggested that they can be conveniently explained away by using the notion of "exclusion" and "otherness." Again, this is not pure nominalism.

It is true that the so-called non-perceptual awareness of a cow is sequentially connected with the sensory perception of a particular. But, for the Buddhists, this is a contingent connection, the latter awareness being contingent upon our desire, purpose, inclination, etc., as has already been emphasized. The same thing, for example, can be called a doorstopper, a brick, an artefact, a work of art, or a murder instrument, depending upon the motivation of the speaker. The cow-appearance, or the cow-form, the common factor, becomes part of the latter "non-perceptual" awareness only when our perception becomes contaminated by some such motivation or other and thereby becomes impregnated with conceptions and latent speech-potentials. If we are motivated to obtain milk we call it a cow, if we are motivated otherwise we call it a beast, and if we are motivated, for example, to protect our flower-beds we may call it a nuisance.

Word-application or concept-application is an important part of our mental faculty. It is called by Diṅnāga (and others) *vikalpa* or *kalpanā*, "imagination," "conceptual construction," "imaginative construction." This is a means for identifying and distinguishing the percept or the "representation" of the object in perception. This distinguishing activity is performed with the help of words (or concepts, if one wishes). Conception, for the Buddhist, is a negative act. It is the exclusion or rejection of the imagined or supposed possibilities. Concept-application should thereby be reinterpreted as rejection of contrary concepts, and word-application similarly as rejection of contrary words. Noncontrary words need not be excluded. Therefore we can apply "cow" and "white" to what we call a white cow, "fire" and "hot" or "fire" and "substance" likewise to a fire-body. For these are not contrary pairs. Application of words makes us presuppose contrary possibilities only in order to reject them later. We may apply "a product" to remove the doubt whether the thing under consideration is a non-product or not, and we may apply "impermanent" to the same thing in order to eliminate the possibility of its being permanent. Hence the two terms "a product" and "impermanent" are not synonymous in spite of their being applied to the same object or objects. In fact, true synonymy is a hard thing to achieve in this theory. Two words can be synonymous not because there is some common objective universal that they mean, but because they may serve to exclude the same contrary possibilities (see *Tattva-saṃgraha* of Śāntarakṣita, verses 1032–3).

Dharmakīrti and his followers developed a theory of dual object for each awareness, perceptual or nonperceptual. One is what is directly grasped and called the "apprehensible" (*grāhya*) and the other is what is ascertained through the first and is called the "determinable" (*adhyavaseya*). In a perceptual awareness the apprehensible object is the datum or the particular whereas the determinable object is such a concept as cowhood, and therefore we pass the verbal judgement "It is a cow." In a non-perceptual (inferential or linguistic) awareness the apprehensible object is the concept cowhood, and the "determinable" is a particular. In the awareness arising from the utterance of the word "cow" what we apprehend is cowhood or cow-appearance or cow-form and what we determine through it is the (external) object "out there" whereupon we superimpose the cow-appearance or cowhood.

This cow-appearance or cowhood is to be interpreted as exclusion of non-cows. Thus in the so-called perceptual judgement "It is a cow" we determine that it is not a non-cow or that it excludes our non-cow supposition. In the inference or in the knowledge from the linguistic sign "cow," we likewise apprehend (directly) the exclusion of non-cows, which is then attributed or superimposed (confer *āropa*) upon the "determinable" object, the external thing, that we determine as excluding our non-cow supposition. In other words, hearing the word "cow" we not only apprehend cowhood but also determine an external object as being excluded from non-cows and such determination in its turn prompts us to act, that is, to proceed to get hold of the cow-particular that will give us milk, and so on. This answers the question about how are we prompted to act from simply a word-generated knowledge of the phoney universal.

To sum up: it must be admitted that the Buddhist substitute, *anyāpoha* (exclusion of the other) has a clear advantage over the Naiyāyikas' objective universal such as cowhood. Since "exclusion" is not construed as a separate reality, we need not raise the question of how it is related to what by its own nature excludes others. Exclusion of non-cows is a shared feature of all cows and therefore can very well be the "basis" for the application of the general term "cow." It is not absolutely clear whether talking in terms of the "exclusion" class, that of non-cows, has any clear advantage over our talking about the class of cows, that is, the positive class. It is, however, clear that formation of the "exclusion" class, that of non-cows, is *ad hoc* and dependent upon the occasion of each use of the general term. It is more clearly an artificially-formed class without any illusion about any underlying common property (a positive one) to be shared by its members. Furthermore, there is the denial rather than assertion of the membership of this artificially-formulated class in the final analysis of the use of such general terms. It seems to me that this device satisfactorily explains the use of the general terms at least without necessarily assuming objective universals. But whether or not we usually learn the use of such terms in this way is, however, another matter. Diṅnāga has said:

> The theory that the meaning (*artha*) of a word is exclusion of other "meanings" (*artha*) is correct because there is an excess of advantage (*guṇa*) in this view. For the characters of the objective universal, e.g. being a unity, being manifested fully in many (distinct things), can apply to "exclusion" since such exclusions are also nondistinct (a unity) in each case, and they do not have to vanish (being supportless) when the objects (individuals) vanish, and they are manifested fully in many. (Quoted by Kamalaśīla under verse 1000, in Śāntarakṣita, 1968: 389).

Notions such as "exclusion," "otherness," or "similarity" are not, however, dispensable even in this theory.

It may be noted here that the Naiyāyikas would also maintain that not all general terms would need objective universals as the "basis" for their application. The term "chef," for example, can be applied to different persons and the so-called basis for such application can be easily identified as similar objective particulars in each case, training in the culinary art, the action of cooking, and so on. Objective universals are posited sometimes to account for natural kinds, water, cows, and so on. Sometimes it helps to explain causal connections (compare *kāraṇatāvacchedaka*, and *kāryatāvacchadaka* in Navya-nyāya) such as the one between seedhood and sprouthood (to explain the fact that from each seed comes out some sprout or other). Sometimes admission of objective universals helps scientific taxonomy. Besides, objective universals are posited when we reach certain fundamental concepts such as substance, quality, and action. Objective universals can be treated as "unredeemed notes" as Quine has called them: "the theory that would clear up unanalyzed underlying similarity notions in such cases is still to come" (1977: 174). In Quine's view, they remain disreputable and practically indispensable and when they become respectable being explained by some scientific theory they turn in principle superfluous.

4.8 The "Wheel of Reason:" Diṅnāga and Uddyotakara

Chapter 1 outlined Diṅnāga's wheel of reason (*hetucakra*). The word "wheel" used as a translation of "*cakra*" does not mean a circular wheel in this context. It means a group, a set, a multitude. The word "reason" is denoting the property called *hetu*. Two well-known studies of this wheel of reason are available, one by Richard S. Chi, *Buddhist Formal Logic* (1968), the other by Richard P. Hayes, *Diṅnāga on the Interpretation of Signs* (1988). I shall here follow Hayes, for his exposition is the more elegant. Diṅnāga's seminal text is a systematic assessment of the state of a reason that might be put forward in support of given conclusions along with the indication why each one is or is not a good reason. Hayes understands Diṅnāga's inference as involving a process of confirmation or disconfirmation by making a comparison of two classes of individuals, with the aim of discovering the relation that the two classes have to one another. The reason or the *hetu* can then be called the evidence confirming the presence of *sādhya* or *sādhya-dharma* (inferable property) in a particular locus or location, called the *pakṣa*. Instead of going into the details (for they are already to be found in chapter 1) I shall use the following symbolic relations. Let the class H stand for the loci of the reason or *hetu*, and the class S for the loci of the property to be confirmed. To compare H with S we can easily note the following four possibilities: (1) there are those individuals that belong to both H and S; (2) there are those that do not belong to H but do belong to S; (3) there are that do belong to H but do not belong to S; (4) and there are those that belong to neither H nor S.

Hayes calls these four "sub-domains or compartments of the induction domain" (1988: 114). Using this convention the sixteen possible configurations of the induction domain can be represented in table 4.1.

TABLE 4.1
CONFIGURATIONS OF THE INDUCTION DOMAIN

	HS	*~HS*	*H~S*	*~H~S*
1	1	0	1	0
2	1	0	0	1
3	1	0	1	1
(4)	1	0	0	0
5	0	1	1	0
6	0	1	0	1
7	0	1	1	1
(8)	0	1	0	0
9	1	1	1	0
10	1	1	0	1
11	1	1	1	1
(12)	1	1	0	0
(13)	0	0	1	0
(14)	0	0	0	1
(15)	0	0	1	1
(16)	0	0	0	0

Here I have used the convention of representing an empty domain or sub-domain by 0 and a non-empty sub-domain by l. The tilde before H or S represents the complement of the class for which H or S stands. Of these sixteen, Diṅnāga mentioned only nine, those not bracketed. Uddyotakara (c. 550–625), after criticizing Diṅnāga for this, expanded the table to sixteen. There are further possible expansions of this scheme. For example, Uddyotakara noted that if we bring in such considerations as whether the locus-property is present in some, all or none of the options, then this table of sixteen can be easily expanded to a table of sixty-four or even further. However, although these are logical possibilities, most of these cases cannot be properly illustrated with examples. For a good representation of the sixteen cases, with the help of Venn diagrams, one should consult Hayes (1988, chapter 4).

CHAPTER 5

Dharmakīrti and the Problem of Induction in India

5.1 Three Kinds of Inference in Dharmakīrti's System

Dharmakīrti (c. 600–660) was a commentator on Diṅnāga. However, he was more than a commentator, he was an original thinker, a brilliant logician, and an astute thinker. His best-known book is called the *Pramāṇavārttika*, which is supposed to be an elaborate commentary on Diṅnāga's magnum opus, the *Pramāṇasamuccaya*. Like his master, Dharmakīrti wrote several manuals on logic, including the *Nyāyabindu*, the *Vādanyāya* and the *Hetubindu*. I shall concentrate here, however, on the *Pramāṇavārttika* and the *Nyāyabindu*.

Diṅnāga divided inference under two headings, *svārtha* and *parārtha*. The first is inferring for one's own sake, and the second is inferring for the sake of others. Inferring for one's own sake covers all the general problems, epistemological, logical and psychological, connected with the process of inference. Inferring for the sake of others involves the demonstration in language of the process of inference, so that others may be persuaded to accept the conclusions. There is, however, no essential difference in principle between these two types of inference.

Diṅnāga's classification became standard, not only for the Buddhist but also for the non-Buddhist. However, Dharmakīrti, in his *Nyāyabindu*, gives another classification of inference which seems to be more useful. Inference, he said, can be of three kinds. One is based upon the *svabhāva* (own-nature) or essential nature of the reason. The second is based upon a reason which is causally related to the property to be confirmed (*tad-utpatti*). The third is a reason which shows that some property is not present in the given locus (*anupalabdhi*).

Dharmakīrti illustrated the three kinds as follows. (1) Inference based on own-nature:

This is a tree because it is an oak tree.

The argument is based here upon the fact that the property of being an oak cannot characterize an object unless that object is also characterized by the property of being a tree. Another justification is given in this way: whatever is causally responsible for the property of being an oak cannot exclude the property of being a tree. Sometimes this inference has been described by modern scholars as being based upon the relation of class inclusion, sometimes as an analytical inference, but such explanations do not capture Dharmakīrti's full intention. Dharmakīrti uses another term to describe the relation involved: *tādātmya*, identity. The idea is that whatever is identical with an oak is necessarily identical with a tree. An oak cannot be but a tree at the same time.

Inference based upon (2) causal relation is illustrated as follows:

There is fire here because there is smoke here.

The explanation of this inference is given along the same lines as the previous one. It is in the nature of smoke that it cannot but be caused by some fire or other. Hence, smoke cannot be there without fire being there. The difference between this one and the previous one, however, is that, in the previous case, the two properties are in some sense identical, for whatever is an oak is also a tree. Here, the two properties, smoke and fire, are non-identical but causally related.

An inference based upon (3) non-perception is illustrated by:

There is no pot here because no pot is perceived here.

Dharmakīrti notes several varieties of this type of inference. I shall discuss each of these types of inference more in §§5.3–5.5, but first some general remarks.

5.2 PREDICTIVE INFERENCE VERSUS EXPLANATION

To understand Dharmakīrti's contribution to the development of the theory of inference in India, it would be useful to compare it with the notion of causal or scientific inference found in K. Hempel (1965). The model of inference to be studied could be written as:

q because *p*.

This should be read as an assertion that "p" is the case, and that there are laws, not explicitly specified, such that "q" follows logically from these laws in conjunction with the statement that "p." We can rewrite Dharmakīrti's model in a similar fashion, as:

G(*a*) because F(*a*).

This type of inference seems to be predictive rather than explanatory for it does not explain why must it be the case that G(*a*) rather than not. Rather, it states why it is the case that G(*a*), given that it is the case that F(*a*).

In the formula above, "F" stands for the indicator-reason (*hetu*), and hence, must fulfill, in accordance with Diṅnāga's doctrine, three conditions. The first condition is just that *a* is known to be f. The second and third conditions might be stated as:

It is known that all Fs are Gs, and
It is known that all non-Gs are non-Fs.

This reading, however, makes the second and the third condition logically equivalent, for one becomes the contrapositive of the other. In the last chapter, we have seen how this reading created puzzlement in the tradition. There is, however, another alternative reading, in which the second condition states that:

All known Fs are known to be G,

and the third condition that:

All known non-Gs are known to be non-F.

The above shows that the condition is that F and G are known to be nomologically related. The upshot of all this is that there should be no observations that falsify the putative laws. A law-like statement is thereby confirmed.

In the inference of the kind studied by Dharmakīrti, we move from the examined to the unexamined cases through a process of projection. The question is, what guarantees that the end-product of this process of projection will be knowledge? Dharmakīrti thinks that we can get such a guarantee by following a "method of association and dissociation" as reflected in conditions 2 and 3. In other words, our task is first to find a case where the two properties, the reason and the confirmable consequence, are associated, and second to be certain that there is no case where they are dissociated (F present but G absent). This second requirement can be supported if we cite a case where both properties are absent.

Dharmakīrti depends upon a notion of metaphysical necessity to resolve our doubts about the induction process. What makes an inference valid or sound is the claim, implicit in Dharmakīrti, that it deals with what may be called, in some sense, genuine properties. They also causally interact. The relation between such genuine properties can be either identity or causal dependence. These relations between genuine properties, on Dharmakīrti's view, hold necessarily but are knowable only *a posteriori*. We will now consider in detail each of Dharmakīrti's three types of inference.

5.3 ON INDUCTION: CAUSALITY

Dharmakīrti claims that if we know either of the two natural relations, identity and causality, we have a sufficient guarantee for making such universal claims as "all Fs are Gs." It is not very clear from his writing how our knowledge of the identity relation comes about. However, Dharmakīrti and his followers say a lot about how our knowledge of the relation of causation can be gleaned from a number (three, or possibly five) of observations of things failing to have the properties that are causality-related. Whether we need to call upon three observations or five observations is a matter that has been apparently disputed. It was known as the "consideration of three or five" (*trika-pañcaka-cintā*). I shall skip the details of the dispute over "three or five" (for which, see Y. K. Kajiyama, 1963). In either case, the idea is to achieve a sort of certainty about the causal relation between Gs and Fs. The fact of the matter is this. We have a hunch about their being causally related, if we observe them together in a place and then see the absence of one accompanied by the absence of the other. Dharmakīrti arranges these observations and non-observations in such a way as to induce at least a sort of certainty about the causal relation.

However, the problem of induction has always remained a problem for philosophers. Nobody has been able to claim that the problem has been solved. As J. L. Mackie has claimed, "if anybody claims today to have solved the problem, we may think of him as being mildly insane." The situation is not very different with Dharmakīrti or with Indian philosophers in general. There are some *ad hoc* rules they resort to to avoid the problem of induction, but not all questions can be satisfactorily answered. For example, in this context one may ask: how can the very same type of perception that fails to establish the truth of simple universal claims, nevertheless establish the truth of causal claims when they themselves imply simple universal claims?

There is one cautionary note that needs to be added here with regard to the expression "cause." According to the Buddhist, a cause is the immediately preceding event that, by virtue of its being there, makes the effect happen in the same location. But even this does not resolve our problem of induction about causality.

5.4 ON INDUCTION: ESSENTIAL IDENTITY

Dharmakīrti's idea about the notion of essential identity as yielding knowledge of concomitance took its final shape in the course of a series of books he wrote—*Pramāṇavārttika*, *Nyāyabindu*, *Hetubindu* and *Vādanyāya*. This is claimed by E. Steinkellner, who has studied the issue in great detail (see his paper in Steinkellner, ed. 1991). It seems that the final form of Dharmakīrti's view is to be found in his last major work, *Vādanyāya*. While discussing the so-called "defeat situations" (see above, chapter 3) in philosophical disputations (*vāda*), Dharmakīrti gave the final formulation of his theory of logical reason. He states his point briefly thus. There are three logical reasons for establishing something not perceived or confirming the property not recognized: essential identity, effect, and nonperception. To justify such a reason one must show (1), the reason's presence in the given locus of inference, and (2), the reason's being concomitant with the property confirmed. Having said this, Dharmakīrti gave a detailed description of how these reasons are ascertained to be concomitant with their confirmable properties.

How do we show that the logical relation, that is, inference-yielding relation, by now known widely as *vyāpti* or *pratibandha*, can be known to us, and in what way? Dharmakīrti thinks that by his doctrine of non-observation of the contrary or contradictory properties he can demonstrate that such knowledge is possible. The centerpiece in the demonstration concerns particularly the reason of essential identity (*svabhāvahetu*).

According to Steinkellner (1991), Dharmakīrti in this regard was reacting against his teacher, Īśvarasena, who faced the problem of induction and tried to solve it by developing a theory of non-perception and by introducing a fourth condition to Diṅnāga's triple condition. The fourth condition is "uncontradictedness of the reason" (*abādhitaviṣayatva*). This means that the possibility of the confirmable property being present in the "problematic" locus (*pakṣa*) should not be contradicted by any strong evidence. Later on the Naiyāyikas and other non-Buddhist logicians adopted this fourth characteristic and added one more, "absence of a contradictory reason" (*asat-pratipakṣitva*). According to Steinkellner, Īśvarasena might even have talked about six characteristics.

Dharmakīrti, however, rejected his teacher's idea of non-perception. For it does not guarantee the certainty of our cognition of concomitance. He argued that the absence of the reason in a locus of the absence of the inferable property is not established by the mere non-perception (*adarśanamātra*) of people like us, for we are non-omniscient beings and cannot see certain things even though they exist (*Vādanyāya*, 9, 1–2). What Dharmakīrti suggested instead was the following:

> Here the ascertainment of the concomitance involves demonstration of an evidence contrary to the presence of the reason in cases where the presence of the inferable property has been repudiated. (*Vādanyāya*, 6)

Our doubt regarding the concomitance cannot be ruled out as long as such a contradictory evidence has not been demonstrated. The argument given seems to consist in showing the absence of an opposition between the reason and the confirmable consequence. If a contradictory evidence is adduced then our doubt would be removed. Here contradiction or opposition should be understood either as mutual exclusion or incompatibility.[1] How do we establish the presence of a contradictory or opposite evidence, which will show the absence of the reason? Epistemically speaking, we discover a contradictory property, cold touch, say, which excludes the inferable property, fire, and thereby the reason, smoke. Logically speaking, the absence of the pervading property serves as a reason for the absence of the pervaded property. This pervaded property is nothing but our initial logical reason.

5.5 Inference Based on Non-Perception

The third kind of inference is what Dharmakīrti calls inference based on non-perception. There are several varieties noted by Dharmakīrti in various writings. The exact number varies. I shall here follow the *Nyāyabindu* classification. The eleven varieties of inference based upon non-perception mentioned there have been illustrated by Dharmakīrti in the following manner.

1 Non-Perception of the Essential Nature of the Property (Svabhāvānupalabdhi), for example,

> There is no smoke here, because a body of smoke being a perceptible object, is not perceived here.

---

1. Thus, a contradictory evidence is adduced just in case a property incompatible with the reason-property is shown to occur in those places where the inferable property has been shown not to occur. From this it follows that, wherever the inferable property is absent, so is the reason property (compare condition 3 above).

The idea of perceptibility presented some problems. Dharmakīrti avoids them by saying that *x* is perceptible if and only if all the conditions for our perception of *x* are present and *x* is still not perceived. The presence of all causal factors needeed for *x* to have been perceived is called the "perceptible condition." We have to assume a psychological condition here, namely that the person is looking for *x*.

2 Non-Perception of the Effect (Kāryānupalabdhi):

> There are no causal factors for smoke present here, because there is no smoke.

Here, from the absence of the effect, we infer the absence of causal factors. But some causal factors may be present even without the effect being there. For example, we might have wet fuel but no fire and therefore there cannot be any smoke there. Hence, we need to have here another qualification, as Dharmakīrti himself noted: the causal factor must be invariably connected with smoke. Jayanta supplies a simpler example: there is no smoke here because no fire is perceived.

3 Non-Perception of the Pervader-Property (vyāpakānupalabdhi):

> It is not an oak because it is not a tree.

This is based upon the contraposition of the relation of pervasion. The pervader-entity is present wherever the entity pervaded by it is present. It follows, therefore, that if the pervader is not present the pervaded entity cannot be present.

4 Perception of What Is Contrary to the Essential Nature of an Entity (Svabhāva-viruddhopalabdhi):

> There is no cold touch here because there is fire.

Here, fire is contrary to the nature of the property of having cold touch.

5 Perception of the Contrary Effect (Viruddhakāryopalabdhi):

> There is no cold touch here because there is smoke.

Smoke is the effect of fire and fire is what destroys the property of cold touch.

6 Perception of the Entity that Is Pervaded by What Is Contrary to the Entity (Viruddhavyāptopalabdhi):

> It is not the case that a created entity would not be destroyed for certain, for it depends upon another cause.

The perception of the factor that is pervaded by what is contrary to the entity justifies the negation here. This is rather a roundabout way of negating something by finding a factor that is concomitant with (pervaded by) the contrary item. Here, it seems that certainty itself is being repudiated. If it is possible to have separate and independent causal factors for destruction, then certainty about non-destruction would be lost.

The structure of this argument may be analysed as follows:

Opponent: A created entity is never destroyed.

Proponent: No. We deny this because there may be other factors causing destruction of such entities.

Awareness of such a possibility destroys the certainty. There may be other ways of interpreting this argument. But we need not go into them here.

7 Perception of What Is Contrary to the Effect (Kāryaviruddhopalabdhi):

> There is no source of cold because there is perception of fire.

This is self-explanatory.

8 Perception of What Is Contrary to the Pervading Property (Vyāpakaviruddhopalabdhi):

> There is no cold touch from snow here because fire is present.

Varieties beginning from 4 to 8 are being described as perception rather than nonperception. The reason is that for Dharmakīrti here, according to the Buddhist view, nonperception is actually perception of something else for, unlike Naiyāyikas, they do not say that we can perceive a blank—an absence. Non-perception of the cup must be, by the same token, perception of something else, such as the table. Hence, this is only a stylistic variation. The remaining three, 9–11, are self-explanatory.

9 Nonperception of the Cause (Kāraṇānupalabdhi):

There is no smoke here because no fire is perceived.

10 Perception of What Is Contrary to the Cause (Kāraṇaviruddhopalabdhi):

There is no horripilation (in this person) here because some fire is perceived to be nearby.

11 Perception of the Effect that Is Contradictory to the Cause (Kāraṇaviruddhakāryopalabdhi):

This place does not have a person who is suffering from horripilation (due to cold) in this place because a body of smoke is perceived here.

Dharmakīrti was a naturalist in his approach to the solution of the problem of induction. How do we jump from the examined cases to the unexamined ones? The materialists (Cārvākas) in India upheld that we can never have knowledge of the unexamined cases. Hence, an inference based upon the examination of the particular cases will never certify the knowledge of universal concomitance. We have to depend upon guess-work and probabilities. Dharmakīrti seems to have been sympathetic to the stance of the Cārvāka materialist and argued that purely observation-based induction cannot generate inferential knowledge. His answer to the problem is to depend upon some natural relation between properties and object. Such natural relations would make one item, the *hetu*, or the indicator-reason, concomitant with the other, the *sādhya* or the property to be inferred.

Dharmakīrti's celebrated verse, often quoted by his successors, states the view in a straightforward manner:

> Invariable concomitance between two items cannot be known from simple observations of things having or failing to have the required properties. It can be known by such a regulator or determiner as the relation between cause and effect or essential identity. (*Pramāṇavārttika, svārthānumānapariccheda, 34)*

Dharmakīrti argues here that knowledge of either of the two natural relations, identity (*tādātmya*) and causality (*tadutpatti*), is sufficient to guarantee our knowledge of universal concomitance.

5.6 UDDYOTAKARA'S THREEFOLD CLASSIFICATION OF INFERENCE

Nyāya-sūtra 1.1.5 divides inference into three types: "*pūrvavat*" (inference from a present event to a past event?), "*śeṣavat*" (inference from a present event to a future event?), and "*sāmānyato-dṛṣta*" (co-temporal inference?). The exact meaning of each type is obscure (compare Matilal 1985: 29–42 for a survey of possible interpretations and a defense of the interpretation given). Uddyotakara (circa 550–625), in his *Nyāyavārttika,* reformulated the old threefold division of inference found in *Nyāya-sūtra* 1.1.5, as "*kevalānvayin*" (universally positive inference, that is, one in which the inferred property is ever-present), "*kevala-vyatirekin*" (universally negative inference, that is, one in which the inferred property occurs at best only in the subject-locus), and "*anvaya-vyatirekin*" (inference based on both positive and negative examples, where the inferred property is present in some examples and absent in others). Of these three, the last one is the most commonly accepted form of inference: the hill has fire on it because there is smoke; the positive example is a kitchen and the negative example is a lake full of water. The other two forms of inference were not accepted by the Buddhists. Diṅnāga, in his system, could have accommodated (as he indirectly acknowledged in another context of the *Pramāṇasamuccaya*) the first one, that is, the universally positive. However, the second one was explicitly declared by him to be a wrong or inconclusive inference. It is included in what is called "*asādhāraṇa,*" the uniquely-inconclusive inference. It occupies the fifth place in his wheel of reason. It lacks both a positive example and a negative example.[2] How can you infer that an individual A has a property G on the basis of its having a unique property F (or A-ness) where the second property is such that, by definition, it does not exist in any individual other than A. It could clearly be an arbitrary claim: the sound is eternal because it has soundness. For one can equally claim that sound is non-eternal for it has soundness. It is like saying, "John is good, because he is John."

Of the two valid inferences in Diṅnāga's "wheel" of nine reasons, one is: "Sound is impermanent, for it is a product" and the other is: "Sound is impermanent, for it is made by human effort." Here the first type can easily be assimilated into a *kevalānvayin* (universally positive) form. For if we accept the Buddhist metaphysics, there is nothing that is neither impermanent nor a product. Hence, just as in the case of a "universally positive" form of inference, an example is nowhere to be found where both the inferable feature (for example,

---

2. That is to say, there is neither any *sapakṣa* nor any *vipakṣa* where the reason-property is present. The uniquely inconclusive inference, may, however, have negative examples, that is, *vipakṣas* where the reason-property is absent.

knowability) and the inferential mark (for example, nameability) are absent. Similarly, in Buddhist parlance, we cannot find a (non-fictional) example where both impermanence and being a product are absent. Such an example in Buddhism would have to be a fictional entity.

The universally positive form is discussed further in §7.6. There is, however, one exegetical problem, that may be explained with a little ingenuity (I owe the explanation to Professor Hattori). One of the three necessary conditions says that the *hetu* or inferential mark should be absent from any place that lacks the inferable property. Can this condition be met if, in actuality, there is no such place? Perhaps, however, the condition is automatically or trivially fulfilled (that is, *vipakṣo nāsti* > *vipakṣe nāsti*: the condition "absence of the *hetu* from the *vipakṣa*" includes the case of "absence of *vipakṣa*"; compare Matilal, 1985: 132). In this way, the problem about this condition is avoided. According to Hattori, this could have been Diṅnāga's explanation.

A major problem is created in this theory of inference, however, by the notion of *kevala-vyatirekin*, "universally negative" form of inference. An example is: "Earth (or any solid substance) is nothing but earth because it has smell" or "An equilateral triangle is equiangular because it is equilateral" or "A triangle is nothing but a triangle because it is a plane figure bounded by three sides." All these seem to be correct forms of inference, but it is difficult, if not impossible, to declare them to be legitimate by following the above theory of inference. For one condition in the above theory is that we find an example where the inferential mark, *a*, and the inferable, *b*, must be present together. But such an example cannot be found in these cases outside the problematic cases, that is, the *pakṣa*. Hence, such apparently legitimate inferences would not be covered by the triple-condition theory. This led the Buddhist to doubt the correctness of the Naiyāyikas' defense of "universal negative" forms of inference. Let us therefore examine this mode of inference in more detail.

5.7 DHARMAKĪRTI ON THE UNIVERSAL NEGATIVE FORM OF INFERENCE

Let us introduce three abbreviations for the three types of inference: "+E" for "*kevalānvayin*" (universally present), "±E" for "*anvaya-vyatirekin*" (positive-negative), and "– E" for "*kevala-vyatirekin*" (universally negative). The problem arises with the last-named: "– E." Read "±E" as "an inference where both types of example are available—one illustrating togetherness of *a* and *b* (*hetu* and *sādhya*), and the other where both are absent, and further none illustrating presence of *a* along with absence of *b*." Similarly, "+ E" is an inference where all examples illustrate presence of both *a* and *b* (there being no case where *b* is absent), and "– E" is "an inference where no examples illustrate the presence of *b* along with the presence of *a* (that is, in all examples, both *b* and *a* are jointly absent). By "all," I mean any example excluding the *pakṣa*, the location or the actual case under consideration.

The Buddhist (Dharmakīrti) rightly objects to "– E" as follows. What can give certainty to the conclusion of the following inference:

> Something has *b*,
> because it has *a*,
> and nowhere is there an *a* where no *b* is observed?

For example, if mangoes are never seen in any tree where mango-blossoms do not grow, could we then infer without doubt that that tree with mango-blossoms must have mangoes later on? This is uncertain because bad weather may destroy the blossoms, as it often does. (It should be noted, however, that Dharmakīrti, perhaps, took "*śeṣavat*" to mean inference from cause to effect, but his criticism is general and thus applicable to the *kevala-vyatirekin* also.) Dharmakīrti's own example is: *dehād rāgānumānavat* (PV II.11). It is usually seen that the embodied existence of a (human) being is the causal factor of such qualities as attachment, love, hatred, and so on. But our inference of such attachment and so on. from the observation of the body will not be correct or (absolutely) certain. As I have noted, certitude is the goal of Diṅnāga's theory of inference. For example, when an Arhat or a Buddhist saint regularly practices different types of meditation to get rid of such qualities as attachment, our inference in the above manner will fail.

Dharmakīrti sums up his argument in the next three verses (PV II.12–14):

> Since our teacher (Diṅnāga) has said: Mere non-observation of the reason in the example where *sādhya* is absent delivers a pseudo-reason, not a proper cognition of reason, as in the case of attachment in the body; we conclude that invariable concomitance (between *sādhya* and *hetu*) cannot be established simply on the basis of non-observation. For, deviation is possible just as one grain of rice may by chance remain uncooked in a rice-cooking pot. Hence our teacher has illustrated the *śeṣavat* (universally negative) inference as a doubtful case because here simple non-observation of the reason is taken to be proving the correctness of the inference.

Kumārila has also indirectly supported such an argument:

> If one may have one hundredth part of a doubt about lack of concomitance how can the reason have the power to prove the correctness of the inference (*Ślokavārttika*, *Anumānapariccheda)*.

Why then did the Naiyāyika accept as legitimate such "universally negative" inferences?

5.8 Induction Again

It is obvious that we are here closely concerned with one of the most vexing problems in logic—the defense of induction. It is generally agreed that the problem is probably insoluble, or, at best, that induction can be defended only probabilistically. If anyone claims more certainty regarding induction, then he "risks the suspicion of being mildly insane." We are of course not concerned here with the problem of induction as a whole. Were we to take induction here as the problem of generalization or extrapolation alone, we might at least defend it along with Mackie, by making use of what has been called "the inverse probability argument" (Mackie, 1985: 159). We, however, are concerned here, as is clear from the above, with a different set of problems—problems that bothered the classical Indian philosophers more than their Western counterparts. Our main problem, therefore, is to see why the Buddhist did not accept the "universally negative" as a correct form of inference, which they rejected, not simply because it cannot give certainty, but also because it was said to suffer from the fault of tautology and redundancy in the qualifications that form part of the inferable property (*sādhya*). And we should also investigate why the Naiyāyikas, while they are well aware of these faults, still accept the "universally negative" inference.

Although the two types of inferences, +E and –E, seem to be quite different from each other, there is a line of agreement between them. They may even be said to be validated by a similar principle. The invariable concomitance of *a* (*hetu*) with *b* (*sādhya*) is proven in the first case, +E, by the supporting example where both *a* and *b* exist together, and sometimes this *can* be a part of the *pakṣa* (for example, "a cloth (or anything) is nameable because it is knowable"). Similarly, the same relation between *a* and *b* in the case of the second type of inference, –E, is supported by a positive example where *a* and *b* may exist together and this example *has* to be a part of the *pakṣa*. This may be the reason why some Buddhist philosophers would not distinguish between the two types. In fact, if, as Dharmakīrti once emphatically claimed (PV II.27), citation of supporting examples is not an essential part of the sophisticated formulation of the inference, then the distinction between +E and –E does not seem to be important.

The later Naiyāyikas explained the "–E" type of inference more as illustrative of "definitional sentences" (*lakṣaṇa-vākya*). Hence, the typical example was given as:

> Earth is different from what is not earth, because it has the earth universal (or, because it has smell).

A definitional sentence is something like this: a block of stone is a piece of earth (an earthly substance), because it has the earth universal. One may wonder why it is that, since "different from what is not earth" is equivalent to "a piece of earth," we not say, "a piece of earth is a piece of earth . . ."? This is true. But, for the Naiyāyika, the conclusion of an inference is a piece of knowledge, and a piece of knowledge must have an element of "novelty," so a tautologous sentence cannot represent knowledge. "*A* is *A*" is thus not a piece of knowledge according to them (it was obvious that they were not concerned with such *a priori* knowledge.) To avoid this quandary, the Naiyāyikas formulate the said inference as:

> A is different from whatever is not A, because. . . .

Although "*A* is *A*" and "*A* is different from whatever is not *A*" both mean the same thing, that is, they imply each other, the second expression nevertheless represents some novelty in the predicate (for it involves an awareness of double negation and so forth). Hence, the –E inference is formulated in this manner:

> A is different from whatever is not A, because it has a,

where the definition sentence is: "Each *A* has *a* (by definition)." The Buddhist opponent, it may be noted, faults this inference because it has redundant qualifiers in the *sādhya*.

We face now at least two problems. The first concerns the definition of a *sapakṣa* "positive example." An example (which is not to be included in the *pakṣa*) is a *sapakṣa* if it has *b* (= *sādhya*) in it. This is in accord with one view. But according to another view, an example is to be called a *sapakṣa* if *b* (= *sādhya*) is *known* to be present there. If we accept the above definition of the "–E" inference, then the second definition of *sapakṣa* given here should be taken into account; otherwise the threefold classification of inference for Nyāya would run into problems. Any piece of earth (solid substance) may be known to be different from water, air, and so on. But that it is different from the rest of the things in the whole universe (from the other thirteen categories or *padārthas*: eight substances plus five other *padārthas* or categories in the Vaiśeṣika scheme of categories) may not be known for certain. Therefore, on this view, we would not have any example that would be known to have the *sādhya* (= *b*) in it. If, on the other hand, we accept the first definition of *sapakṣa*, then when we take one piece of stone as our *pakṣa* (that is, we want to establish that a piece of stone is a piece of stone, not different from earth) then any other piece of earth could be its *sapakṣa*. In that case, the alleged inference will not fall under the category of *kevala-vyatirekin* ("universally negative") inference as defined here. (To wit: "–E" is an inference where there is no *sapakṣa*.)

Part of the second problem has already been mentioned. Our knowledge of the concomitance between *a* and *b* has to depend here only upon the absence of any (known) counter-example (an example where *a* is present but *b* is not.) It is thus very close to the example of a pseudo-reason (*hetvābhāsa*) called *a-sādhāraṇa anaikāntika*, "uniquely inconclusive." To repeat the example:

Sound is eternal because it is audible,

or

Sound is eternal because it has soundness.

I have already indicated briefly how Dharmakīrti has argued that simple non-observation of a counter-example does not validate the conclusion, that is, does not make the conclusion a piece of knowledge or a certainty. What did the Naiyāyikas have to say about this?

5.9 NYĀYA ON THE "UNIQUELY INCONCLUSIVE" REASON

The Naiyāyikas held two different views about the nature of the "uniquely inconclusive" pseudo-reason. One is said to be the view of the older Naiyāyikas and the other the view of the later Naiyāyikas.

The old Naiyāyikas call a reason *a* a "uniquely inconclusive pseudo-reason" provided that it is found to be non-concurrent with *b* (= *sādhya*) (for example, soundness is not concurrent with a non-eternal thing, say, a pot). Co-occurrence of *a* (= *hetu*) with *b* (= *sādhya*) is an essential part of the definition of what we call *vyāpti* "invariable concomitance." Now, in this case of pseudo-reason, this part of the supporting concomitance is violated, and hence it is a pseudo-reason.

The later Naiyāyikas define the same type of pseudo-reason as one where the alleged reason, *a*, is absent from both the *sapakṣa* and the *vipakṣa* (where *sapakṣa* = examples where *b* is present, and *vipakṣa* = examples where *b* is absent). In this case, however, a correct reason, the "universally negative," will be very similar to an incorrect (unsound) reason (a pseudo-reason), the one that is called the "uniquely inconclusive." For instance, in the—E inference, "Earth is different from what is not earth, for it has earth-hood," not only there is no *sapakṣa* (for any thing that is different from what is non-earth is part of the *pakṣa*, that is, the problematic case under consideration for the inference in question), but also there are no *vipakṣas* (examples that are non-earth) where the alleged reason, earth-hood, does exist. Since "absence of any *sapakṣa*" may entail, in the above manner, "absence of the reason from the *sapakṣa,*" we may say that the reason is absent from both *sapakṣa* and *vipakṣa*. Thus, how are we to distinguish between the universally negative reason and the uniquely inconclusive reason (a pseudo-reason)?

The ancient Naiyāyikas point to the lack of co-occurrence of *a* (the *hetu*) and *b* (the *sādhya*) as the main fault of this pseudo-reason, for it thereby invalidates part of the invariable concomitance relation. But later Naiyāyikas take a different line here. A thing (an example) that is non-earth, that is, a *vipakṣa*, need not bother us. But a *sapakṣa*, an example that is a piece of earth, is generally a member of the *pakṣa* class, or a part of the *pakṣa*. Now, can we use such a case as a supporting positive example to strengthen the concomitance relation? Ordinarily we cannot do such a thing on this theory, because tautology and redundancy in the predicate expressions are considered to be unacceptable faults. However, the criticism of Dharmakīrti as well as early Naiyāyikas persuaded the later Naiyāyikas to admit that a merely negative case cannot strengthen the concomitance relation enough to make the conclusion a certainty. Hence, the following suggestion was accepted as adequate. The *pakṣa* in most such cases of inference is a class term that has many individual members. (Or, it may be a mass term, for example, water or earth, that has many small parts). Now, if we believe in the argument that a positive example is necessary to support the Nyāya theory of inference, then a member of the *pakṣa* class (a piece of stone, say) may be chosen as the relevant example. Thus, we will have a stronger positive support for the invariable concomitance relation that will validate the inference under consideration.

There is a further difference of opinion among the later Naiyāyikas that underlines another subtlety here. Some say that just as the (positive) example illustrating the co-occurrence of *a* and *b* strengthens the positive side of the concomitance relation, the example illustrating the co-occurrence of the absences of *a* and *b* strengthens the negative side of the same concomitance relation. But others hold that the positive concomitance relation is the most useful one in the theory of inference, and the (negative) example illustrating the absences of *a* and *b* does not support the "negative side" of the concomitance, but it indirectly supports the accurate positive version of the concomitance relation, and it is the latter version which has the adequate power to validate the conclusion of the inference concerned. For us there is no special preference for either of these two views. But it seems that the latter view has more plausibility and, hence, receives more support.

We may now face the other important question. The Buddhist, as I have already noted, does not accept the soundness of the "universally negative" inference. It has also been pointed out that, under Dharmakīrti's theory of inference, the distinction between the "universally positive" and the "universally negative" almost collapses. After Diṅnāga, Dharmakīrti mainly emphasises the threefold inference-yielding relations: *svabhāva* (natural presence), *kārya* (effect, that is, causal relation) and *anupalabdhi* (non-observation). They generally cover all types of sound inferences. In fact, Dharmakīrti goes so far as to say that the citation of the supporting example (positive or negative) is not very important as long as the inference-yielding relations are well understood by the other (opponent) side. Citation of the reason would be enough. Therefore, in the Buddhist theory we do not face the problems that we have faced in the Nyāya theory.

5.10 ON "INTERNAL" CONCOMITANCE

There is another post-Dharmakīrti development in the Buddhist logical theory that squarely meets the issue we have been discussing here. This is the division of concomitance into *antar-vyāpti* or "internal concomitance" and *bahir-vyāpti* or "external concomitance" (although the distinction was not originally meant to solve the problem of the uniquely-negative inference).

The relation of concomitance between *a* and *b* is usually known to us from our observation of examples. Both the Nyāya and the Buddhist agree in this regard. The examples where *a* (the *hetu*) coexists with *b* (the *sādhya*) are called *sapakṣa*. The examples where they are both absent are called *vipakṣa*. None of these examples should usually form any part of the *pakṣa*. However, where the *sapakṣa* example forms a part of the *pakṣa*, it is called a case of *antar-vyāpti*, internal concomitance. But where the *sapakṣa* example does not form a part of the *pakṣa* itself (as in the case of fire and smoke where the kitchen is the example and the hill is the *pakṣa*) we have a case of *bahir-vyāpti*, external concomitance.

Regarding the origin of the distinction between "external" and "internal," there is a difference of opinion among scholars. Some say that it originated in the Jaina tradition (compare K. Bhattacharya's article, "Some Thoughts on *Antarvyāpti*, *Bahirvyāpti*, and *Trairūpya*," in Matilal and Evans eds., 1986). But this has not been conclusively established. The later Buddhists accepted the distinction, and Ratnākaraśānti wrote a short tract on this issue (published in Sastri, 1910). It is, however, quite clear from what I have said above that Dharmakīrti himself was to some extent responsible for the origin of this idea. Here I agree with E. Steinkellner (1967).

If we wish to infer that everything is momentary because everything exists, then we would not be able to find an example which is outside the *pakṣa*, that is, "everything." In such cases, our concomitance can be supported only by an internal example. Of course, there are other ways of getting around this difficulty, and the Buddhist logicians, those who rejected "internal" concomitance, never tired of pointing them out. My point here, however, is different. I have tried to show that sometimes even the Naiyāyikas accepted *sapakṣa* examples from the domain of the *pakṣa*. They redefined their notion of *sapakṣa* to fit their theory of inference. Those later Naiyāyikas who were emphatic about the role of the positive example in supporting the concomitance relation, perhaps unconsciously, followed the Buddhist way in accepting part of the *pakṣa* as a *sapakṣa* example supporting the concomitance relation.

The great Naiyāyika Udayana (circa 975–1050) has given an elaborate defense of the theory of *kevala-vyatirekin* or universally-negative inference, in his well-known book, the *Kiraṇāvalī*. I shall conclude by giving a brief account of it here.

5.11 UDAYANA ON DEFINITION

In the *Kiraṇāvalī* (1971:28), Udayana makes his Buddhist opponent pose the following question: what is the use of *lakṣaṇa* or definition? Udayana answers: "A definition is nothing but the special reason (*hetu*) of what is called the 'universally negative' inference." Udayana adds, quoting most probably Śrīdhara (whom he calls the reverend Ācārya, "teacher"): "the purpose of a definition is to differentiate the object from its similar and dissimilar classes." Here, a serious objection is raised by the Buddhist. Both sides admit that, since tautology does not constitute knowledge, the inferable property and the subject-locus or *pakṣa* cannot be expressed by the same expression. They also admit that a general notion of the inferable property should be available to both arguers, the proponent and the opponent, before the inference is formulated. This means that if some unfamiliar or unknown element is used as the inferable property or as part of its qualifications, then there will arise a fault which will invalidate the inference. Technically, this fault will be the one called *aprasiddha-sādhaka* ("having an unknown inferable property"), or the one called *aprasiddha-viśeṣaṇatā* ("the fault of unestablished or unknown qualifications").

Now, the Buddhist argues that the inferable property in the universally negative inference, namely "different from non-earth," suffers from the second defect. For if there is no *sapakṣa* or example where such an inferable property is present, the prior notion of the inferable property would remain unestablished. Udayana gives a sophisticated answer to this rather technically formulated question. The notion of the inferable property may be first well-established and then be connected, by the inference, to the *pakṣa* or the actual case under consideration. It is not necessary that the property's connection with the *pakṣa* should be established prior to the inference in question here.

The Buddhist asks a further question: "Let us accept that every bit of earth, such as a pot, is different from non-earth, and this is established perceptually. Hence, it may be all right to use such a pot as the supporting positive example and then infer that the earthly atoms are different from non-earth, and so on. This will, of course, mean that we do not need the category of inference called the universally negative." Thus, the Buddhist question is: why accept the universally negative? Udayana answers with a touch of irony: "Save your friendly advice, for the definition of universally negative can be made faultless" (1971: 29). The Naiyāyikas regard the category of the universally negative inference as an important one and are reluctant to give it up, for it helps us to understand the necessity as well as the nature of definition (*lakṣaṇa*) in philosophy through logic (for more on this, see Matilal, 1985: 176–209).

The philosophical method in India is heavily dependent upon what they call a "*pramāṇa,*" a "means of knowing or establishing" an object or a theory. What they call "*lakṣaṇa*" or "definition" forms also an essential part of this method. Now, the opponent, says Udayana, wants to retain the method of definition as an acceptable device while rejecting the *pramāṇa* derived from it, the universally-negative inference. Udayana says that this type of opponent is like a person who condemns drinking while continuing to drink themselves!

CHAPTER 6

The Jaina Contribution to Logic

6.1 Origins of the Doctrine of Non-Onesidedness

A metaphysical thesis, in the context of classical Indian philosophy at least, usually takes the form of such a proposition as "Everything is F" or "Nothing is F." Philosophical rivalry springs from the varieties of such proposed positions, that is, varieties of such Fs. For example, the Advaita Vedāntin says: "Everything is Brahman;" the Mādhyamika, "Everything is empty of its own-being or own-nature;" and the Yogācārin, "Everything is a *vijñapti* 'making of consciousness.' " We may add to the list even such positions as "Everything is non-soul, impermanent, and suffering" (the Buddhist in general), and "Everything is knowable and nameable" (the Nyāya-Vaiśeṣika). If we have to add the Jainas to the list, then we can say theirs is: Everything is "non-one-sided" (*anekānta*). However, I shall argue that at least on one standard interpretation, the Jaina thesis is held at a slightly different level. If the others are called metaphysical, this one may be called meta-metaphysical. The sense of it will be clear later on. I do not wish to claim this to be the "one-up-manship" of the Jainas. The claim here is a modest one; it harks back upon the historical origin of the position.[1]

It is rather hard to see how such metaphysical theses as illustrated above, in the form of "Everything is F," can be proven in a straight-forward manner. They are often presuppositions, sometimes accepted as an axiom

1. This chapter is somewhat tangential to the main thread in the book. The reader whose main interest is in the development of the notion of an inference-warranting relation and associated concepts may wish to skip it and move directly to chapter 7.

of a system. The argument, if there is any, must be indirect or *reductio-ad-absurdum*; it is persuasive and suggestive. It may be pointed out at this stage that according to the later Nyāya school, any argument that has a conclusion (a thesis) of the form "Everything is F" is fallacious, because it would be inconclusive. To use their technical vocabulary, the inferred conclusion of the form "Everything is F" (where "Everything" is the subject term, playing the role of the *pakṣa*), is faulty because it suffers from the defect called *anupasaṃhārin*. Such a defect occurs when and only when the *pakṣa* (the subject locus) is *kevalānvayin*, which corresponds to a universal class. Strictly speaking, we should say that the property that qualifies the subject-locus here, that makes it what it is, a subject-locus, is a universal (or everpresent) property. Such being the case, we cannot compare or contrast it with anything else. The Indian theory of inference, on the other hand, depends essentially upon the possibility of such comparison (by the citation of a *sapakṣa*) and contrast (by the citation of a *vipakṣa*). This does not make the Indian or the Nyāya theory a theory of inference based upon analogy. It only certifies its empirical, that is its non-*a priori*, character. Proving something to be the case here means to make it intelligible and acceptable by showing how (1) it is similar to other known cases and (2) what it does differ from, and in what way. This demand on the proof is much stricter than usual. Otherwise, the Indians will say that something may actually be the case but it cannot be claimed or established as such. Hence, the inconclusiveness (*anaikāntika*) of the said type of inference was regarded as a defect, a *hetvābhāsa*.

A metaphysical thesis was usually expressed in the canonical literature of Buddhism and Jainism in the form of a question, "Is A B?" or "Is everything F?"—to which an answer was demanded, either *yes* or *no*. If *yes,* the thesis was put forward as an assertion, that is, the proposed position "A is B" or "Everything is F" was claimed to be true. If *no,* it was denied, that is, it was claimed as false. Therefore, *yes* and *no* were substitutes for the truth-values, true and false. The Buddhist canons describe such questions as *ekāṃśa-akaraṇīya*, those that can be answered by a direct *yes* or *no*. However, both the Buddha and the Mahāvīra said that they were followers of a different method or style in answering questions. They were, to be sure, *vibhajya-vādin*, for they had to analyze the significance or the implications of the questions in order to reach a satisfactory answer. For it may be that not everything is F, although it may not be true that nothing is F.

The followers of the Mahāvīra developed their doctrine of *anekānta* from this clue found in the canonical literature. This is the clue of *vibhajya-vāda*, which originally meant, in both Buddhist and Jaina canons, a sort of openness—lack of dogmatic adherence to any view-point exclusively. The philosophy of Jainism has been called "non-dogmatism" or "non-absolutism."

I prefer the literal rendering "non-onesidedness," for it seems to retain the freedom of the interpreter as well as its openness.

A metaphysical puzzle seems to have started in the early period in India (as it did in Greece too) with a dichotomy of basic predicates or concepts such as being and non-being, permanence and change, is and is-not, substance and modes, identity and difference. Although these five pairs just cited are not strictly synonymous, they are nevertheless comparable and often interchangeable, depending, of course, upon the context. The first member of these pairs used to be captured by a common denominator, à la the Buddhist canons called Eternalism or *śāśvatavāda*, while the second member constituted the opposite side, Annihilationism or *uccheda-vāda* (sometimes, even Nihilism). Indulging in the same vein, that is, the vein of rough generalization, we put the spirituality of reality on one side and the materiality of reality on the other. Looking a little further, we can even bring the proverbial opposition between Idealism and Realism, in their most general senses, in line with the above pairs of opposites.

Avoidance of the two extremes (*anta* = one-sided view) was the hallmark of Buddhism. In his dialogue with Kātyāyana, the Buddha is said to have identified "it is" as an "*anta*" (= extreme) and 'it is not' as the other extreme, and then he said that the Tathāgata must avoid both and resort to the middle. Hence Buddhism is described as the Middle Way. The Mahāvīra's *anekānta* way consisted also in not clinging to either of them exclusively. Roughly, the difference between Buddhism and Jainism in this respect lies in the fact that the former avoids by *rejecting* the extremes altogether, while the latter does it by *accepting* both with qualifications and also by reconciling them. The hallmark of Jainism is, therefore, the attempted reconciliation between opposites.

6.2 WHAT IS NON-ONESIDEDNESS?

It would be better to start with some traditional descriptions of the concept of *anekānta*. An alternative name is *syādvāda*. Samantabhadra (flourished seventh century) describes it as a position "that gives up by all means any categorically asserted view" (*sarvathaikāntatyāgāt*) and is dependent (for its establishment) upon the method of "sevenfold predication" (*Āptamīmāṃsā*, 104). Malliṣeṇa (flourished 1290) says that it is a doctrine that recognizes that each element of reality is characterized by many (mutually opposite) predicates, such as permanence and impermanence, or being and non-being. It is sometimes called the *vastu-śabala* theory (1933: 13), one which underlines the manifold nature of reality. Manifoldness in this context is understood to include mutually contradictory properties. Hence on the face of it, it seems to be a direct challenge to the law of contradiction. However, this seeming challenge should not be construed as an invitation to jump into the ocean of irrationality and unintelligibility. Attempts have been made by an array of powerful Jaina philosophers over the ages to make it rationally acceptable. We will see how.

Guṇaratna Sūri, in his commentary on Haribhadra's *Ṣaḍdarśana-samuccaya*, says that the Jaina doctrine is to show that mutually-opposite characterizations of reality by rival philosophers should be reconciled, for, depending upon different points of view, the same reality can be discovered to have both natures, being and non-being, permanent and impermanent, general and particular, expressible and inexpressible. The Jainas argue that there are actually seriously held philosophical positions that are mutually opposed. For example, we can place the Advaita Vedānta at one end of the spectrum, as they hold Brahman, the ultimate reality, to be a non-dual, permanent, substantial, and all inclusive being. This is where the "being" doctrine culminates. The Buddhists on the other hand are at the other end of the spectrum. Their doctrine of momentariness (as well as emptiness) is also the culmination of the "non-being" doctrine, which can also be called the *paryāya* doctrine. Traditionally, in Jainism, *dravya* ("substance," "being") is contrasted with *paryāya* "modification," "change," or even "non-being." One should be warned that by equating Buddhism with the "non-being," I am not making it nihilistic. For "non-being" equals "becoming." *Paryāya* is what is called as process, the becoming, the fleeting or the ever-changing phases of reality, while *dravya* is the thing or the being, the reality which is in the process of fleeting. And the two, the Jainas argue, are inextricably mixed together, such that it does not make any sense to describe something as exclusively "permanent," a *dravya*, without necessarily implying the presence of the opposite, the process, the fleetingness, the impermanence, the *paryāya*. Being and becoming mutually imply each other, and to exclude one or the other from the domain or reality is to take a partial (*ekānta*) view.

The idea is not that we can identify some elements of reality as "substance" and others as "process" or *paryāya*. Rather, the claim is that the same element has both characteristics alternatively and *even simultaneously*. It is the last part—". . . even simultaneously"— that would be the focus of our attention when we discuss the sevenfold predication (see below, §6.4). The challenge to the law of contradiction discussed earlier can be located, in fact, pin-pointed, in this part of the doctrine. The *anekānta* has also been called *ākulavāda*, a "precarious" doctrine. The idea is, however, that it challenges any categorically asserted proposition, ordinary or philosophical. Its philosophical goal is to ascribe a "precarious" *value* to all such propositions. It condones changeability of values (that is, truth-values). However, it does not amount to skepticism, for the manifoldness of reality (in the sense discussed above) is non-skeptically asserted. It is also not dogmatism, although it can be said that they were dogmatic about non-dogmatism!

6.3 RATIONALITY AND THE PRINCIPLE OF CONTRADICTION

How do the Jainas argue in favor of their position and answer that charge of irrationality and unintelligibility? Traditionally, their method *sapta-bhaṅgī* or "sevenfold predication" and their doctrine of "standpoints" (*nayavāda*), supply the material for the constructive part of the argument. To answer criticism, however, they try to show how contradictory pairs of predicates can be applied to the same subject with impunity and without sacrificing rationality or intelligibility. This may be called the third part of their argument. I shall comment on the last by following an outstanding Jaina philosopher of the eighth century AD, Haribhadra. In another section, I shall discuss the first part, the sevenfold predication before concluding with some general comments.

In his *Anekāntajayapatākā* (= "The Banner of Victory for *Anekānta*"), Haribhadra formulates the opponents' criticism as follows (we will be concerned with only a few pages of the first chapter). He first selects the pair: *sattva* "existence" or "being" and *asattva* "non-existence" or "non-being." The opponent says (p.11):

> Existence is invariably located by excluding non-existence, and non-existence by excluding existence. Otherwise, they would be non-distinct from each other. Therefore, if something is existent, how can it be non-existent? For, occurrence of existence and non-existence in one place is incompatible . . .
>
> Moreover, if we admit things to be either existent or non-existent, existence and non-existence are admitted to be properties of things. One may ask: are the property and its locus, the thing, different from each other? Or are they identical? Or, both identical and different? If different, then, since the two are incompatible, how can the same thing be both? If identical, then the two properties, existence and non-existence, would be identical . . . And if so, how can you say that the same thing has [two different] natures? (pp. 11–12)

The main point of the argument here depends on reducing the Jaina position to two absurd and unacceptable consequences. If the properties (or the predicates) are incompatible (and different), they cannot characterize the same entity. And if they are somehow shown to be not incompatible, the

Jainas lose their argument to show that the same entity is or can be characterized by two incompatible properties. Haribhadra continues:

> If they are both, identical and different, we have also two possibilities. If they are different in one form or one way and identical in another way, then also the same entity cannot be said to have two different natures. However, if they are different in the same way as they are identical with each other, this is also not tenable. For there will be contradiction. How can two things be different in one way, and then be identical in the same way? If they are identical, how can they be different? (pp. 12–13)

This is the opponent's argument. The formulation is vintage Haribhadra. Now the answer of Haribhadra may be briefly given as follows:

> You have said "How can the same thing, such as a pot, be both existent and non-existent?" This is not to be doubted. For it [such dual nature of things] is well-known even to the [unsophisticated] cowherds and village women. For if something is existent in so far as its own substantiality, or its own location, or its own time, or its own feature is concerned, it is also non-existent in so far as a different substantiality, a different location, a different time or a different feature is concerned. This is how something becomes both existent and non-existent. Otherwise, even such entities as a pot would not exist. (p. 36)

The existence of an entity such as a pot, depends upon its being a particular substance (an earth-substance), upon its being located in a particular space, upon its being in a particular time, and also upon its having some particular (say, dark) feature. With respect to a water-substance, it would be non-existent, and the same with respect of another spatial location, another time (when and where it was non-existent), and another (say, red) feature. It seems to me that the indexicality or the determinants of existence is being emphasized here.

To make this rather important point clear, let us consider the sentence: It is raining. This would be true or false depending upon various considerations or criteria. It would be true if and only if it is raining, but false if it happens to be snowing. This may correspond to the "substantiality" (*dravyataḥ*) criterion mentioned by Haribhadra. Next, the same would be true if and only if it is raining at the particular spot where the utterance has been made, otherwise false (at another spot, for instance). It would be likewise true if and only if it is raining now when it has been uttered, but false when the rain stops. Similarly, it would be again true if and only if it is raining actually from rain-clouds, for instance, not so when it is a shower of water from artificial sprinklers. It is easy to see the correspondence of these criteria with those other three mentioned by Haribhadra.

Haribhadra, in fact, goes a little further to conclude that a statement like "It is raining" or even "The pot exists" has both truth-values; it is both true and false in view of the above considerations. In fact, it is better to talk in terms of truth-values (as will be clear below), rather than in terms of contradictory pairs of predicates. For the law of contradiction, as it is usually stated in ordinary textbooks of logic, requires that the denial of a predicate, *F*, of a subject, *a*, be the same as the affirmation of the contradictory predicate of the same subject, and vice versa. Besides, saying *yes* and *no* to such a question as "Is *a F*?" is equivalent to assigning truth or falsity respectively to the statement "*a* is *F*."

One may argue that discovery of the indexical elements on which the determinants of a truth-value depends, that is, of the indexical determinants for successfully applying a predicate, may not be enough to draw such a radical conclusion as the Jainas want, namely, co-presence of contradictory properties in the same locus or assigning of both truth and falsity to the same proposition. Faced with such questions where indexical elements play an important and significant role, we may legitimately answer, "Yes and no. It depends." However, to generalize from such evidence and conclude that the truth or falsity of all propositions suffers from this indeterminacy due to the presence of the indexical or variable elements, and further that all propositions are therefore necessarily and omnitemporally (*sarvathā* and *sarvadā*) both true and false, may be an illicit jump. The successful application of any predicate to a thing on this view, depends necessarily upon a variable element such that it can or cannot be applied according as we can substitute one or another thing for these variable elements. These elements which may remain hidden in a categorically asserted proposition, are sometimes called a "point of view" or a "standpoint." It also amounts to a view which announces that all predicates are *relative* to a point of view: no predicates can be *absolutely* true of a thing or an object in the sense that it can be applied unconditionally at all times under any circumstances. Jainas in this way becomes identified with a sort of facile relativism.

If the points in the above argument are valid, then it would be a sound criticism of Jaina philosophy. However, let us focus upon two related points. First, relativism. The reflexes of relativism are unmistakable in Jainism as they are in many modern writers. The familiar resonance of Jainism is to be found in Nelson Goodman's *The Ways of World-Making*. A typical argument is to show how the earth or the sun can be said to be both in motion and at rest depending upon the points of view. An obvious criticism of the facile relativism (though not that of Goodman) is that it can be shown to be self-inconsistent, for in trying to argue that all truths are relative to some point of view or other, it makes use of an absolute notion of truth. Will this charge hold against Jainism? I do not think so. For Jainism openly admits an absolute notion of truth that lies in the total integration of all partial or conditionally arrived at truths, and is revealed to the vision of an omniscient being such as Mahāvīra. The emphasis here is on the conditionality and limitedness of human power and human vision and therefore it applies to all humanly constructible positions. The concern is somewhat ethical. Rejection of a seriously held view is discouraged lest we fail to comprehend its significance and underlying presuppositions and assumptions. The Jainas encourage openness.

Are the Jainas guilty of illicit generalization? This is another point of the above critique. All predicates for which there is a contradictory one, are indeterminate as regards the truth or falsity of their application. In fact by claiming that the contradictory pairs are applicable they take the *positive* way out as opposed to the Buddhists, the Mādhyamikas, who take the *negative* way. Of the familiar four Buddhist alternatives, *yes, no, both,* and *neither,* the Jainas may prefer the third, both *yes* and *no,* while the Mādhyamikas reject all four. If unconditionality and categoricality of any predication, except perhaps the ultimate one, *anekānta* in this case, is denied, then this is a generalized position. The only way to counter it would be to find a counterexample, that is, an absolute, unconditionally applicable, totally unambiguous and categorically assertible predicate, or a set of such predicates, without giving in to some dogma or have some unsuspected and unrecognized presupposition. The Jainas believe that this cannot be found. Hence, *anekānta.*

Haribhadra and other Jaina philosophers have argued that we do not often realize, although we implicitly believe, that application of any predicate is guided by the consideration of some particular *sense* or criterion (excessive familiarity with the criterion or sense makes it almost invisible, so to say). This is not exactly the Fregean *Sinn.* In the Indian context, there is a well-entrenched tradition of talking about the "basis" or the "criterion" for the application of a predicate or a term. This can be called the *nimitta* theory (the "basis" or the "criterion" theory). A predicate can be truly applied to something *x* in virtue of a particular or a specific basis. The philosopher, when he emphasizes the particularity or specificity of such a basis, indirectly and implicitly commits himself to the possibility of denying that predicate (that is, of applying the contradictory predicate) to the same thing, *x*, in virtue of a different basis or criterion. Haribhadra says (p.44):

> (The Opponent says:) The lack of existence in virtue of being a watery substance etc., belongs to a particular earth-substance, a pot; however, this is because the locus of non-existence of something cannot be a

> fiction. We admit therefore that it is the particularity of the earth-substance, the pot, that excludes the possibility of its being existent as a water substance (this does not amount to admitting the co-presence of existence and non-existence in one locus).
>
> (The Jaina answers:) Oh, how great is the confusion! By your own words, you have stated the *anekānta*, but you do not even recognise it yourself! Existence in virtue of being an earth-substance itself specifies its non-existence in virtue of being a water-substance (you admit this). But you cannot admit that the thing has both natures, existence and non-existence. This is a strange illusion! No object (or thing) can be specified without recourse to the double nature belonging there, presence of its own existence in it, and absence from it, the existence of the other.

The general point of the Jainas seems to be this. Any predicate acts as a qualifier of the subject and also a distinguisher. That is, its application not only refers to or, in the old Millian sense, connotes, a property that is present in the subject, but also indicates another set of properties that are *not* present in it at all. In fact, insistence, that is absolute insistence, on the presence of a property (an essential property) in a subject, lands us invariably into making a negative claim at the same time, absence of a contradictory property, or a set of contrary properties from the same subject-locus.

At this stage the opponent might say, with some justification, that the conclusion reached after such a great deal of arguing tends to be trivial and banal. All that we have been persuaded to admit is this. Existence can be affirmed of a thing, *x*, in virtue of our fixing certain determinants in a certain way, and if the contrary or contradictory determinants are considered, existence may be denied of that very thing. This is parallel to assigning the truth-value to a proposition when all the indexical elements in it are made explicit or fixed, and being ready to accept the opposite evaluation if some of their indexicals are differently fixed or stated. Realists or believers in bivalence (as Michael Dummett has put it), would rather have the proposition free from any ambiguities due to the indexical elements—an eternal sentence (of the kind W. V. Quine talked about) or a Thought or *Gedanke* (of the Fregean kind)—such that it would have a value, truth or falsity—eternally fixed. However, the Jainas can reply to the charge of banality by putting forward the point that it is exactly such possibilities that are in doubt. In other words, they deny that we can without impunity talk about the possibility of clearly and intelligibly stating such propositions, such eternal sentences, or expressing such Thoughts. We may assume that a proposition has an eternally fixed truth value, but it is not absolutely clear to us what kind of a proposition that would be. For it remains open to us to discover some hidden, unsuspected determinants that would force us to withdraw our assent to it.

6.4 Jaina Seven-Valued Logic

A more serious criticism of Jainism is that if the senses change, and if the indexicals are differently interpreted, we get a new and different proposition entirely, and hence the result would not be an affirmation and denial jointly of the same proposition. If this is conceded then the main doctrine of Jainism is lost. It is not truly an *anekānta*, which requires the mixing of the opposite values. This critique, serious though it is, can also be answered. This will lead us to a discussion of *saptabhaṅgī*.

The philosophical motivation of the Jainas is to emphasize not only the different facets of reality, not only the different *senses* in which a proposition can be true or false, not only the different determinants which make a proposition true or false, but also the contradictory and opposite sides of the *same* reality, the dual (contradictory) evaluation of the same proposition, and the challenge that it offers to the doctrine of bivalence or realism.

Let us talk in terms of truth predicates. The standard theory is bivalence, that is, two possible valuations of a given proposition, true or false. The first step taken by the Jainas in this context is to argue that there may be cases where joint application of these two predicates, true and false, would be possible. That is, given certain conditions, a proposition may be either (1) true, or (2) false, or (3) both true and false. If there are conditions under which it is true and there are other conditions under which it is false, then we can take both sets of these conditions together and say that given these, it is both. This does not mean, however, the rejection of the law of contradiction. If anything, this requires only non-compliance with another law of the bivalence logic, that of the excluded middle (the excluded third). It requires that between the values, true and false, there is no third alternative. The law of contradiction requires that a proposition and its contradictory be not false together. This keeps the possibility of their being true together open. Only the law of excluded middle can eliminate such a possibility. This is at least one of the standard interpretations of the so-called two laws of bivalence logic. In a non-bivalence logic, in a multiple valued logic, the law of contradiction is not flouted, although it disregards the excluded third. The Jainas likewise disregards the mutual exclusion of *yes* and *no*, and argues, in addition, in favor of their combinability in answer to a given question. We have shown above how such opposite evaluations of the same proposition can be made compatible and hence combinable.

It is the sameness of the proposition or the propositional identity that is open to question here. If the change of determinants, of point of view, of the indexical element, introduces a different proposition, then change of truth-values from true to false could not be significant enough. However, we may claim that the proposition, whatever that is, remains the same and that it has both values, true and false depending upon other considerations. This would still be a non-significant critique of the classical standard logic of bivalence. The Jainas therefore go further, in order to be true to their doctrine of "precarious" evaluation (*ākulavāda*), and posit a separate and non-composite value called "*avaktavya*" ("inexpressible"), side by side with true and false. I shall presently comment on the nature of this particular evaluation. First, let us note how the Jainas get to their seven types (ways) of propositional evaluation. If we admit combinability of values, and if we have three basic evaluable predicates (truth-values), true, false and "inexpressible" (corresponding to *yes, no* and "not expressible by such *yes* or *no*") then we have seven and only seven alternatives. Writing "+," "–" and "o" for the these values respectively, the seven alternatives are:

+, –, +–, o, o+, o–, o+–.

For the proper mathematical symmetry, we may also write:

+, –, o, +–, o+, –o, o+–.

This is following the principle of combination of these basic elements, taking one at a time, two at a time and all three. The earlier arrangement reflects the historical development of the ideas. Hence in most texts, we find the earlier order.

The "inexpressible" as a truth-like predicate of a proposition has been explained as follows. It is definitely distinct from the predicate "both true and false." For the latter is only a combination of the first two predicates. It is yielded by the Jaina idea of the combinability of values or even predicates that are mutually contradictory. Under certain interpretations, such a combined evaluation of the proposition may be allowed without constraining our intuitive and standard understanding of contradiction and consistency. "It is raining" can be said to be both true and false under varying circumstances. However, the direct and unequivocal challenge to the notion of contradiction in standard logic comes when it is claimed that the same proposition is both true and false at the same time in the same sense. This is exactly accomplished by the introduction of the third value "inexpressible," which can be rendered also as paradoxical. The support of such an interpretation of the "inexpressible" is well-founded in the Jaina texts. Samantabhadra and

Vidyānanda both explain the difference between the "true and false" and the "inexpressible" as follows: the former consists in the gradual (*kramārpaṇa*) assigning of truth-values, true and false, while the latter is a joint and simultaneous ("in the same breath") assigning of such contradictory values (c.f. *sahārpaṇa*). One suggestion is that the predicate is called "inexpressible" because we are constrained to say in this case both "true" and "false" in the same breath. Something like "truefalse" or "yes-no" would have been better, but since these are only artificial words, and there are no natural language words to convey the concept that directly and unambiguously flouts non-contradiction. The Jainas have devised this new term "inexpressible" to do the job—a new evaluation predicate, non-composite in character, like "true" and "false."

This metaphysical predicate "inexpressible" as a viable semantic concept has been acknowledged in the discussion of logical and semantical paradoxes in modern times. Nowadays, some logicians even talk about "para-consistent" logics, where a value like "both true and false simultaneously" is acknowledged as being applicable to the paradoxical propositions, such as "this sentence is false" or "I am lying." The third value is alternatively called "paradoxical" or "indeterminate" (this is to be distinguished from "neither true nor false" which is also called "indeterminate;" see Priest 1979). With a little bit of ingenuity, one can construct the matrices for Negation, Conjunction, Alternation, and so on, for the system. The Jainas, however, do not do it.

I shall now emphasise the significant difference between the philosophical motivations of the Jainas and those modern logicians who develop multiple-valued logics or the para-consistent logic. First, the logicians assign truth to the members of a certain set of propositions, falsity to another set, and the third value, paradoxicality to the "problem" set, that is, the set of propositions that reveals the various versions of the Liar paradox and the other paradoxes. The Jainas on the other hand believe that each proposition, at least each metaphysical proposition, has the value "inexpressible" (in addition to having other values, true, false, and so on). That is, there is some interpretation or some point of view under which the given proposition would be undecidable so far as its truth or falsity is concerned, and hence could be evaluated as "inexpressible." Likewise, the same proposition, under another interpretation, could be evaluated "true," and under still another interpretation, "false."

Second, my reference to the non-bivalence logic or para-consistent logic, in connection with Jainism, should not be over-emphasized. I have already noted that Jaina logicians did not develop, unlike the modern logicians, truth matrices for Negation, Conjunction, and so on. It would be difficult, if not totally impossible, to find intuitive interpretations of such matrices, if one were to develop them in any case. The only point that I wanted to emphasize here is to show that the Jaina notion of the "inexpressible," or the notion of *anekānta* in the broader perspective, is not an unintelligible or an irrational concept. Although the usual law of non-contradiction, which is by itself a very nebulous and vague concept, is flouted, the Jainas do not land us into the realm of illogic or irrationality.

Last but not least, the Jainas in fact set the limit to our usual understanding of the laws of non-contradiction. There are so many determinants and indexicals for the successful application of any predicate that the proper and strict formulation of the ways by which this can be contradicted (or the contradictory predicate can be applied to the same subject) will always outrun the linguistic devices at our disposal. The point may be stated in another way. The notion of human rationality is not fully exhausted by our comprehension of, and the insistence upon, the law of non-contradiction. Rational understanding is possible of the Jaina position in metaphysics. In fact, one can say that the Jaina *anekānta* is a meta-metaphysical position, since it considers all metaphysical positions to be spoiled by the inherent paradoxicality of our intellect. Thus, it is a position about the metaphysical positions of other schools. It is therefore not surprising that they were concerned with the evolution of propositions, with the general principle of such evaluations. In this way, their view rightly impinged upon the notions of semantics and problems with semantical paradoxes. And above all, the Jainas were non-dogmatic, although they were dogmatic about non-dogmatism. Their main argument was intended to show the multi-faceted nature of reality as well as its ever elusive character such that whatever is revealed to any observer at any given point of time and at any given place, would be only partially and conditionally right, ready to be falsified by a different revelation to a different observer at a different place and time. The Jainas think in our theoretical search for understanding reality, this point can hardly be overstated.

CHAPTER 7

NAVYA-NYĀYA: TECHNICAL DEVELOPMENTS IN THE NEW SCHOOL SINCE 1300 AD

7.1 THE BEGINNING OF NAVYA-NYĀYA

Navya-nyāya is rather an odd name given to a system of logic that was foreshadowed in the writings of Udayana (circa 975–1050), then developed and flourished in the post-Udayana writers such as Maṇikantha, Śrīvallabha, and Śaśadhara, but most spectacularly in Gaṅgeśa's magnum opus, *Pramāṇatattvacintāmaṇi*. In the development of Navya-nyāya, the contributions of the Vedāntin Srīharṣa and the criticisms of the Buddhists Jñānaśrīmitra and Ratnakīrti should also not be forgotten. For a history of the school, see (Matilal, 1980).

Gaṅgeśa (c. 1325) is often regarded as the father of the Navya-nyāya school. His *Tattvacintāmaṇi* was the most influential text of Navya-nyāya. What D. C. Bhattacharya (1958: 96) observed seems to be quite correct:

> Gaṅgeśa's achievement is quite unique in the history of philosophical literature of India. There is not another scholar in the whole mediaeval period who had such a spectacular success through one single book. The *Tattvacintāmaṇi*, a treatise of about 12000 *granthas* in extent [one *grantha* = 32 syllables] appeared like a flash to dispel the gloom of centuries succeeding Udayana and laid the solid foundation of Indian dialectics.

This elaborate text[1] deals exclusively with the *pramāṇas* or "means of knowledge," and is divided into four parts. Each part deals with one of the

1. For a very detailed summary of this text, see Potter and Bhattacharya (1993).

four *pramāṇas* of the Nyāya school—perception, inference, analogical identification, and testimony. There are forty-six (12 + 17 + 1 + 16) sections in these four parts. The first part on perception is very important, but it did not become popular with the later writers. Only two sections of this part, *Maṅgalavāda* ("benediction") and *Prāmāṇyavāda* ("theory of truth"), were commented upon and elaborated by them. The part on inference is the largest of all. It also contains an elaborate section on the problem of God as an appendix. On the whole this was a comprehensive book, and Gaṅgeśa's style, precision, and uniformity, his logical ordering of thoughts and arguments, became the model for all later writers. Most of these later writers earned their fame by writing a commentary or a sub-commentary on any section or sub-section of the *Tattvacintāmaṇi.* Sometimes Gaṅgeśa's style was so concise that even a single sentence of his book was later developed and elaborated by his commentators into a separate work of considerable length.

Part II, the chapter on inference, was indeed the most important and influential. It was also the most profound portion of the whole book. Later Navya-nyāya tradition, which produced series of commentaries and sub-commentaries on this part, divided it into two broad sections: *vyāptikāṇḍa*, the section dealing with the definition of inference and pervasion as a principle underlying inference, and *jñānakāṇḍa*, the section dealing with *pakṣatā* (subjecthood), deduction, and classification of fallacies. For about three or four centuries after Gaṅgeśa, Navya-nyāya scholarship in India "flowed through a large number of channels cut by single sentences or phrases of this part of Gaṅgeśa's work and by far the widest channel emerged from the general definition of fallacy" (DC Bhattacharya, p.108).

To illustrate how Gaṅgeśa formulates different alternative definitions of *vyāpti* "pervasion" let me quote below what is usually called the group of five definitions (*pañca-lakṣaṇī*):

> 27.2-31.2. What is pervasion in that knowledge of a pervasion which is the cause of a conclusion? It is not [the reason's] non-deviation [from the probandum]. For that cannot be (l) [the reason's] non-occurrence in the loci of absence of the probandum, (2) [the reason's] non-occurrence in the loci of absence of the probandum which are different from locus of the probandum, (3) [the reason's] having no common locus with a mutual absence whose counterpositive is locus-of-the-probandum, (4) [the reason's] being the counterpositive of an absence resident in all loci of absence of the probandum, or (5) [the reason's] non-occurrence in what is other than locus of the probandum, since it would then fail to apply in the case of universal positives." (Transl. C. Geokoop, 1967: 60)

Part III, the chapter on *upamāna* (analogical identification), is the shortest in the book. It has generally been neglected by later scholars. Only two scholars, Pragalbha and Rucidatta, are known to have written commentaries on this part. Part IV deals with verbal testimony, with the problems of grammar, language, and meaning. Like part II, part IV has also been very popular. Many Navya-nyāya authors either wrote commentaries on it or produced independent works dealing with the concepts discussed in this part. It goes without saying that the overwhelming popularity of Gaṅgeśa's work on *pramāṇa* pushed the works of the old Nyāya school gradually into the background, if not into oblivion.

Although Gaṅgeśa quoted a verse from Jñānaśrīmitra, the well-known Buddhist philosopher, his main opponents were not the Buddhists but the Prabhākara Mīmāṃsakas. It is significant that no notable Buddhist philosopher appeared after Mokṣākaragupta (twelfth century AD). Udayana, in his *Ātmatattvaviveka*, called the Prabhākaras "friends of the Buddhists." Thus, from the twelfth century onwards, philosophic activity in India was kept alive through the debates and counter-arguments of the Prabhākaras and the Naiyāyikas.

Gaṅgeśa belonged to Mithilā. His probable date is c. 1325 AD. He called his own book a "jewel" (*maṇi*), and later writers used to refer to him as Maṇikāra ("the jeweller"). In the introductory verses, he said that his book was meant for the decoration of scholars, and opponents who would be refuted in his book would no longer be able to press their views cleverly in debates. This claim proved to be true.

7.2 A Refined Theory of Inference

In the reformulation of the theory of inference, Gaṅgeśa chooses two major concepts—(i) the notion of concomitance, and (ii) the clear characteristics that characterize the concept of the subject-locus or the *pakṣa*. The idea is that there is an underlying causal theory here. Inference is the resulting knowledge caused by the cognition with the concomitance as the qualifier of the indicator-reason (*hetu*, *liṅga*) while the same concomitant reason must also be present in the subject-locus. This is a complicated way of defining inference, but carries the intended implications that we need to have in a causal definition of inference.

The general causal theory implicit here can be made explicit as follows. Let an arrow "→" denote a causal relation such that what precedes the arrow sign would denote the cause and following it would denote the effect of the cause. Thus

"A → B"

would denote that A, a mental event, causes or gives rise to B, another mental event. "A" may be a complex event which may be represented as

A = (P + Q).

In an inference, P represents, for example, a mental event according to which there is fire in the kitchen and Q represents another mental event according to which fire is concomitant with smoke. Then the combined event, A, called the *parāmarśa*, generates the conclusion event B, that is, there is fire on the mountain (compare Matilal, 1990: 51).

Obviously the most important concept here is *vyāpti*, variously called in English by such names as concomitance, pervasion, invariant relation, and so on. Gaṅgeśa devotes almost half of his energy to define the concept of concomitance. He offers thirteen of fourteen definitions of concomitance, all of which he rejects as suffering from one fault or another. Most of these definitions fail because of the admittance of "partially locatable" properties (*avyāpyavṛttidharma*) in the system. The final definition uses the notion of a property's having both a presence range and absence range (see below). The definition-sentence needs a lot of insertions and additions and subtractions in order to be flawless. However, I shall not discuss all these problems.

One of the simpler definitions of concomitance is given as follows. All smoke-possessing places are fire-possessing. This should be understood as that there is no place where fire is absent but smoke is not. That means that a place that contains the absence of fire will be the locus of the absence of smoke. Somebody might ask why people in India chose such a roundabout way of explaining concomitance. Why did the simpler statement, such as that all *a*s are *b*s did not satisfy them? The only answer is that this is how the meaning of "all" is to be understood. So, this can be taken as an explanation of the meaning of universal quantification. The matter can be understood if we follow the method developed below.

7.3 THE NAVYA-NYĀYA LOGIC OF PROPERTY AND LOCATION

A judgmental cognition in Navya-nyāya is analyzed in terms of property and location. Negation is always construed as term-negation. Sentential negation is usually transformed into term-negation of some kind or other. Negation of a property generates another (negative) property. A negative statement is analyzed as attribution of a negative property. Properties, here, are to be understood not simply as universals. They would include any occurrent or attributable, specific features which may even be particulars (compare §1.7).

The universe U is peopled with loci or locations where properties are locatable. The presence-range of a property is the set of loci where it is locatable. The absence-range is the set of loci where it is not locatable.

A property with an empty presence-range is unlocatable. It is ruled as fictitious (for example, the golden mountain). Properties with empty absence-ranges are admitted as real (non-fictitious), for example, knowability. They are called ever-present (see next section). Both the fictitious (unlocatables) and the ever-present are ruled as unnegatable, for the negation of them does not generate real (locatable) properties. A property is unreal if it is not locatable.

Most properties are *wholly* locatable, such that they are not co-locatable with their absences in the same set of loci. But some properties are partially locatable, such as chair-contact. Such a property is apparently co-locatable with its absence in the same locus. This infringes upon the generally understood law of negation. For we can say, with regard to the same locus, that it has as well as does *not* have a particular property (in the given sense). Thus, a device is used to reparse the partially locatable properties as wholly locatable, so that the standard notion of negation may not be "mutilated" in this system.

Non-deviation and pervasion are two important logical relations that generate inference in the system. The Navya-nyāya formulation of these relations will be given here. Navya-nyāya's insistence on the non-emptiness of the presence-range of properties serves the purpose of making the existential import of general statements explicit. In this respect, non-deviation can be contrasted with the A-relation of Aristotle.

To explain the notion of the unnegatable as well as the negation of the partially locatable, some concepts of a multiple-valued system may be used with an entirely different interpretation of the values. The negation matrix has been given at the end of this section. I shall continue the discussion of the unnegatables (that is, the ever present properties) in the next section. Despite the peculiarities mentioned above, Navya-nyāya tries to work with the standard notion of negation in a two-valued logic.

With this as a prelude let me describe some features of what has been called "Navya-nyāya logic" or just "Navya-nyāya"—the system that developed within the new Nyāya tradition. It absorbed the Buddhist criticism of the earlier Nyāya school and reformulated its older theory of inference. In the remainder of this section, I shall first outline the Navya-nyāya concept of property and location and the logical relations formulated in terms of property and location. I shall then (§7.4) make some observations to show the relevance of some Navya-nyāya theories to certain modern concerns in the philosophy of logic.

Cognitive States. Navya-nyāya analyzes cognitions in terms of property and location or locus. More correctly, Navya-nyāya analyzes what I have elsewhere called judgmental or qualificative cognitive states in terms of qualifiers and qualificands (1968: 12). Such a cognitive event is usually represented by a sentence. Because of the use of the term "cognitive" or "cognition" here, a logician trained in the tradition of Frege and Carnap may immediately bring the charge of "psychologism" against Navya-nyāya. But I have argued elsewhere that this charge is not always relevant (1986: 118–127). Navya-nyāya is concerned with the "objective" content of a cognitive event and analyzes the sentence that is supposed to represent the structure of such a content. It is not concerned with the psychological act of cognition as such. Thus, in Navya-nyāya logic when one cognitive event is said to be contradictory to another, it is not just their psychological impossibility that is appealed to. In other words, what is appealed to here is the impossibility that is completely determined by the logical relation between *p* and not-*p*.

Diṅnāga suggested a *dharma-dharmin* ("property and locus") analysis of a qualificative (judgmental) cognitive event. In Diṅnāga's terminology, however, such a cognitive event is called "constructive"; for, Diṅnāga like the British empiricists, emphasized a distinction between the data (immediately "given" in consciousness) and the constructs based on the data. Existence or reality is ascribed only to the data (*svalakṣaṇa*, "unique particular"), and the constructs are products of imagination (*kalpanā*). Navya-nyāya rejected this ontology of data of the Buddhists, but accepted the *dharma-dharmin* analysis of a cognitive event that is propositional.

Properties. A cognitive event is usually said to locate a property in a locus: the form is "x has *p*" or "*p* (is) in x." Simple predicate formulations, such as "x is F" are noted, but only to be rephrased as "x has F-ness" (where "F-ness" stands for the property derived from "F"). Thus, we have here two types of individuals–properties and locations or loci. Correspondingly, we can talk about two sorts of individual constants: property-terms (*r, s, t, u, w, h*. . . .) and location-terms (*l, m, n, o, p* . . .). The best example of a property-term is "blue-color" which is locatable in a cup that is blue, or the property expressed by "cowness" that is locatable in a cow (in any cow). Such physical materials as a cup, fire, smoke, water, and a pot are also treated in Navya-nyāya as properties, inasmuch as they are locatable in such loci as a table, a mountain, ground, the kitchen, and the plate. Hence, terms expressing such physical materials are treated as property-terms in the specific sense, of being about a property-particular, that I have alluded to in the first chapter. The apparent oddity of treating such things as properties can be resolved if we conceive anything to be a property that purports to have a location and allow a sort of stipulative identity between having-a-cup-on-it and cup-property. In other words, we have to stipulate a sort of referential identity between such expressions as "cup-possessorhood" and "cup" (used as a property). One may even suggest a distinction here between two uses of the expression "cup;" one use of "cup" ("a cup" or "the cup") is to refer to the locus of properties, the other use ("a cup" or "the cup") is to refer to a property. Both refer to the same ontological entity but to different logical constructs.

It may further be noted that even a so-called relation (a connector) may sometimes be treated as a property in Navya-nyāya. If a relation is tied in one end to the relatum, then the whole complex can be treated as a particular qualifier of the other relatum. Thus, the cup-contact in the case of a cup being placed on a table can be treated as a property or a qualifier of that table, provided we can take the cup-contact as a particular locatable on the table, the locus.

Negation. Navya-nyāya basically recognizes two types of negation: absence and difference. Most peculiar features of Navya-nyāya emerge in connection with its interpretation of negation of properties. Sentential negation is usually avoided. A negation is construed as a term-negation in either of the following ways. We get an absence when it is a negation of occurrence or location, a difference when it is a negation of identity. When a negation or a negative statement negates location or occurrence of a property in a locus, it is construed as ascribing the absence of a property to that locus. Thus, absence of a property is treated as another property. "The pot is not blue" is first rephrased here as "the pot does not have blue color" which is further rephrased as "the pot has the absence of blue color." Using the complement sign "–" for term-negation, we can represent the above statement:

"m has $-s$," where (m = the pot, s = blue color).

When a statement negates an identity between, say, a table and a cup, it is construed as "a table is different from a cup" ("$s \neq t$"). Navya-nyāya argues that to say that a table is different from a cup is equivalent to saying "a table lacks the essence of a cup, or simply, lacks cupness." In other words, "difference from a cup" is said to be extensionally equivalent to "the absence of cupness" (which means that both these properties are locatable in the same set of loci).

World of Loci: Presence-Range and Absence-Range. Let us conceive of a universe U, which is peopled with loci or locations. Locations are so called because they accommodate "properties," in our specific sense of the term, that is, in the peculiar sense that we have tried to develop here. And similarly, properties are properties as long as they are locatable in some locus or other. Henceforth, I shall use the term "property" unabashedly in this specific sense.

Given a particular property *t*, we can find a set of locations or loci where *t* is locatable or present, and another set of loci where *t* is not locatable. Let us call the former set the presence-range of *t*, and the latter the absence-range of *t*. Let us use the notation "$t+$" for the presence-range of *t*, and "$t-$" for the absence-range of *t*. Thus, ordinarily, the two sets, $t+$ and $t-$, are supposed to exhaust the universe of loci U.

The Unlocatables. Navya-nyāya demands that the presence-range of a non-fictitious (real) property should be non-empty. Navya-nyāya argues that if the presence-range be empty then the property in question would be unlocatable. An unlocatable property is a suspect in Navya-nyāya. It is regarded as a fictitious property which cannot be located in our universe of loci. It is called an *a-prasiddha* property, "unexampled" property, that is, "unestablished," imaginary property (compare Ingalls, 1951: 61). Using modern terminology, we may say that it is a property that has location in a possible world, but not in the actual world. (I shall come back to this problem in the last chapter). Navya-nyāya hesitates to perform logical operations on such a property. For example, one cannot negate such a property and thereby obtain or derive another (negative) property for they would not be locatable in the actual world! Thus, we have the following restriction on negation: if *s* is a property with a non-empty presence-range, then by negating it we get another property, a negative property $\tilde{s}$; but if *s* is unlocatable, it cannot even be successfully negated.

Properties in Navya-nyāya are either atomic (or "simple") or composite. A composite property is formed out of atomic ones, and, hence, such a property is analyzable into atomic components or "simple" properties. A "simple" property is regarded as fundamental. It is not analyzable into components. (For more on the notation of "simple" property, see Matilal, 1971: 83–91). An example of a simple property is: cowness. The absence of cowness is a composite property. All fictitious properties like the property of being a flying horse, that of being a unicorn, a golden mountain, and the son of a barren woman, are composite properties, being analyzable into a number of "simple" properties. And, it is argued, such "simple" components are always real properties in the sense that they are locatable in some locus or other in our actual world.

The Unnegatables. If the presence-range of a property is empty, it is unlocatable. Nyāya calls such a property fictitious. What about properties whose absence-range is empty? Nyāya admits such properties as real, that is, non-fictitious. They are called ever-present properties (compare *kevalānvayin*).

They are said to be locatable in all loci of U. Examples of such properties are: knowability, expressibility, and provability (see §7.5).

An ever-present property is non-fictitious in Navya-nyāya, for, its presence-range is non-empty (in fact, the presence-range is the whole universe U). We have to assume that such a property is locatable also in itself, for, it must belong to the universe U. But since its absence-range is empty, Navya-nyāya regards such a property as unnegatable! In other words, just as an unlocatable property is said to be not negatable in Navya-nyāya, an ever-present property is also regarded as not negatable. For, we cannot derive a real, non-fictitious (negative) property by negating an ever-present property. Thus, we have another restriction on the operation of negation: If *e* is an ever-present property, it is locatable (that is, real), but it is, nevertheless, unnegatable.

It is obvious that the introduction of ever-present properties in the system involves many logical difficulties. Thus, some pre-Gaṅgeśa Nyāya logicians were definitely not in favor of using such a concept. They argued that a true property should have a non-empty presence-range as well as a non-empty absence-range. If we rule the unlocatable as fictitious, we might as well rule the ever-present properties as fictitious, for, both, as we have seen, cannot be successfully negated. But Gaṅgeśa rejected this view and argued that even if we do not accept such properties like knowability as non-fictitious, we cannot escape from admitting other kinds of ever-present properties. If we believe that each locus in the universe of loci is distinct from another, then this property, distinctness, can be construed as an ever-present property (for more on this argument, see §7.5).

Sondaḍa, a pre-Gaṅgeśa Navya-Naiyāyika, disputed the position that the unlocatables are unnegatable. If we admit an ever-present property as real (non-fictitious), that is, accept such a property to be real as is locatable in all loci, then, one might argue, by negating a so-called unlocatable property, we obtain only a negative property that should be locatable in all loci. In other words, such a negative property has to be admitted as real because its presence-range is non-empty (it is an ever-present property). Thus, if the property of being a golden mountain is unlocatable, then the absence of such a property is to be located everywhere! For, it makes perfect sense to say that there is no golden mountain, or that all loci in our actual world lack the property of being a golden mountain.

But Gaṅgeśa refuted Sondaḍa's contention. An unlocatable property, according to Gaṅgeśa, resists the operation of negation. Negation is restricted to the locatables and again only to such locatables whose absence-ranges are non-empty. To say, "there is no golden mountain" means, for Gaṅgeśa, that no mountain is golden, that is, made of gold. But "the property of being a golden mountain" as expressing a composite property is unlocatable.

Partial Location. We face a further oddity about negation when Navya-nyāya introduces the notion of partial location (compare *avyāpya-vṛtti*, Ingalls: "incomplete occurrence") of properties. Most properties are wholly or pervasively occurrent or locatable in their loci, but some properties are said to be only partially or non-pervasively occurrent or locatable in their loci. (We may imagine a "property" *dharma* in this sense to be a paint-coating, with which the locus is besmeared partly or wholly.)

To explain this notion, we have to develop some further logical vocabularies. Let us use a two place predicate (that is, a relational term), "L" for "located in;" we then define some other (logical) predicates or connections in terms of this "L." First, let us define the connection of co-location, "C." We can say that *s* is co-located with *t* provided there is a locus where both *s* and *t* are locatable. Thus, co-location is symmetrical. In other words, one property is co-locatable with another just in case their presence-ranges intersect or overlap. Using the convention of modern logic, we can say that *s* is co-locatable with *t* provided the logical product of *s*+ and *t*+ is non-empty. Lotus-hood and blue are co-locatable in things we call "blue lotuses." If such things did not exist in our actual world, the said logical product would have been empty.

In the above we have noted that if *s* is a locatable property then *s*+ and *s*- exhaust the universe of loci U. But we have not required the presence-range and the absence-range of *s* to be disjoint. In other words, we have left open the possibility of one intersecting the other. According to Navya-nyāya conception of negation, this is not impossible: in other words, a property and its absence may both be locatable in the same locus. Navya-nyāya calls such properties partially or non-pervasively locatable.

A property is pervasively (wholly) locatable provided it is not co-locatable with its absence. But when a property is co-locatable with its absence, it is called a partially locatable property. To put it in another way, if the absence-range of a property overlaps or intersects its presence-range, it is only a partially locatable property.

Physical contact is the best example of a partially locatable property. When I am sitting on a chair, there are places in the chair where my body-contact is absent. Thus, the same chair is said to be the locus of my body-contact (as a property) and also of the absence of my contact. Obviously it clashes with our general notion of negation to say that the same locus is characterized by a property and its absence at the same time. (Remember that absence of a property means only the negation of that property. How can we affirm and negate the same property of the same locus?) Thus, this doctrine of partial location requires some reformulation of the usual notion of contradiction. A property and its absence cannot be "contradictory" in this sense (compare *sahānavasthāna*) unless their loci or places of occurrence are specifically qualified in detail (using "delimitors," and so on).

An example may illustrate some further problems involved in the notion of partial location. Suppose, w is a partially locatable property. Now the absence-range of w will include not only those loci where w is absent (wholly) but also those loci where w is partially present. In other words, the presence-range of $\bar{w}$ includes the presence-range of w. Thus, the presence-range of $\bar{w}$ is the whole universe of the loci U. This means that if w is a partially locatable property, then $\bar{w}$ is an ever-present property, for, the formal character of an ever-present property will undoubtedly apply to it. Now, if we negate further $\bar{w}$, we are supposed to derive an unlocatable property. (Remember the previous point: negation of the ever-present generates the unlocatable). However, Navya-nyāya accepts the law of double negation. Udayana formulated the law as follows: the negation of the negation of a property is identical with the property itself (*Nyāya-kusumāñjali*, 3.2). Thus, we must have: the absence of $\bar{w} = w$. We face here an apparently paradoxical situation: if w is a partially locatable property, then w can be shown to be unlocatable!

Gaṅgeśa avoids this apparent problem by pointing out that there are two kinds of ever-present property, one of which is to be treated as unnegatable but the other is negatable. It is all right to say that when w is partially locatable, $\bar{w}$ becomes an ever-present property in the above manner, for it is present not only where w is absent but also where w is present. But $\bar{w}$ is also partially locatable with regard to some of its loci. In other words, the presence-range of $\bar{w}$ is actually a combination of the two: its pure presence-range (where w is not present) and a mixed range where $\bar{w}$ is co-locatable with w. Thus, $\bar{w}$ is a partially locatable ever-present property, and as such, it is negatable. The absence-range of $\bar{w}$ is non-empty; it coincides with the presence-range (which is a "mixed" range) of w. Thus, we have a formal restriction on the formal restriction of negation: not all ever-present properties are unnegatable.

Gaṅgeśa saved the law of double negation by resolving the oddity in the above manner. Some Navya-nyāya writers differed from him in this regard. Raghunātha, for example, suggested that the law of double negation be given up in the given context, for, it is based upon only extensional identity (their presence-ranges and absence-ranges being equal). Intensionally, w and the absence of $\bar{w}$ are distinguishable.

Mathuranātha suggested a different method of resolving the above oddity. According to him, instead of treating $\bar{w}$ as ever-present, we should treat the expression "$\bar{w}$" as ambiguously referring to two distinct (negative) properties: one that is partially locatable in its loci, the other wholly locatable in its loci. The presence-range of the first is disjoint from that of the second. The first is actually co-locatable with w, but the second is locatable where and only where w is not locatable. Thus, the problem of negating an ever-present property will not arise in this case.

Deviation and Pervasion. In the above we have defined co-location. Let us define some more logical predicates, such as deviation (D), non-deviation (N), and pervasion (V). We can say that h deviates from s just in case the absence-range of the latter overlaps (intersects) the presence-range of the former (compare *sādhyābhāvavad-vṛttitvaṃ vyabhicāraḥ*). Using the modern logical, that is, the Boolean convention (in which "." stands for intersection), we can write:

$h\mathrm{D}s$ iff $h+ \cdot s- \neq 0.$

Similarly, h non-deviates from s if and only if s- does not overlap $h+$ (*sādhyābhāvavad-avṛttitvam avyabhicāraḥ*):

$h\mathrm{N}s$ iff $h+ \cdot s- = 0.$

The relation of pervasion (*vyāpti,* V) is an important relation in Navya-nyāya, since it allows valid inference of one property from another. Thus, if h is pervaded by s then from the presence of h in a particular locus, we can validly infer presence of s in it. The rule is:

$(h\mathrm{L}p.\ s\mathrm{V}h) \supset s\mathrm{L}p.$

The relation "pervaded by" is identifiable with non-deviation (defined above) as long as we talk of such properties whose absence-ranges are non-empty. (For, we have used the absence-range of s in the above definition of non-deviation.) However, if s is unnegatable, the above definition, according to Navya-nyāya, becomes inapplicable. There are also several ever-present properties, according to Nyāya, and, hence, one can be inferable from another. Thus, Gaṅgeśa reformulates the definition of pervasion that will be inclusive of pervasion between ever-present (unnegatable) properties (compare *hetuman-niṣṭhābhāvāpratiyogi-sādhya-sāmānādhikaraṇyaṃ vyāptiḥ*). Thus, we may say: s pervades h if and only if (1) s is co-located with h and (2) if the absence-range of any property t intersects the presence-range of h, then t is non-identical with s.

$s\mathrm{V}h$ iff $s+ \cdot h+ \neq 0$ and if $(t- \cdot h+ \neq 0)$, then $t \neq s.$

A further problem arises when s becomes a partially locatable property. For, we have seen that, by definition, the presence-range and the absence-range of such a partially locatable property do intersect. Thus, when *s* is partially locatable, its absence-range includes its presence-range, and thereby its absence-range intersects the presence-range of *h*. Thus, the second component of the above definition may not be satisfied by such an *s*. Gaṅgeśa avoids this quandary by suggesting further qualification of the above definition:

$$sVh \text{ iff } s+\cdot h+\neq 0 \text{ and if } (t+\cdot t-=0 \text{ and } h+\cdot t-\neq 0) \text{ then } t\neq s.$$

There will arise some further problems even in this formulation, and commentators of Gaṅgeśa discussed them in detail. But I shall move on to the next section without going into such details.

7.4 NAVYA-NYĀYA AND MODERN LOGIC

In the following general observations I try to connect the problems discussed above with the explicit concern of modern logicians. This is by way of answering a criticism, viz., why these theories would form part of a study that has been called "logic." Let us note, first, that non-deviation and pervasion relations may be compared with the A-relation of Aristotle, for all three share a common logical feature, that is, transitivity. For contrast, we may say that the Navya-nyāya formulation of non-deviation (or pervasion relation), while it is narrower in its scope, does not suffer from the same ambiguity that the A-relation of Aristotle seems to have suffered from.

It is often pointed out, for example, that the existential import of the A-proposition should be assumed, in order that all the laws of the traditional (Aristotelian) system might be satisfied. Strawson (1952) has discussed three possible interpretations of the four propositions of Aristotle, and has shown that all the traditional laws can be satisfied under the third. In the context of Indian logic, we are primarily concerned with a general (affirmative) proposition that is used as the major premise. Richard S.Y. Chi (1969: xxx–xxxi) has rightly pointed out (against the common misinterpretation of many modern writers on Indian logic) that the "exemplified major in the Indian variety of syllogism is actually to be interpreted as 'an existential major premise.' " By "an existential major premise," Chi has obviously meant a general affirmative proposition where the non-emptiness of the class denoted by the subject term is presupposed.

The contrast between non-deviation (or pervasion) on the one hand and the A-relation of Aristotle on the other can be brought about in the following way. Navya-nyāya says that non-deviation of *h* from *s* holds when the following conditions are satisfied:

i) h and s have non-empty presence-ranges;
ii) s is not unnegatable, that is, its absence-range is non-empty; and
iii) the absence-range of s does not intersect the presence-range of h.

And pervasion of s with h holds when:

i) the non-empty presence-ranges of s and h intersect; and
ii) if h is locatable in the absence-range of any t, then $t \neq s$.

Following Strawson, we can represent the three interpretations of the A-relation and contrast them with non-deviation and pervasion as follows:

xAy (lst inter.) $\alpha\ \overline{\beta} = 0$

(2nd inter.) $\alpha\ \overline{\beta} = 0.\ \alpha \neq 0$

(3rd inter.) $\alpha\ \overline{\beta} = 0 \cdot \alpha \neq 0 \cdot \overline{\beta} \neq 0$

hNs $(h+ \cdot s- = 0) \cdot h+ \neq 0 \cdot s- \neq 0 \cdot s+ \neq 0$
sVh $(h+ \cdot s+ \neq 0) \cdot$ Not $(h+ \cdot t- \neq 0 \cdot t = s)$.

From the above it is clear that the third interpretation of the A-relation is closer to the concept of non-deviation in Navya-nyāya except for the fact that the latter requires an additional condition. Navya-nyāya's insistence on the non-emptiness of the presence-range or absence-range pays dividend in the long run, inasmuch as it makes the presupposition of a general statement (involving non-deviation or pervasion) explicit. It should, however, be noted that both non-deviation and pervasion are much stricter relations compared to the A-relation.

Second, let us note that most inferences studied in Navya-nyāya try to locate a property (called *sādhya*, "inferable property" s) in a particular locus (called *pakṣa*) with the help of another property (called *hetu*, "reason" h). Thus, the predominant inference-pattern of Navya-nyāya corresponds to what W. V. Quine (1962: 196) has called "singular inference." Hence, contrary to the belief of some modern interpreters of Indian logic, the Navya-nyāya inference is not exactly a *Barbara*, but a singular inference. Chi (1969: 13ff) has distinguished the standard *Barbara* from the singular inference by calling the latter *Barbara-A* and the former *Barbara-B*. Navya-nyāya, however, allows inferences corresponding to *Barbara-B*, for it notes that the "pervasion" relation is transitive (compare *tad-vyāpaka-vyāpakasya tad-vyāpakatvam, tad-vyāpya-vyāpyasya tad-vyāpyatvam*).

The Navya-nyāya restrictions on negation are instructive in many ways. To recapitulate briefly the Navya-nyāya position on negation: a property with an empty presence-range is called fictitious or unreal. We have called it unlocatable. Negation is viewed as an operation on real (non-fictitious) properties generating further real (that is, locatable but negative) properties. Thus, a property with an empty absence-range is considered unnegatable in this system. For, although such a property is held to be real (since it is locatable), its negation would not generate a real (that is, locatable) property.

It is possible to use some notions of multiple-valued logic under a special non-standard interpretation in order to represent the domain of properties in Navya-nyāya. Using "property" in the widest sense, we can construct the following tree to represent the branching of properties.

FIGURE 7.1
FIRST CLASSIFICATION OF PROPERTIES

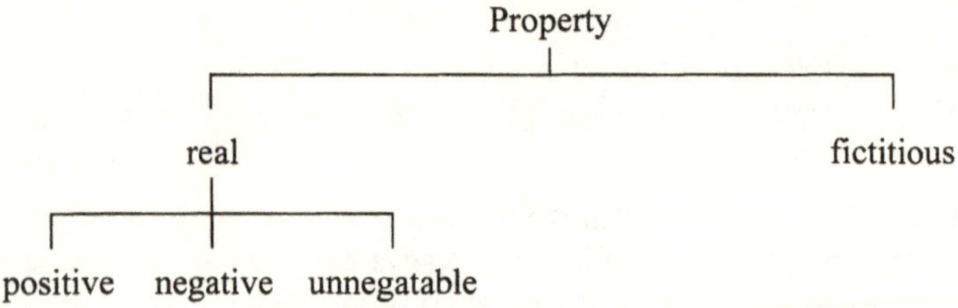

In ordinary three-valued system, such values as *T*, *F* and *I* are usually interpreted as "truth," "falsity," and "intermediate" (or, "undecided" or "neither true nor false"). Let us propose a completely different interpretation of values for the representation of the so-called real properties of Navya-nyāya. Our proposed three values are: P (for "positive"), N (for "negative"), and U (for "unnegatable"). Now, we can have a standard three-valued negation as table 7.1 shows:

TABLE 7.1
FIRST TRUTH-TABLE FOR NEGATION

w	not-w
P	N
N	P
U	U

This has the desirable outcome, viz.,

The presence-range of w = The absence-range of $\tilde{w}$,

The absence-range of w = The presence-range of $\tilde{w}$.

But, by negating an unnegatable we get only another unnegatable (a fictitious one). Further, since combination of an unnegatable with a positive yields, for Navya-nyāya, a positive property (and disjunction of a positive with an unnegatable yields an unnegatable), the corresponding tables for "AND" and "OR" can be constructed accordingly. But these tables will differ from the standard tables in some respects.

The problem of negation of the partially-locatable properties can be tackled in another way. Let us construe the negation of a partially-locatable property as both partially and wholly locatable. Then, we can agree with the following fourfold classification of properties:

FIGURE 7.2
SECOND CLASSIFICATION OF PROPERTIES

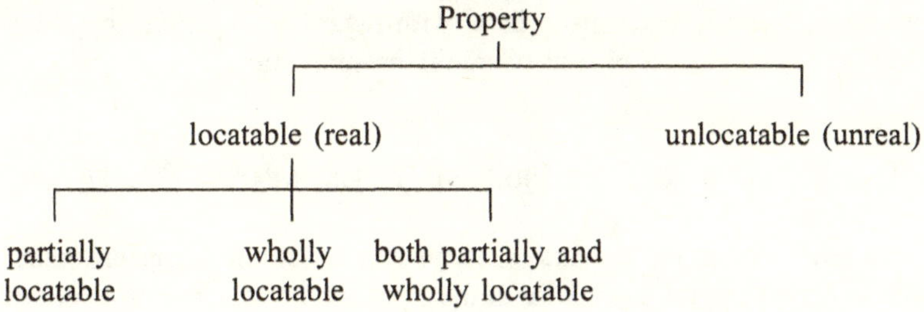

We have seen, for example, that negation of the body-chair-contact (a partially locatable property) yields a (negative) property that is both partially locatable (in the same loci, for example, my body) and wholly locatable in other loci. Here, using the notion of a multiple-valued system, we can assign value 1 for the wholly locatable, 2 for the partially locatable, 3 for those which are both partially locatable and wholly locatable, and 4 for the unlocatable. Thus, we can construct a four-valued system with non-standard interpretation of all values, and the negation matrix can be written as:

TABLE 7.2
SECOND TRUTH-TABLE FOR NEGATION

w	not-*w*
1	1
2	3
3	2
4	4

Finally, we may note that despite the above oddities, the Navya-nyāya doctrine of negation is not very different from what is usually called "classical" or standard negation. The law of double negation, which roughly combines the law of contradiction and the law of excluded middle, is always satisfied by what Nyāya calls wholly-locatable properties. (Only Raghunātha, a commentator of Gaṅgeśa, disputed this position, as I have mentioned above.) Thus, within the domain of wholly-locatable properties, our standard notion of negation is not "mutilated" (to use a term used by Quine).

Since the notion of partial location creates difficulty in interpreting negation in the standard fashion, Navya-nyāya recommends the use of the technique of delimitors (compare *avacchedaka*), by which a partially locatable property can be parsed as a wholly locatable one so that negation can be given the desirable standard interpretation. By declaring the unlocatables as un-negatable, Navya-nyāya solves another problem that may possibly arise due to what is called "truth-value gaps" of such propositions as: "There is no golden mountain" or "The son of a barren woman does not speak" (Udayana's example). Thus, despite the oddities encountered in Navya-nyāya theories, an attempt has constantly been made here, with regard to negation, to follow what Quine has called the maxim of minimum mutilation.

7.5 The Problem of Ever-Present (*Kevalānvayin*) Properties

We have seen in the previous sections that certain problems are rather peculiar to Navya-nyāya. They arise in the discussion of the Nyāya-Buddhist logical theories because of certain particular doctrines that were already propounded in the tradition. The concept of universal or ever-present properties is one such doctrine. As I have already noted, these universal properties cannot be equated with the notion of the universal class. For, to be sure, knowability and nameability are held to be non-identical properties, although they are said to occupy the same set of entities as loci.

That certain properties could be present in everything was an idea that was already implicit in the "wheel of reasons" (*hetucakra*) of Diṅnāga and the theory of inference propounded therein. If inference is the establishment of an object (or property in our sense described before) through an already known object occurring in a subject-locus (which is again another object), then what we have is a three-term operation. The first object is what we prove (to be precise, whose presence or occurrence we prove) by inference, and it is, accordingly, called *sādhya*. The second is what proves (or to be precise, whose presence in the third object as well as its relation with the first, proves), and, hence, it is called *sādhana* or *hetu*. The third object is called the *pakṣa*. (In this way of putting the matter, no distinction will be made between "object" and "property," for, both are alike members or items of the so-called universe of discourse.) Due to the above reason, most modern writers have translated "*sādhya*" as "probandum" and "*hetu*" as "probans," and I have sometimes followed them. However, obviously, the terms "probandum" and "probans" are not at all familiar to those who today write and read philosophical treatises in English. There is, therefore, some argument in favor of retaining these terms, *sādhya* and *hetu*, in the English versions. My advice is this, if probandum and probans seem almost as opaque as *sādhya* and *hetu*, one may very well leave these two terms untranslated. In what follows, if the reader finds the probans-and-probandum pair unacceptable, he may substitute it by the *sādhya*-and-*hetu* pair.

Now, to sketch Diṅnāga's "wheel of reasons," we can define the class of agreeing instances (*sapakṣa*) as the class α of all objects x such that the probandum is present in x. Similarly, the class of disagreeing instances (*vipakṣa*) can be defined as class β of all objects x such that the probandum is absent from x. Thus, any member of α is a *sapakṣa* and any member of β is a *vipakṣa*. Now, the probans as a property can be present in all, some, or no members of α. Similarly, the probans can be present in all, some, or no members of β. Combining these two sets of cases we get nine possibilities, of which only two cases are cases of valid inference (compare §1.2 and chapter 4).

The above is a rough sketch of Diṅnāga's system of logic as found in his *Hetucakraḍamaru*. For our purpose it is important to note here that one of the nine possibilities demands that the probans be present in all members of α as well as β. Now, if α and β are taken to be two complementary classes in the sense that taken together they exhaust the whole universe of discourse, then the probans in the above case will be a universal property that is present everywhere. Uddyotakara argued that in some cases of inference even our probandum can be a universal, that is, an ever-present (*kevalānvayin*) property. This implies that with regard to certain cases of inference, class β may be a null class, class α being a universal class.

In the Navya-nyāya school, however, the concept of ever-present property appears to have been taken very seriously. Navya-nyāya writers like Vallabha, Maṇikaṇṭha and Gaṅgeśa, rejected all such definitions of *vyāpti* (invariable concomitance between the probans and the probandum) as based on the notion of non-deviation (*avyabhicāritatva*) because such definitions would be inapplicable to cases of inference with an ever-present property as the probandum. The *siddhāntalakṣaṇa*, "conclusive definition," of *vyāpti* is formulated in such a way that it becomes logically applicable to all cases of inference including those in which some ever-present property is the probandum. I have presented my version of this definition of *vyāpti* in the previous section.

First, an ever-present property, in the sense I am using it here, cannot be identified with the notion of universal class for the following reason. Using the convention of modern class logic we can say that classes with the same members are identical. Thus, " $\omega = \omega'$" may be written as a convenient abbreviation of "(x)(x ∈ ω ≡ x ∈ ω')". But a property or attribute, in its non-extensional sense, cannot be held to be identical with another attribute, even if they are present in all and only the same individuals (compare Quine, 1953: 107). Properties are generally regarded by the Indian logicians as non-extensional, inasmuch as we see that they do not identify two properties like *anityatva* (non-eternalness) and *kṛtakatva* (the property of being produced or caused), although they occur in exactly the same things. In Udayana's system, however, such properties as are called *jāti* (generic characters) are taken in extensional sense, because Udayana identifies two *jāti* properties if only they occur in the same individuals. This is the significance of the condition called *tulyatva* (equipollence) found in the list of six *jāti-bādhakas* (impediments to generic characters) mentioned by Udayana.

Following the older tradition of the Nyāya school (notably Uddyotakara—see §5.6), Gaṅgeśa classified the types of inference as follows: 1) *kevalānvayin*, cases in which the probandum is an ever-present property, 2) *kevalavyatirekin*, cases in which the probandum is a property unique to the subject (*pakṣa*) so that no agreeing instances are available, 3) *anvaya-vyatirekin*, cases in which the probandum is a property present in some examples but absent in others. The third type includes the commonest forms of inference where both classes α and β (that is, *sapakṣa* and *vipakṣa*) are neither the universal nor null classes. We are concerned here mainly with the first type, in which there cannot be any *vipakṣa*, that is, class β is a null class.

Uddyotakara's example (taken from Diṅnāga) of *anvayin* inferences (corresponding to the first type here) was "Sound is noneternal because it is a product (*anityaḥ śabdaḥ kṛtakatvāt*)." Here the probandum non-eternalness will be a universal property for those thinkers who hold to the doctrine that everything is non-eternal. Note here that the universe of discourse for the Buddhist will include only non-eternal things and hence class β will be a null class (see §5.6). Vācaspati cited a better example of this type of inference: *viśeṣa* (particularity) is nameable because it is knowable. In a slightly modified form, this example was accepted as a paradigm in later Nyāya school: the pot is nameable because it is knowable.

Gaṅgeśa defined this kind of inference as one with no disagreeing instances (*vipakṣa*). Since everything in the universe of discourse is (at least, theoretically) nameable or expressible in language, the property nameability (*abhidheyatva*) is a universal property and in no individual is there an absence of nameability. To cite an instance where namability is absent is *ipso facto* to demonstrate that this instance is not inexpressible. If, however, the opponent does not cite such an instance where nameability is absent, but, nevertheless, believes it to be existent, then as far as the logicians' inference is concerned it is as good as non-existent, since inferential procedure demands the use of language. The opponent may argue that although a disagreeing instance in this case is not expressible in language, it can still be a communicable concept in the sense that it is conveyed by the meaning of some linguistic expression. But this would run counter to the Nyāya thesis that there cannot be any instance that is not nameable.

Gaṅgeśa argued that from the opponent's viewpoint, the notion of ever-present property invites the following paradox. If p is asserted to be an ever-present property then one can infer validly from this premise that p is not ever-present. It is observed that with regard to each property (*dharma*) it is legitimate (according to the Indian theory) to assert that each property is such that it is absent from something. Using quantificational notation and interpreting "Fx" as "x is a property" and "Oxy" as "x is present in y" we may represent this premise as:

$$(x)\ (\exists y)(Fx \supset -\ Oxy).$$

Now, since p is a property (that we have assumed to be ever-present), it follows (by universal instantiation and truth-functional tautology) that p is such that it is absent from something. In other words, the conclusion is "$(\exists y)(-Opy)$." This implies that there is an instance y where p (that is, knowability) is not present. Thus, our original assumption that p is an ever-present property is contradicted.

Gaṅgeśa tried to answer this objection as follows. If the property "to be absent from something," that is, the property represented by the propositional function "$(\exists y)(-Opy)$," is said to be a property which is not absent from anything, then the same property becomes ever-present. If, however, this property (that is, "to be absent from something") happens to be not present in something x then that x becomes, in fact, ever-present. Let us try to understand the implication of this argument. Let class ω be defined as $\hat{x}(\exists y)(-Oxy)$. Now, if we assume that $-(\omega \in \omega)$, it means that the statement "$(\exists y)(-Owy)$" is false, that is, "$-(\exists y)(-Owy)$" is true. This implies that the class property of ω is something that is not absent from anything, that is, it is ever-present. In an indirect way, this means that ω is a universal class. If, on the other hand, we assume that $\omega \in \omega$, then the statement "$(\exists y)(-Owy)$" becomes true. This means that there is something y from which the class-property ω is absent. But to deny the class-property ω of something y means to admit y as an ever-present property. (Notice that no type-difference of properties is being admitted here).

Gaṅgeśa's argument was exactly similar to this, although he did not use the notion of class. Instead, he used his notion of constant absence (*atyantābhava*) and its counterpositive-ness or the absenteehood (*pratiyogitā*). A constant absence is arrived at by hypostatizing the negation illustrated in the matrix "there is no x in y" or "x is not present in y." Thus, y is said to be the locus that possesses constant absence of x, and x is said to be the counterpositive or absentee of an absence that is present in locus (for the notions of counterpositive and constant absence, see Ingalls, 1951: 54–58, and Matilal, 1968: 52–61, 94–95). In fact, the constant absence of x may conveniently be regarded as a class-property of the class which is defined as $\hat{y}(\exists x)(x \text{ is not present in } y)$. The mutual absence of x (illustrated by the matrix "y is not x") may likewise be regarded as a class-property of the class that is defined (using usual symbols for identity and negation) as $\hat{y}\ (\exists x)\ (x \neq y)$. This interpretation of absences in terms of the class-concept of modern logic gets indirect support from the fact that Navya-nyāya, in most cases, identifies two absences that occur in the same loci.

Gaṅgeśa argued as follows. If the property of being the absentee of a constant absence does not become the absentee of any constant absence then the same property can be taken to be ever-present. And if, on the other hand, that property is regarded as the absentee of some constant absence say, the constant absence of x in locus y, then the locus y where such a constant absence resides becomes itself an ever-present property. The upshot of Gaṅgeśa's argument is that if something x is a property it does not necessarily follow that there is something else y wherefrom x will be absent. This is so because there are ever-present properties that will not be absent anywhere. An ever-present property can now be defined as:

> D1. x is an ever-present property if and only if x is not the absentee of any constant absence.

To develop the next point in Gaṅgeśa's discussion we have to understand what Navya-nyāya calls a non-pervasive (*avyāpyavṛtti*) property (see §7.4). A property is called non-pervasive if and only if it occupies only a part of the locus such that in remaining parts of the locus there is the constant absence of that property (Ingalls, 1951: 73; Matilal, 1968: 53, 71–2). Thus, properties like a pot or contact-with-a-monkey (in fact, almost all properties except certain abstract ones like cow-ness), with respect to their loci, such as a piece of ground or a tree, behave as non-pervasive properties. Now, the constant absence of a property p is regarded as another property, say q, which is present in all things except where p is present. But the constant absence of any non-pervasive property, it has already been argued, will become an ever-present property simply because such an absence is not only present in all loci except where the non-pervasive property in question is absent but also in locus where the same non-pervasive property is present. This follows from the very definition of non-pervasive property. However, Gaṅgeśa pointed out that as soon as we introduce the notion of delimitors (*avacchedaka*) in our discourse the constant absence of a non-pervasive property (say, a pot) can no longer be, strictly speaking, an ever-present property. Thus, a pot cannot be said to be absent from the locus ground if it is actually present there. In simple language, this only means that right in the space of the ground occupied by the pot there cannot be any constant absence of the pot. Hence, such a constant absence is not ever-present. There is a locus, as we have just referred to, where pot-absence is not present. Note that the notion of delimitor here serves to dispel the vagueness of ordinary uses of "locus (*adhikaraṇa*)" and "occurrence (*vṛtti*)."

Another suggestion for constructing an ever-present property can be given as follows. The ubiquitous physical space (*gagana*) in the Nyāya-Vaiśeṣika system of categories is held to be a non-occurrent entity in the sense that it does not occur in any locus. All entities of the Nyāya-Vaiśeṣika system are properties (in the sense that they occur in some locus or other) except entities like the ubiquitous space. Thus, since there is no entity where the space might occur as a property, the constant absence of the space becomes ever-present. But this procedure eventually leads to some difficulties. Technically speaking, the constant absence of the space can very well be the absence (*pratiyogin*) of another constant absence, viz., the constant absence of the constant absence of the space (which, according to Nyāya, is just identical with the space itself). Thus, the above definition of ever-present property cannot be applied to the constant absence of the space. This eventually landed Gaṅgeśa into the puzzling discussion of the Navya-nyāya school, viz., what constitutes the absence of an absence? (see Ingalls, 1951: 68, 71–2; Matilal, 1985: 145–64).

The constant absence of x is constantly absent from all things except those that have no x. Hence, the constant absence of the constant absence of x is present in all and only those things where x is present. Applying the principle of identification of the indiscernibles, Udayana, and following him Gaṅgeśa, identified the constant absence of the constant absence of x with x on the ground that:

A. (y) (y has the constant absence of the constant absence of $x \equiv y$ has x).

The mutual absence of or difference from pot is constantly absent from all things that are called "pot," that is, from all things that have pot-ness. Thus, the constant absence of the mutual absence of pot is present in all and only those things that have pot-ness. Therefore, as above, one can identify the constant absence of the mutual absence of pot with pot-ness on the principle that:

B. (y) (y has the constant absence of the difference from pot $\equiv y$ has pot-ness).

Note that we are identifying here two class-properties on the ground that the corresponding classes are identical by virtue of their having the same members. This indirectly supports my earlier suggestion that absences in many contexts can conveniently be taken to be class-properties suitably chosen. Properties, in such contexts, are used in their non-intensional sense. I have discussed these issues further in (Matilal, 1985: 145–64).

Navya-nyāya, however, regards the constant absence of the ubiquitous space as an ever-present property, and, accordingly, Gaṅgeśa developed a technical sense of "ever-present property" by rephrasing D1 as follows:

> D2. *x* is ever-present if and only if *x* is not the absentee of any occurrent (*vṛttimat*) constant absence.

Although the constant absence of the space may be said to be the absentee of the constant absence of the constant absence of the space, the second absence is not occurrent because it is to be identified with the space and the space is, by definition, not occurent anywhere. Properties like knowability and nameability are not the absentee of any occurrent constant absence and hence they can be called ever-present. This is one of many possible interpretations of Gaṅgeśa's rephrasing (which was ambiguous in the original). But, according to Raghunātha, this was just Gaṅgeśa's way of being polite to the opponent (compare *abhyupagamamātram*). Actually, the constant absence of the constant absence of the space cannot be identified with the space because the above principle A is not applicable here. Since in the Nyāya-Vaiśeṣika system there is no entity that has the space as a property, we cannot identify it with the constant absence of the constant absence of the space under principle (A). The significance of the adjective "occurrent (*vṛttimat*)" was explained by Raghunātha as follows. When something is said to be present in something else, it is present there always through some relation or other. Thus, in speaking of something as ever-present one should specify the relation through which it is considered present everywhere:

> D3. *x* is ever-present through relation *r* if and only if *r* is the delimiting relation of the absenteehood of some constant absence and *x* is never the counterpositive of such absence.

To expose another logical difficulty involved in the notion of ever-present property, we have to go back to the definition of *kevalānvayin* inference (type 1 above). First, it is odd to say that the probans does not reside in disagreeing instances, when there is, in fact, no disagreeing instance. It is further odd to say that there is no disagreeing instance, when "disagreeing instance" (*vipakṣa*) is a mere indesignate or empty (*nirupākhya*) term, for one tends to argue that to make such denials meaningful our acceptance of the existence of such non-entities is in order. Vācaspati puzzled over this problem because, according to the Nyāya theory, each negation, in order to be meaningful, must negate a real entity and must denote an absence that usually behaves as a property occurring in some locus. Thus, an absence is always determined by its absence (that is, the negatum) on the one hand and by the locus (*ādhāra*) on the other. Vācaspati tried to solve the above puzzle by saying that the prudent course is silence, that is, not to deny or affirm anything (including existence) of the non-existents. The denial sounds odd because its contradictory, that is, affirmation, sounds odd too. Udayana suggested a better method of answering such problems. According to him, a statement like:

1. The rabbit's horns do not exist,

does not affirm or deny existence of anything, but simply expresses an absence *not* of the rabbit's horns but of horns, an absence that occurs in a rabbit. Note that having horns is a real property such that one can meaningfully speak of its absence (another real property for the Naiyāyikas). This analysis is related to the epistemological theory of error of the Nyāya school which is technically known as *anyathākhyāti*. The structure of this analysis may remind one of B. Russell's analysis of similar statements with his theory of descriptions (for further details, see Matilal, 1985: 85–112).

Applying Udayana's principle of analysis, Gaṅgeśa tried to make sense of the statements that make use of such indesignate expression as "the absence of an ever-present property like knowability," viz.,

2. "the absence of knowability is *not* present in *y*" (a true one)
3. "the absence of knowability is present in *y* (a false one).

Note that "the absence of knowability" is, as it stands, an empty term and on par with "the present king of France." According to Gaṅgeśa, we can rephrase (2) and (3) as:

4. Knowability is not the absence of any absence that may occur in *y*.
5. Knowability is the absentee of an absence that occurs in *y*.

Here, (4) predicates of knowability the absence of the property of being the absentee of any absence occurring in *y*, while (5) predicates of knowability the absenteehood of an absence occurring in *y*. Thus, (4) expresses a trivial truth (see Dl before) while (5) expresses a falsehood. Note that "an absence which occurs in *y*" will denote a real absence occurring in the thing substituted for "y" and that its absentee will be a real entity. Hence the property of being such an absentee is also a real property that characterizes certain things (viz., things that are really absent from *y*) but not knowability.

Gaṅgeśa used this method of analysis in order to make sense of the doubt or uncertainty (*saṃśaya*) of the form "perhaps it is knowable, perhaps it is not." This statement expresses a doubt and can be said to be a meaningful statement if it is rephrased in the above manner so as to avoid the use of any empty term-complex such as "the absence of knowability" (which refers to nothing as in (3) above). Note that the second part of the statement expressing doubt, viz., "it is not (knowable)," would have contained such an empty term-complex, if it were straight-forwardly analyzed in its logical form: it has the absence of knowability.

It should be noted in this connection that, according to the Navya-nyāya theory of inference, an inference (as an effect, that is, *kārya*) must be preconditioned by what Navya-nyāya calls *pakṣatā*. The condition of *pakṣatā*, according to the view of the old Nyāya, involves in the presence of a doubt or uncertainty which should be expressed in the form "perhaps the subject possesses the probandum, perhaps it does not." This postulate is based upon the simple fact that we do not infer something that we already know with certainty unless we wish to prove it again. Now, if inference of an ever-present property like knowability has to be an actual event, it should be pre-conditioned by an uncertainty of the form described above. Thus, the statement that expresses this uncertainty or doubt must be a meaningful statement so that the required doubt (*saṃśaya*) may, in fact, arise. Gaṅgeśa pointed out that when the second part of the statement expressing doubt is interpreted as (5) above, we can retain its meaningfulness and avoid using empty terms that refer to nothing.

While studying Indian logic, scholars will find themselves concerned with issues of two different kinds. The first are those problems that are bounded by the Indian tradition itself, that is, those that arise out of the peculiar yet rich tradition of India's scholastic past. They are partly conditioned by the Sanskrit language and partly by the fundamental concepts and philosophical attitudes that Indian logicians inherited. The second set of problems we face here could be called universal. They are, in essence, the very same problems faced by the Western tradition, although often, because of the parochial and tradition-bound interest of both sides, this fact has been either ignored or badly misunderstood.

7.6 INFERENCE AND CONCOMITANCE (VYĀPTI)

With the advent of Navya-nyāya methodology, the notion of invariable concomitance or pervasion (*vyāpti*) became increasingly the center of interest of most Naiyāyikas in India. Even before the time of Gaṅgeśa, there were numerous definitions of pervasion offered by different writers, the difference of one definition from the other being at times very subtle and theory-bound and at other times trivial. Even a cursory glance at Gaṅgeśa's text (he notes as many as twenty-one definitions, all of which he rejects for some reason or other, and then goes on to give seven or eight more definitions, each of which he seems to accept) will convince one how much interest was created regarding the explication of the concept of pervasion. This interest continued even after Gaṅgeśa with much gusto, and as a result, we find numerous commentaries and sub-commentaries written particularly upon this portion of Gaṅgeśa's text. It is no wonder, therefore, that in the traditional seminaries of India today a beginner in Navya-nyāya usually starts with one or two sub-commentaries on some section of the *Vyāpti* section of Gaṅgeśa. Why do we find this rather unusual interest in the definition of this concept among the Indian logicians? The history of logic in India has its own unique nature of development, as we have seen. A brief review may be enlightening.

Early attempts to study the inferential relation can be found in the *Vaiśeṣika-sūtras* 3.1.8 and 9.18, as well as in the Sāṃkhya school (viz., *Ṣaṣṭitantra*). The former speaks of four types of inferential relation beginning with causal relation (in the Vaiśeṣika sense of the term "cause"), while the Sāṃkhya speaks of seven types of relation beginning with part and whole (*mātramātrikābhāva*). It was felt at the time of Praśastapāda and Diṅnāga that this type of classification was not exhaustive or could not have been so.

Kumārila used the term *vyāpti* "pervasion" for the inferential relation and tried to develop a sort of logic based upon the relation of class inclusion and extension of terms. The pervaded (*vyāpya*), that is, the middle term, is either co-extensive with (*sama*) or included in (*nyūna*) the extension of the pervader (*vyāpaka*), that is, the major term. Inductive generalization, according to Kumārila, is based upon multiplication of empirical evidence, and an undiscovered or unnoticed "associate condition" (*upādhi*) may falsify the supposed generalization.

Dharmakīrti provided a much neater scheme for classifying pervasion (see §5.1). Pervasion or inferential relation may be based upon identity relation, which is actually a relation of class inclusion (viz., it is a plant, because it is an ivy). This is called identity, because the two terms here refer to the same thing. Pervasion may also be based upon causal relation, which should be an inseparable relation (effect being inseparably connected with its cause) between two different entities (viz., there is fire there, because there is smoke). In fact, in the former case we get what we may call today an analytic judgement as our major premise, the whole argument taking purely a deductive character. In the latter case we get a synthetic judgement (in some sense) as our major premise which combines two different entities through causal relation.

Whether Dharmakīrti envisioned a real distinction similar to the one that we make today between analytic and synthetic propositions is, however, very difficult to say. The matter is not easily decidable.[2] Dharmakīrti also noted various other types of inseparable relation, which were, in essence, ramifications of these two major relations combined with negation and contradiction.

This neat scheme of Dharmakīrti was severely criticized by the Naiyāyikas as being insufficient on obvious grounds. Some very common forms of inference (for example, inference of sunrise tomorrow from today's sunrise) can hardly be assimilated under this neat scheme. Trilocana, the Naiyāyika, thought it proper to define pervasion as the *natural* (*svābhāvika*) relation. A *natural* relation is explicated as an "unconditional" relation (*anaupādhika*), a relation that is uncontaminated by an "associate condition," *upādhi*. Udayana favored a modified version of unconditionality as a definition of pervasion. Vallabha registered a note of caution. For him, pervasion means accompaniment of all the cases of the middle term with the major term. The differentiating mark (*lakṣaṇa*) of pervasion relation is, however, the absence of *upādhi*, "associate condition." An "associate condition" is defined, according to Vallabha, as the property that accompanies all cases of the major term, that is, what is to be inferred (*sādhya*), but only some cases of the middle term, for example, the *hetu* or the "reason."

By the time Navya-nyāya method was developing and greater attention was being paid to the precise formulation of the definition of different concepts, there were several alternative definitions of the concept of pervasion as well as several alternative formulations of the definition of *upādhi* "associate condition" (which was well-recognized by this time as a negative mark of pervasion). Thus, Maṇikaṇṭha Miśra (who preceded Gaṅgeśa) mentioned as many as eleven different definitions of pervasion, each of which was

---

2. Note, however, that in §5.2, which was written much later than the present section, Matilal argues that inferential relations based on the identity relation are necessary but *a posteriori* truths. He records his change of mind about this point in Matilal and Evans, 1986: 23–4, where he says that:

> In an earlier paper I had described the "natural" connection as based upon an analytical proposition. This was inaccurate, as some (e.g. E. Steinkellner, 1974) have pointed out. This cannot be strictly described as analytical. However, I still believe that Dharmakīrti, probably unlike Diṅnāga, wanted a sort of *necessary* connection to obtain between the sign and the signified, obviously in order to avoid the contingencies of an inductive generalisation based purely upon observation. . . . If analyticity is regarded as a linguistic notion, we need not connect it with the present issue. It may be said that the natural invariance . . . is a necessary proposition which we know *a posteriori*.

rejected by him on various grounds. He accepted what seems to be a modification of his eleventh definition.

Gaṅgeśa's twenty-nine different formulations of the definition of pervasion (twenty-one of which being unacceptable and eight being acceptable to Gaṅgeśa) were largely based upon Maṇikaṇṭha's and Śaśadhara's discussions of pervasion. The following are the eleven alternative definitions of pervasion found in Maṇikaṇṭha: Pervasion 1 is "any kind of relation," *sambandha-mātra* (the view of Bhūṣaṇakāra = Bhāsarvajña?); Pervasion 2 is "non-deviation," *avyabhicāritatva* (found in Śrīdhara's *Nyāya-kandalī* and in many other places); Pervasion 3 is "the property of not occurring without (the other)," *avinābhāva* (Diṅnāga, Praśastapāda and many others); Pervasion 4 is "natural relation," *svābhāvikasambandha* (Trilocana); Pervasion 5 is "relation of the effect to its efficient cause," *nimitta-naimittika-bhāva* (the Sāṃkhya view?); Pervasion 6 is "identity," *tādātmya* (Dharmakīrti); Pervasion 7 is "relation of the qualifier to the qualified," *viśiṣṭa-vaiśiṣṭya* (?); Pervasion 8 is "the property of being the counterpositive of an absence which (absence) is pervasive of the absence of the major term," *sādhyābhāva-vyāpakābhāva-pratiyogitva*; Pervasion 9 is "accompaniment of all cases of one term with the other term," *kārtsnyena sādhana-sādhya-sahabhāva* (Vallabha); Pervasion 10 is "unconditional relation," *anaupādhikasambandha* (Udayana and others); Pervasion 11 is "co-occurrence with something that is never the counterpositive of a constant absence which (absence) is co-occurrent with the other term (the *hetu*) in the same locus" *sādhanatvābhimatasamānādhikaraṇātyantābhāva-pratiyogisāmānādhikaraṇya*.

Gaṅgeśa first takes the second definition of Maṇikaṇṭha's list, viz., non-deviation, and gives seven different formulations of this definition then rejects each of them mainly on the ground that it fails to include the pervasion relation existing between two "ever-present" *kevalānvayin* properties, such as knowability and nameability. An incidental discussion is introduced here on the point whether the absence of "unactualized possible" entities could be regarded as an ever-present property or not. I have noted the question already in the previous discussion. This is followed by four different ramifications of the definition of pervasion, some of which can be located in Śaśadhara's *Nyāyasiddhāntadīpa*. Then Gaṅgeśa examines two different formulations of the notion of unconditionality (definition 10 of Maṇikaṇṭha) and four different formulations of the pervasion relation by making use of a universal quantifier (*kṛstna*, *yāvat*; definition 9 above). Next we find brief mention of definition 4 (*svabhāvika-sambandha*), definition 3 (*avinābhāva*) and definition 1 (*sambandha-mātra*) from the above list.

The *siddhānta-lakṣaṇa*, that is, the definition acceptable to Gaṅgeśa, is only a modified version of Maṇikaṇṭha's final definition. This formulation takes care of the cases where the major term is such that both its absence and its presence can be truly asserted of the same locus (that is, *avyāpyavṛtti-sādhyaka*). A similar definition is also found in the list of Śaśadhara. This definition does not use any universal quantifier, but makes use of a generic absence, for example, an absence whose absentee is qualified by a generic property. Gaṅgeśa inserts here a discussion to show how and why the generic absence must be regarded as separate from the integration of specific absences. Gaṅgeśa next offers three different formulations of the definition of pervasion where no use of the notion of generic absence is made. Gaṅgeśa finally accepts definition 10, that is, "unconditionality" or pervasion, as an alternative definition, and gives four acceptable formulations of this definition. This is followed by three different formulations of the notion of "associate condition," *upādhi*.

The quest for good reasons that generate dependable and acceptable conclusions is almost universal. Indian logic, by which I mean a combined tradition of the Buddhist, Nyāya, and the Jaina, is only another instantiation of this universal quest in the intellectual history of mankind. It represents an independent tradition of studying inference and its soundness. Just because of its difference as well as independence from the Western tradition, the inference theory developed here should prove extremely interesting for both logicians and philosophers. The Indian theory of inference shows a continuous development from the pre-Christian era up to the seventeenth century AD. It lacks, it is true, some of the familiar logical (and mathematical) notions that logicians of today have come to expect. But then it offers a contrast in these areas with Western logical theories that developed primarily during the last two centuries. It is also instructive in that it shows, at least, what other ways are left to us for solving some logical problems in case certain familiar devices are not available.

Philosophers Discussed

Nyāya-Vaiśeṣika

Akṣapāda Gautama, c. 150. Naiyāyika, author of the *Nyāya-sūtra*.

Vātsyāyana, c. 350–425. Naiyāyika, author of *Nyāya-bhāṣya* on the *Nyāya-sūtra*.

Praśastapāda, c. 450–500. Vaiśeṣika, author of *Padārthadharmasaṃgraha*.

Uddyotakara, c. 550–625. Naiyāyika, author of *Nyāyavārttika* on the *Nyāya-bhāṣya*.

Vācaspati, f. 980. Naiyāyika, author of *Nyāyavārttika-tātparyaṭīkā*, and other works.

Udayana, c. 975–1050. Naiyāyika, author of *Pariśuddhi* on Vācaspati's *Nyāyavārttika-tātparyaṭīkā*, *Lakṣaṇāvalī*, and other works.

Gaṅgeśa, f. 1325. Navya-naiyāyika, author of *Tattvacintāmaṇi*.

Buddhist

Upāyahṛdāya, author and date uncertain.

Nāgārjuna, c. 150–250. Mādhyamika, author of *Mulamādhyamikakārika*, *Vigrahavyāvartanī*, and other works.

Tarkaśāstra, author and date uncertain.

Vasubandhu, f. 320–350. Abhidharma author of the *Vādavidhi* and other works.

Buddhaghoṣa, f. early fifth century. Abhidharma author of a commentary on the *Kathāvatthu* (second century BC), and other works.

Diṅnāga, c. 400–480. Author of *Pramāṇasamuccaya*, *Hetucakraḍamaru*, *Nyāyamukha*, and other works.

Dharmakīrti, c. 600–660. Interpreter of Diṅnāga, author of *Pramāṇavarttika*, *Nyāyabindu*, *Hetubindu*, *Vādanyāya*, and other works.

JAINA

Sthānāṅga sūtra, c. 100 BC? A Jaina canonical text.

Samantabhadra, seventh century. Author of *Āptamīmāṃsā*.

Haribhadra, c. 700–770. Author of *Anekāntajayapātaka*, *Ṣaḍdarśanasamuccaya* and other works.

Hemacandra, 1088–1172. Author of *Pramāṇamīmāṃsā*, *Anyayogavyavacchedadvātriṃśika*.

Malliṣeṇa, f. 1290. Author of *Syādvādamañjarī* on Hemacandra's *Anyayogavyavacchedadvātriṃśika*.

OTHERS

Caraka. c.100. Medical theorist, author of the *Caraka-saṃhitā*.

Bibliography

Akalaṅka (1939). *Akalaṅka-grantha-traya*, ed. M.K. Sastri. Singhi Jain Series 12. Ahmedabad: Sañchālaka-singhī Jaina Grathamālā.

Akṣapāda Gautama (1936). *Nyāyasūtra*, with Vātsyāyana's *Bhāṣya*, Uddyotakara's *Vārttika*, Vācaspati Miśra's *Tātparyaṭīkā* and Viśvanātha's *Vṛtti*. Ed. Taranatha Nyayatarkatirtha and Amarendramohan Tarkatirtha. Calcutta: Calcutta Sanskrit Series nos. 18-19.

Akṣapāda Gautama (1967). *Nyāyadarśana*, with Vātsyāyana's *Bhāṣya*, Uddyotakara's *Vārttika*, Vācaspati Miśra's *Tātparyaṭīkā* and Udayana's *Nyāyavārttika-tātparya-pariśuddhi*. Vol. 1, chapter 1. Ed. A. Thakur. Mithila: Mithila Institute Series.

Aristotle. (1941). *The Basic Works of Aristotle*, ed. R. McKeon. New York: Random House.

Aung, S. Z. (1915). *Points of Controversy, or, Subjects of Discourse: Being a Translation of the Kathāvatthu from the Abhidhammapītaka*, eds. S. Z. Aung and C. A. F. Rhys Davids. Pali Text Society. London: Routledge and Kegan Paul.

Bagchi, S. (1953). *Inductive Reasoning: A Study of Tarka and its Role in Indian Logic*. Calcutta: Calcutta Oriental Press.

Bhattacharya, D. C. (1958). *History of Navya-Nyāya in Mithila*. Mithila Institute, series 3, no. 2. Dharbhanga: Dharbhanga Press.

Bochenski, J. M. (1956). *A History of Formal Logic*. Freiburg. Second edition, trans. I. Thomas, New York: Chelsea Publ. Co. (1961).

Caraka (1981). *Caraka-saṃhitā*. Ed. and trans. P. Sharma. Varanasi: Chaukhambha Orientalia.

Cartwright, H. (1970). "Qualities." *Philosophical Review*, 79: 25–42.

Chakrabarti, K. K. (1977). *The Logic of Gotama*. University of Hawaii Society for Asian and Comparative Philosophy Monograph, no. 5. Hawaii: University Press of Hawaii.

Chi, R. S. Y. (1969). *Buddhist Formal Logic: A Study of Dignāga's Hetucakra and K'uei-chi's Great Commentary on the Nyāyapraveśa*. London: The Royal Asiatic Society of Great Britain.

Dharmakīrti (1968). *Pramāṇavārttika*, ed. Swami Dwarkidas Sastri. Varanasi: Bauddha-Bharati.

Dharmakīrti (1972). *Vādanyāya and Sambandhaparīkṣa*, ed. Swami Dwarkidas Sastri. Varanasi: Bauddha Bharati. Vādanyāya is critically edited and translated in Gokhale P. P. (1993) *Vādanyāya of Dharmakīrti: The Logic of Debate*. Delhi: Sri Satguru Publications.

Evans, J. D. G. (1977). *Aristotle's Concept of Dialectic*. Cambridge: Cambridge University Press.

Geokoop, C. (1967). *The Logic of Invariable Concomitance in the Tattvacintāmaṇi*. Dordrecht: Reidel.

Goodman, N. (1978). *The Ways of World-Making*. Indianopolis: Hackett.

Granoff, P. (1978). *Philosophy and Argument in Late Vedānta: Śrī Harṣa's Khaṇḍanakhaṇḍakhādya*. Studies of Classical India, vol. 1. Dordrecht: Reidel.

Haribhadra (1940). *Anekāntajayapatākā*, ed. H. R. Kapadiya. Baroda: Gaekwad Oriental Series, no. 88.

Haribhadra (1905-14). *Ṣaḍdarśanasamuccaya*, with Guṇaratna Sūri's commentary. Calcutta: Bibliotheca Indica. Reprinted by the Asiatic Society, Calcutta (1986).

Hayes, R. (1980). "Diṅnāga's Views on Reasoning," *Journal of Indian Philosophy*, 8: 219–277.

Hayes, R. (1986). "An Interpretation of *Anyāpoha* in Diṅnāga's General System of Inference," in B. K. Matilal and R. D. Evans (eds) (1986).

Hayes, R. (1988). *Diṅnāga on the Interpretation of Signs*. Studies of Classical India, vol. 9. Dordrecht: Kluwer.

Heijenoort, J. van (1974). "Subject and Predicate in Western Logic," *Philosophy East and West* 3: 253–268.

Hempel, K. (1965). *Aspects of Scientific Explanation*. New York: Free Press.

Hoffman, F. J. (1982). "Rationality in Early Buddhist Four-Fold Logic," *Journal of Indian Philosophy*, 10: 309–337.

Ingalls, D. H. H. (1951). *Materials for the Study of Navya-Nyāya Logic*. Harvard: Harvard University Press.

Kajiyama, Y. K. (1963). "*Tripañcakacintā*: Development of the Buddhist Theory of Determination of Causality," *Miscallenea Indologica Kiotsena*, 4-5: 1–15. Reprinted in Y.Y. Kajiyama, *Studies in Buddhist Philosophy: Selected Papers*, ed. Katsumi Mimaki et al. Kyoto: Rinsen Books, (1989).

Kajiyama, Y. K. (1966). *An Introduction to Buddhist Philosophy: A Translation of Mokṣākara-gupta's Tarkabhāṣā*. Kyoto: Memoirs of the Faculty of Letters, Kyoto University.

Katsura, S. (1983). "Dignāga on *Trairūpya*," *Journal of Indian and Buddhist Studies*, 32: 15–21.

Kitagawa, H. (1965). *Indo koten ronrigatu no kenkyū: Jinna (Diṅnāga) no taikei*. Tokyo: Suzuki Gakujutsu Zaidan.

Kneale, W. and Kneale, M. (1964). *The Development of Logic*. Oxford: Clarendon Press.

Kumārila (1898). *Mīmāṃsā-śloka-vārttika*, ed. R. S. Tailanga Manavalli. Varanasi: Chowkhamba.

Mackie, J. L. (1985). *Selected Papers: Logic and Knowledge*, ed. J. Mackie and P. Mackie. Oxford: Clarendon Press.

Malliṣeṇa (1933). *Syādvādamañjarī*, ed. A. B. Druva. Bombay: Bombay Sanskrit and Prakrit Series.

Matilal, B. K. (1968). *The Navya-Nyāya Doctrine of Negation*. Harvard: Harvard University Press.

Matilal, B. K. (1971). *Epistemology, Logic and Grammar in Indian Philosophical Analysis*. The Hague: Mouton.

Matilal, B. K. (1976). *Śaśadhara's Nyāyasiddhānta-dīpa, a Critical Edition with Introduction and Notes*. Ahmedabad: L. D. Institute of Indology. Ahmedabad: L. D. Series, no. 56.

Matilal, B. K. (1977a). *Nyāya-Vaiśeṣika (a historical survey)*, vol. VI of *A History of Indian Literature*, general editor: Jan Gonda. Wiesbaden: Otto Harrasowitch.

Matilal, B. K. (1977b). *The Logical Illumination of Indian Mysticism*. Oxford: Clarendon Press.

Matilal, B. K. (1981). *The Central Philosophy of Jainism (anekānta-vāda)*. Ahmedabad: L. D. Institute of Indology, L. D. Series 74.

Matilal, B. K. (1982). *Logical and Ethical Issues in Religious Belief*. Calcutta: University of Calcutta.

Matilal, B. K. (1985). *Logic, Language and Reality: An Introduction to Indian Philosophical Studies*. Delhi Motilal Banarsidass. Second edition under new subtitle, *Indian Philosophy and Contemporary Issues*, 1990.

Matilal, B. K. (1986). *Perception: an Essay on Classical Indian Theories of Knowledge*. Oxford: Clarendon Press.

Matilal, B. K. and Evans R. D. (eds). (1986). *Buddhist Logic and Epistemology: Studies in the Buddhist Analysis of Inference and Language*. Studies of Classical India, vol. 7. Dordrecht: Kluwer.

Milindapañho (1962). Ed. V. Trenckner. London: Pali Text Society.

Parsons, T. (1970). "An analysis of mass terms and amount terms." *Foundations of Language*, 6: 362–388.

Plato (1963). *Collected Dialogues*, eds. E. Hamilton and H. Cairns. New York: Bolligen Foundation.

Potter, K. H. and Bhattacharyya, S. eds. (1993). *Indian Philosophical Analysis: Nyāya-Vaiśeṣika from Gaṅgeśa to Raghunātha Śiromaṇi*. Encyclopedia of Indian Philosophies, volume VI. Delhi: Motilal Banarsidass.

Praśastapāda (1971). *Praśastapādabhāṣya*, with Udayana's *Kiraṇāvalī*. Ed. J. S. Jetly. Baroda: Gaekwad Oriental Series 154.

Priest, G. (1979). "Logic of Paradox," *Journal of Philosophical Logic* 8: 219–241.

Prior, A. N. (1976). *Papers on Logic and Ethics*, ed. P. T. Geach and A .J. P. Kenny. London: Duckworth.

Quine, V. W. O. (1953). *From a Logical Point of View*. Cambridge: Harvard University Press.

Quine, W. V. O. (1960). *Word and Object*. Cambridge, Mass., Technology Press.

Quine, W. V. O. (1962). *Methods of Logic*. Second edition. London: Routledge and Kegan Paul.

Quine, W. V. O. (1977). "Natural Kinds," in S. P. Schwartz (ed.) *Naming, Necessity and Natural Kinds*. Ithaca: Cornell University Press (1977).

Randle, H. N. (1924). "A Note on the Indian Syllogism." *Mind*, vol. 33: 398–414.

Randle, H. N. (1930). *Indian Logic in the Early Schools*. London: Oxford University Press.

Robinson, R. (1953). *Plato's Earlier Dialectic*. Oxford: Clarendon Press.

Robinson, R. H. (1957). "Some Logical Aspects of Nāgārjuna's System." *Philosophy East and West* 6: 291–308.

Samantabhadra (1914). *Āptamīmāṃsā*, ed. G.L. Jain. Kashi: Sanatana Jaina Granthamala.

Śāntarakṣita. (1968). *Tattvasaṃgraha*, with Kamalaśīla's *Pañjikā*. Ed. Swami Dwarikadas Shastri. Varanasi: Bauddha Bharati.

Sastri, H. ed. (1910). *Six Buddhist Nyāya Tracts in Sanskrit*. Calcutta: Bibliotheca Indica, no. 179. Reprinted by the Asiatic Society, Calcutta (1989).

Schayer, St. (1933). "Altindische Antizipationen der Aussagenlogik," *Bulletin International de l'Academie Polonaise des Sciences et des Lettres*, classe de philologies: 90–96.

Searle, J. (1969). *Speech-Acts: an Essay in the Philosophy of Language*. Cambridge; Cambridge University Press.

Sharvey, R. (1978). "Maybe English has no count nouns: Notes on Chinese semantics," *Studies in Language* 2: 345–365.

Sharvey, R. (1979). "The indeterminacy of mass predication," in F. J. Pelletier ed., *Mass Terms*. Dordrecht: Reidel (1979).

Solomon, E. A. (1976). *Indian Dialectics*. Ahmedabad: B.J. Institute.

Śrīharṣa. (1970). *Khaṇḍanakhaṇḍakhādya,* with Śaṃkara Miśra's commentary, ed. N. K. Jha. Varanasi: Kashi Sanskrit Series, 197.

Staal, J. F. (1962). "Negation and the law of contradiction in Indian thought," *Bulletin of the School of Oriental and African Studies*, 25.

Stcherbatsky, Th. (1930). *Buddhist Logic*. Vols 1 and 2, Bibliotheca Buddhica, 26. Leningrad.

Steinkellner, E. (1967). *Dharmakīrti's Hetubinduḥ*. Wien: Hermann Bohlaus.

Steinkellner, E. (1974). "On the reinterpretation of the *svabhāvahetuḥ*." *WZKSO* 18: 117–129.

Steinkellner, E. (1991). "The Logic of the *svabhāvahetu* in Dharmakīrti's *Vādanyāya,*" in E. Steinkellner (ed), *Studies in the Buddhist Epistemological Tradition* (1991). Proceedings of the Second International Dharmakīrti Conference, Vienna, 1989. Wien.

Sthānāṅga-sūtra (1937). With Abhayadeva's commentary. Ahmedabad.

Strawson, P. (1952). *Introduction to Logical Theory*. London: Methuen.

Strawson, P. (1959). *Individuals: an Essay in Descriptive Metaphysics*. London: Methuen.

Strawson, P. (1974). *Subject and Predicate in Logic and Grammar*. London: Methuen.

Swift, J. (1919 edn). *Gulliver's Travels*, ed. P. Colum. London.

Tucci, G. (1929a). "Buddhist Logic before Diṅnāga (Asaṅga, Vasubandhu, *Tarkaśāstras*)." *Journal of the Royal Asiatic Society*: 451–88; corrections: ibid. 870–1.

Tucci, G. (1929b). *Pre-Diṅnāga Texts on Logic from Chinese Sources*. Baroda: Gaekwad Oriental Series, no. 49.

Tucci, G. (1930). *The Nyāyamukha of Dignāga: The Oldest Buddhist Text on Logic.* Materialen zur Kunde des Buddhismus, no. 15. Heidelberg: Otto Harrasowitch.

Udayana. (1911). *Nyāyavārttika-tātparya-pariśuddhi*, with Vardhamāna's *Nyāyanibandhaprakāśa*, eds. L. S. Dravid and V. P. Dvivedin. Calcutta: Bibliotheca Indica.

Udayana (1971). *Kiraṇāvalī.* See Praśastapāda (1971).

Uddyotakara (1915). *Nyāyavārttikam.* Ed. V. P. Dvivedin. Varanasi: Chowkhamba.

Venkatanātha (1901). *Nyāyapariśuddhi.* Ed. R. M. Sastri, in *The Pandit*, vol. 23.

Vācaspati (1936). See Akṣapāda (1936).

Vidyabhusana, S. C. (1921). *A History of Indian Logic: Ancient, Mediaeval and Modern Schools.* Calcutta: Calcutta University.

Warder, A.K. (1963). "The earliest Indian logic," *Trudi Dvadtsat Pyatogo Mejdunarodnogo Kongressa Vostokovedov*, Moscow, Izdatelstvo Vostochnoi Lieraturi, vol. IV.

Warder, A. K. (1971). *Outline of Indian Philosophy.* Delhi: Motilal Banarsidass.

INDEX

A

Abhidhamma, 33
Akalaṅka, 80, 81
Akṣapāda Gautama, 2, 4, 42
analogical identification (*upamāna*), 141, 142
anekānta. *See* non-onesidedness
anumāna. *See* inference
apoha (exclusion, theory of meaning), 98–105
aprasiddha. *See* property, unexampled
Aristotle, 14, 16, 31, 57, 58, 152
asādhāraṇa. *See* property, uniquely deviating
associate condition (*upādhi*), 166–68
Aung, S. Z., 37
avyāpyavṛtti-dharma. *See* property, partially locatable

B

Bhartṛhari, 102
Bhāsarvajña, 5, 10, 167
bivalence, principle of, 135, 136
Bochenski, J. M., 1, 33

C

Candrakīrti, 72
Caraka, 41 passim, 46
Caraka-saṃhitā, 32, 38, 39
Carnap, R., 145
Cartwright, H., 25
Cārvāka/Lokāyata, 116
catuṣkoṭi. *See* negation, four-fold
chala. *See* quibbling
check. *See* defeat situation
Chi, R. S. Y., 106, 152, 153
clincher. *See* defeat situation
concomitance. *See* relation, inference-warranting
contradiction, principle of, 131–39

D

debate, 1, 2, chapter 2 passim; destructive (*vitaṇḍā*), 2, 3, 51 passim, 55, 56; honest (*vāda*), 2, 3, 41, 44 passim; tricky (*jalpa*), 2, 3, 41, 47 passim, 56; and dialectics, 56–59

defeat situation (*nigrahasthāna*), 3, 46, 47, 50, 81 passim
definition, 11, 120, 125–26
delimitor (*avacchedaka*), 156, 160–61
Dharmakīrti, 7, 11, 13, 14, 56, 80, 82, 87, 93, 103, 104, chapter 5; three kinds of inference, 108–109, 124, 165–66
Diṅnāga, 6, 7, 8, 9, 11, 13, 24, 42, 50, 56, 64, 70, 76, 80, 82, 86, 87, chapter 4, 145, 165–67; wheel of reason, 7–11, 97, 105–107, 117, 156–57
Dummett, M., 135

E

Evans, J. D. G., 58

F

false rejoinder (*jāti*), 3, 47, 48 passim, chapter 3 passim, Table 3.1 (p. 62)
Frauwallner, E., 73
Frege, G., 14, 134, 135, 145

G

Gaṅgeśa, 12, 140 passim
Goodman, N., 133

H

Haribhadra, 130, 131 passim
Hayes, R. P., 95, 106–107
Heijinoort, J. von, 25
Hemacandra, 81
Hemple, C. G., 96, 109
heterologue (*vipakṣa*), 6, 17, 92, 122–23
hetu. *See* sign, inferential
hetucakra. *See* Diṅnāga, wheel of reason
homologue (*sapakṣa*), 6, 17, 92, 121, 122–23

I

induction, problem of, 96–98, chapter 5
inference: as a means of knowing, 1, 14, 58; causal theory of, 142–43; for oneself vs. for others, 108; locus of (*pakṣa*), 6, 22, 91 passim, 156; predictive vs. explanatory, 109–11
Ingalls, D. H. H., 149, 161
internal concomitance (*antarvyāpti*), 97, 124–25

J

jalpa. *See* debate, tricky
jāti. *See* false rejoinder
Jayanta, 114
Jayarāśi, 52, 72

K

Kajiyama, Y. K., 111
kathā. *See* debate
Kathāvatthu, 32, 34 passim
Katsura, S., 93, 98
Kitagawa, H., 92
Kumārila, 102, 119, 165

L

lakṣaṇa. *See* definition
language: feature-placing, 24; property-location, 26 passim, 143–51; Sanskrit, 28
"limb" of an inference (*avayava*), 4
liṅga. *See* sign, inferential
logic: and debate, 2; and epistemology, 42, 88, 94; deductive vs.

inductive, 15; formal vs. informal, 1; nature of Indian, chapter 1 passim, 164, 168; paraconsistent, 138
Lukasiewicz, J., 17

M

Mackie, J. L., 111, 120
Malliṣeṇa, 129
Maṇikaṇṭha, 166–67
mass terms, 24 passim; and adjectives, 28
Mathuranātha, 150
means of knowing (*pramāṇa*), 1, 3, 43, 140; and definition, 126; and inferential sign, 42, 44
Mill, J. S., 17

N

Nāgārjuna, 3, 53, 54, 57, 79
Nāgasena, 32, 46
negation, 146–47; four-fold (*catuṣkoṭi*), 53; law of double, 150; meaning of, 95; vs. refutation, 54–56
nigrahasthāna. *See* defeat situation
non-deviation (*avyabhicāritatva*), 144, 151
non-onesidedness (*anekānta*), 81, chapter 6
nyāya method, 4, 5, 13, 58
Nyāya school, 4, 10, 25, 45, 69, 128; Navya-Nyāya, chapter 7
Nyāyasūtra, 2, 3, 4, 5, 7, 12, 23, 32, 39, 42, 43, 44 passim, 58, 60 passim, 74, 77, 80, 81 passim; three kinds of inference, 117

P

pakṣa. *See* inference, locus of
Parsons, T., 25
perception, 102, 141
pervasion. *See* relation, inference-warranting
Plato, 31, 56
pramāṇa. *See* means of knowing
Praśastapāda, 13, 14, 165, 167
predication, seven-fold (*saptabhaṅgī*), 129, 131–39
presumption (*arthāpatti*), 70
Priest, G., 138
Prior, A. N., 25
property: ever-present, 128, 148, 150, 156–64; imposed (*upādhi*), 25; partially locatable (*avyāpya-vṛtti*), 143–44, 149–51, 154–55, 160; simple, 147; to-be-inferred (*sādhya*), 22, 153, 156; unexampled (*aprasiddha*), 147; unlocatable, 144, 147, 154–55; unnegatable, 144, 147–48, 150, 154–55
psychologism, 14, 91, 145

Q

quibbling (*chala*), 3, 47, 48, chapter 3 passim
Quine, W. V., 15, 19, 20, 24, 103, 105, 135, 153, 156

R

Raghunātha, 150, 156, 162
Randle, H. N., 15, 18, 60
rationality, 33, 131, 139
relation, inference-warranting, 12, 18, 49, 141, 143, 151–52, 164–68; conception of in the *Nyāya-sūtra*, 63–64; knowledge of, 112–13
Robinson, R., 56

S

sādhya. *See* property, to-be-inferred
Samantabhadra, 129

Sāṃkhya school, 86
Sānātani, 3, 55
Sañjaya, 52
Śāntarakṣita, 104
sapakṣa. *See* homologue
saptabhaṅgī. *See* predication, sevenfold
Śaśadhara, 167–68
Saussure, 6
scepticism, 52
Schayer, S., 37
Searl, J., 52
Sharvey, R., 25
sign, inferential, 5, 11, 88 passim, 142, 153, 156; pseudo-sign (*hetvābhāsa*), 46, 122, 128; triple-conditioned (*trairūpya*), 6–7, 90–96, 110; uniquely deviating (*asādhāraṇa*), 8, 98, 117, 122–24; universal negative (*kevala-vyatirekin*), 9, 98, 117–19, 124–25, 158; universal positive (*kevalānvayin*), 9, 117, 124, 158, 162
Socrates, 31, 38, 56
Soloman, E., 60, 75, 76
Sondaḍa, 148
sophistical rejoinder. *See* false rejoinder
Śrīdhara, 125, 167
Śrīharṣa, 3, 56, 57, 72, 79
Staal, J. F., 54
Stcherbatsky, Th., 1, 15
Steinkellner, E., 112, 124, 166
Strawson, P. F., 19, 20, 21, 24, 153
syādvāda. *See* non-onesidedness
syllogism, 3, 15, 57, 95, 152

T

tarka (supportive argument), 3, 4, 45, 46
Tarkaśāstra, 58, 59, 61, 73 passim, 83
trairūpya. *See* sign, triple-conditioned
tricks in debate. *See* quibbling and false rejoinder
Tucci, G., 60, 61, 73, 76, 77

U

Udayana, 3, 11, 14, 46, 55, 56, 83, 125, 140, 142, 150, 156, 158, 161, 163, 167
Uddyotakara, 7, 8, 10, 11, 45, 47, 64, 65, 67, 73, 82, 83, 102, 107, 157
upādhi. *See* associate condition
upamāna. *See* analogical identification
Upāyahṛdaya, 58, 59, 61, 73 passim, 86

V

Vācaspati, 79, 80, 85, 158, 163
vāda. *See* debate, honest
Vallabha, 166, 167
Vasubandhu, 47, 56, 77, 80, 82
Vātsyāyana, 3, 42, 45, 51, 57, 63, 64, 68, 71, 72, 77, 82
Veṅkaṭanātha, 84
Vidyabhusana, S. C., 1, 60
vipaksa. *See* heterologue
vitaṇḍā. *See* debate, destructive
vyāpti. *See* relation, inference-warranting

W

Warder, A. K., 36, 37, 43

Y

yukti (causal inquiry), 42

www.ingramcontent.com/pod-product-compliance
Lightning Source LLC
Chambersburg PA
CBHW021758230426
43669CB00006B/123